Acknowledgments

Grateful acknowledgment is made to the following for per-
mission to quote copyright material : to the publishers, Martin
Secker and Warburg, and to Mrs Sonia Brownell Orwell, for
quotations from *The Collected Essays, Journalism, and Letters
of George Orwell*, and from *Burmese Days, A Clergyman's
Daughter, Keep the Aspidistra Flying, Coming Up for Air,
Down and Out in Paris and London, The Road to Wigan Pier,
Homage to Catalonia, Animal Farm*, and *1984*, by George
Orwell; to the publishers, Jonathan Cape, for quotations from
We, by Yevgeny Zamyatin, in the translation by Bernard
Guilbert Guerney.

THE ROAD TO MINILUV

THE ROAD TO MINILUV

George Orwell, the State, and God

by

CHRISTOPHER SMALL

LONDON
VICTOR GOLLANCZ LTD
1975

ISBN 0 575 01848 8

MADE AND PRINTED IN GREAT BRITAIN BY
THE GARDEN CITY PRESS LIMITED
LETCHWORTH, HERTFORDSHIRE SG6 1JS

Contents

Bibliographical Note

The published works of George Orwell are available in a Uniform Edition comprising his novels, autobiographical writings, and his longer political essays (London, 1948–60). *The Collected Essays, Journalism, and Letters of George Orwell*, in four volumes edited by Sonia Orwell and Ian Angus (London, 1968) add a quantity of miscellaneous writing extending in scope over the whole of Orwell's career from boyhood to his death.

Over the quarter-century since Orwell died in 1950 a large number of books have been published about him and his work. No full-length biography has appeared as yet (although an authorised Life is shortly expected), but a detailed study of his early life has been made by Peter Stansky and William Abrahams (*The Unknown Orwell*, London, 1972). In addition reminiscences of the man have been published by many different persons, combined in some cases with comment upon the writer : notably by Richard Rees in *George Orwell: Fugitive from the Camp of Victory* (London, 1961); by Christopher Hollis in *A Study of George Orwell* (London, 1956); by George Woodcock in *The Crystal Spirit, a Study of George Orwell* (London, 1967); and by Orwell's publisher, Fredric Warburg, in the second volume of his memoirs, *All Authors Are Equal* (London, 1973).

To all of these I am indebted, both for the information they provide about Orwell's life and personality and for views of his work which, while I do not necessarily agree with them, have been a stimulus to my own. I owe most, perhaps, to the late Sir Richard Rees, whose discussion of Orwell's character and outlook points to affinities with Simone Weil and Dostoevsky. Among purely critical works I have found the most valuable to be Alan Sandison's *The Last Man in Europe: An Essay on George Orwell* (London, 1974). I would also like to mention an admirable essay on Orwell by D. S. Savage, as yet unpublished, which I have had the advantage of reading in manuscript, which approximates in many ways to my own point of view.

Other works referred to include *The Tales of D. H. Lawrence* (London, 1934); F. M. Mayor, *The Rector's Daughter* (London, 1924); Jack London, *The People of the Abyss* and *The Iron Heel* (London, 1903 and 1907) and *Letters from Jack London*, edited by King Hendricks and Irving Shepard (London, 1966); Yevgeny Zamyatin, *We*, translated by Bernard Guilbert Guerney (London, 1970); Simone Weil, *Gravity and Grace* and *Waiting on God*, translated by Emma Craufurd (London, 1952 and 1951); James Burnham, *The Managerial Revolution* (London, 1941); Karl Marx, *Theses on Feuerbach*, from *Early Writings* of Marx, translated by Rodney Livingstone and Gregor Benton (London, 1973); Arthur Koestler, *Arrival and Departure* (London, 1943); Fyodor Dostoevsky, *The Brothers Karamazov*, translated by Constance Garnett (London, 1912) and *Notes from Underground*, translated by Jessie Coulson (London, 1972).

Man must and will have some religion. If he has not the religion of Jesus, he will have the religion of Satan, and will erect the Synagogue of Satan, calling the prince of this world "God"; and destroying all who do not worship Satan under the name of God. Will any one say: "Where are those who worship Satan under the name of God?" Where are they? Listen! Every religion that preaches vengeance for sin is the religion of the enemy and avenger, and not of the forgiver of sin; and their God is Satan, named by the Divine Name.

William Blake : *Jerusalem*

Man is like a novel: one doesn't know until the very last page how the thing will end.

Zamyatin : *We*, translated by B. G. Guerney

God is not in strength but in truth.

Dostoevsky : *The Brothers Karamazov*

I

Introduction: Pilgrim's Progress

THE YEAR 1984 is within the coming decade; most of us, probably, can expect to see it. Already something like a count-down has started, and as the date with its imaginary horrors draws nearer, we feel an actual relief that events are not going according to plan : that the programme laid down by George Orwell's novel is irretrievably behind time, if not altogether mistaken. Nineteen-eighty-four, we assure ourselves, won't come; or if it comes we shall hardly notice it.

Of course it is absurd to speak of Orwell's satire in this way, as though it were a sort of Nostradamus forecast, to be refuted or confirmed according to a time-table. Nevertheless, it is often done, and is itself an indication of the extraordinary effect of the book and of its continuing hold upon imagination in the quarter-century since it was written. The title has passed into the language as shorthand for the worst that can be imagined in political and social development, and some degree of this feeling, a foreboding transmitted by the author, is hardly to be avoided. The date, loaded with sombre meaning, fascinates us; and though we know quite well that the man who chose it did so more or less arbitrarily (probably as a simple inversion of the year in which he was writing, 1948) the knowledge scarcely diminishes the sinister power that this new Doomsday has over us.

The power lies partly in recognition that much of Orwell's description of affairs is, in terms of satire, accurate and just; how accurate as an account of existing and foreseeable social-political tendencies is a matter of rational argument. But there is another and stronger component in the hold *1984* has over us, which does not arise from any rational assessment and cannot easily be dispelled by reason : it is at this point, where political satire blends into and is swallowed up by nightmare,

that the story Orwell told really takes a grip. It is recognition of
this visionary quality, not so much as pre-vision, rather as the
substance of a very bad dream, that dominates our feelings about
the book, and that has been responsible, indeed, for its
absorption into a modern folk-lore of evil.

1984 is a bad dream : is it therefore "only a bad dream"? So
we are inclined to say, hoping to reassure ourselves of its unreality. But there are no such things as dreams that are "only
dreams"; nightmares, we know, grow out of the dreamer's
whole life and circumstances, and come in turn to affect that
life. The dreams that a writer shares through his work are always
of more than personal significance by the very act of telling, and
the more they affect us the better we know that they are partly
our dreams as well. That in the end is what makes them worth
hearing.

It is possible to look at the work of George Orwell as the
expression of an individual fantasy, and to find, in his last and
most famous book, the summing up of personal emotions and
obsessions traceable backwards through his earlier writings and
also through his life. But, again, that is no sort of comfort for
the fears which the book arouses : it rouses them with such
force precisely because we respond to the personal view. The
obsessions are ours as well. We know, too, that obsessions of this
general kind, the fantasy-life of individuals which is shared by
social groups and whole peoples, are the driving forces of society
at large : of the public world which is the sphere of politics. If
there is anything we have learned about political behaviour in
the past fifty years it is that the drives behind it are not solely
rational; indeed, insofar as they can be called drives, compulsions, they are not rational at all. Even if they are described as
ideology, and thought of as concealing rather than expressing
the true functioning of society, their power to influence political
behaviour must be acknowledged. And in truth the notion that
societies, while expressing their purposes in fantasy, are ruled by
an impersonal, concealed reason, has come to seem no more
than a fantasy itself : more properly, one of the myths which
shape social life. And the power of myths is something we can
no longer deny, or ignore. It is not only that we have seen
entire nations carried away by myths, or systematised dreams :
we have come to realise that all collectives are ruled by the

dreams that they have of themselves, the accumulated substance of individual imaginings.

That is the real warning and, to put it more strongly, the threat of Orwell's *1984*: it is the most thorough-going account in modern literature of a society altogether in the grip of fantasy. The fact that, in its manner of telling, it appears to be one man's fantasy, a single point of view, merely reinforces the effect. It is, notoriously, the unanimity of the society Orwell imagined that makes it so horrible : the story could in fact be described as the merging of a "single point of view" in collective fantasy. Again, we can call the fate of this singular man, Orwell's Winston Smith, a dream; but it is an evil dream which, by the end, everyone in the book shares, by implication the entire population of the world, and from which no one is ever going to wake up.

Nowadays we no longer try to see in dreams the direct equivalents or prognostication of future events. We try to understand them in terms of the dreamer's life, his past and present and therefore only indirectly his possible future. Most studies of Orwell have, however, been of the former kind : that is to say they have interpreted the content of his work, and especially of his last novel, in exterior terms, as description, more or less objective, of the "outside" world, now and to come. There is little doubt that Orwell himself viewed his work in this way : to describe the world as he saw it accurately and "objectively" was certainly what he wished to do and—as testified by many passages in his writings—what he thought he was doing. To a large extent this assumption has been taken over by his readers, who have regarded him principally, perhaps, as an unusually observant and truthful recorder of men and affairs, not a "subjective" writer, though one with a highly individual way of looking. The obvious contradiction in the last words has not troubled readers of this kind, and evidently did not occur to Orwell himself; he knew well enough that he saw the world in a particular way—and his idea of the "exterior" world was essentially solipsist, as we shall see—but he seldom paused to ask himself *why* he saw it so. By his own confession, and by the evidence of all his writing, he was intensely self-conscious, but his consciousness, though it extended to motives, was strictly

limited. There will be more to say about these limitations, and
about his attitude to subjectivity, later on. In the meantime it
may be noted that in some respect he felt subjectivity to be
dangerous, though also an allurement. (For a writer of fiction
to use first-person narrative, the most obviously subjective mode,
he said was "like dosing yourself with some stimulating but
very deleterious and very habit-forming drug.")

Any study of Orwell becomes a study of conflict; even more
than the many other writers who express the contradictions of
the age, Orwell was visibly at odds with himself. Buridan's Ass,
reduced to complete inaction by conflicting urges, was a self-
image Orwell used more than once; although in his case, of
course, the impossible choice "between the water and the hay"
had issue in action of different kinds, chiefly the action of
writing. The conflict that shows in him can be described in
more than one way, and indeed it will be found that, under
examination, it changes its aspect; it may not appear in the
end to be at all what the writer himself and, perhaps, his readers
have assumed. But as a starting point the contradiction already
mentioned is worth looking at more closely, that between a
personal or subjective view of the world and the aim (even if
not achieved) of looking at it objectively.

A passage from Orwell's essay on *The Prevention of Literature*
(1946) illustrates the point, and his awareness of it. The subject
of the essay is the irreconcilable opposition between creative
literature and totalitarian demands upon it; and as a defender
of "intellectual liberty" he urges the essential claim of subjectivity. He says that "so far as freedom of expression is concerned, there is not much difference between a mere journalist
and the most 'unpolitical' imaginative writer. The journalist is
unfree, and is conscious of unfreedom, when he is forced to
write lies or suppress what seems to him important news : the
imaginative writer is unfree when he has to falsify his subjective
feelings, *which from his point of view are facts*. He may distort
and caricature reality in order to make his meaning clearer, but
he cannot misrepresent the scenery of his own mind . . ." (my
italics). The same passage goes on, however, to assert that the
private world, where subjective interpretations and emotions are
facts, necessarily impinges on the public one where facts are,
or are supposed to be, of a different, verifiable kind. The imagi-

native writer, Orwell says, cannot avoid trouble by keeping away from the public or political realm, because "there is no such thing as genuinely non-political literature, and least of all in an age like our own, when fears, hatreds, and loyalties of a directly political kind are near to the surface of everyone's consciousness".

That all writing is in some way "political", that "no book is genuinely free from political bias" was strongly maintained by Orwell, and even if he admitted that at other times political pressures upon literature were not so great, he believed that now they are unavoidable. He at any rate did not avoid but actively embraced them; in the account of *Why I Write* (1946) in which the last remark quoted occurs he roundly asserted that "every line of serious work that I have written since 1936" had been with conscious political purpose, guided by "desire to push the world in a certain direction, to alter other people's idea of the kind of society that they should strive after". At the same time he regretted the necessity and even resisted some of its demands as he saw them, continuing to pursue aesthetic ends (or "to make political writing into an art") and to indulge personal interests: "Anyone who cares to examine my work will see that even when it is downright propaganda it contains much that a full-time politician would consider irrelevant. I am not able, and I do not want, completely to abandon the world-view that I acquired in childhood ... the job is to reconcile my ingrained likes and dislikes with the essentially public, non-individual activities that this age forces on all of us."

The whole of Orwell's apologia in *Why I Write* is replete with contradictions, or rather with ideas which, when examined, seem to run in divergent directions. Two main strands of thought may be distinguished, however, obscurely expressed in a poem, written ten years before, which is quoted in the course of the article. The poem, much commented upon, opens in a mood of frank nostalgia: "A happy vicar I might have been/ Two hundred years ago" but goes on to describe the impossibility of such a life in the present time, the age of all-demanding politics in which dreams are "forbidden"; yet it ends with an ironic evocation of quite a different sort of dream:

> I dreamed that I dwelt in marble halls,
> And woke to find it true;

I wasn't born for an age like this;
Was Smith? Was Jones? Were you?

What the poem seems to be saying, and is reinforced in the article as a whole (the latter having been written later, when Orwell had made a political decision and "knew", as he said, "where I stood") is that the private, subjective world must defer to the public one; with the implication that the public world is one of objective fact concerning which the writer's most important task, just because he is involved in politics, is to tell the truth. Orwell knew very well, of course, that political life is par excellence the realm of untruth, but all the more he insisted that the writer engaged in politics (as, for instance, he felt himself to be in writing his Spanish Civil War account, *Homage to Catalonia*) had an obligation not to tell lies or conceal the truth.

w will disagree with him; and his stubborn attachment to ⎯ath in political affairs, his refusal to be coerced by weight of current opinion, and his defence of minority views, remain among the chief reasons, and surely sound ones, for his high place in our general esteem. Yet elsewhere, as we have seen, it is recognised that subjective feelings have the status of "facts" for a writer, and that it is at least as important for him to be true to them as it is for a reporter to deal faithfully with external events. Dreams, in a word, are facts of a personal kind; and now, returning to the poem, we may note again that there are two kinds of dream alluded to in it. There are dreams of happiness, "girls' bellies and apricots,/Roach in a shaded stream,/Horses, ducks in flight at dawn"—all of which, with meanings for the writer that remain to be investigated, are lost or unreal. And there is the dream of "marble halls", which here, in the satiric tone of the final verse, stand for all the public horrors of "an age like this"; and this dream turns out to be real.

What is the relation between the "marble halls" that exist in dreams, and have only the status of subjective fact and those that exist in the waking or objective world? If to ask this seems to reason too nicely about a poetic device and a facetious reference, there is another place where Orwell, speaking directly of politics, has something to say with a more serious, not to say sinister, bearing on the question. In the same year, 1946, as that of the other two articles referred to, we find him, still speaking of the need to "continue the political struggle", admitting that politics itself is not a reasonable activity : "we shall get nowhere unless we start by recognising that political behaviour is largely non-rational, that the world is suffering from some kind of mental disease which must be diagnosed before it can be cured." He went on, indeed, to attempt a diagnosis himself, postulating a "desire for pure power" which "seems to be much more dominant than the desire for wealth." Why this should be so he could not say, since, though "taken for granted as a natural instinct", the desire for power "is no more natural, in the sense of being biologically necessary, than drunkenness or gambling". But clearly, here, with a view of political life as infected by madness, dominated by desires outside rational control, we are very near the world of *1984*; and what is especially striking is that the passions of politics are compared, just as is the subjectivity of first-person narrative in the remarks quoted earlier, with vices of addiction. The reprehensible indulgence in personal daydream for literary purposes (which is how Orwell thought of this kind of writing) and the pursuit of political power are both likened to habit-forming drugs. A vicious habit of mind can be linked with vicious political practice, the subjective can be expressed in the objective facts of political life.

We seem to have Orwell's own warrant, therefore (not to labour the point further), to treat both the subjective and objective content of his work together, not only the politics but the irrational or so to speak non-political motives behind them; and not these motives alone, divorced from their consequences, but as they have issue in the actualities of political behaviour. To find the origins of a particular set of political beliefs or practices in private and non-rational factors—or, in a word, in dreams—by no means allows us to treat the beliefs in question lightly. On the contrary, they gain in power to make themselves felt, to demand attention, precisely as they are manifestly independent of rational considerations. Because Orwell's fears for the political future can be shown, it may be, to have roots in his personal past is no reason at all to dismiss them. But it does mean that these roots should if possible be examined and understood; the diagnosis which he asked for can perhaps start there.

Some work in this direction has lately been done and the emphasis has shifted from Orwell's status as political satirist to his moral outlook and its personal origins. The process may indeed already have gone too far, in the sense of diminishing interest in what he had to say about politics. It is possible now to say, what would once have seemed entirely paradoxical, that Orwell's significance is primarily moral and religious. But the further paradox remains, that just because he is not to be thought of principally as a political writer (whatever he said himself) his work has real importance for political life; for it is only by going beyond "politics" that anything—and perhaps especially in "an age like this"—can usefully be said about them. This was Orwell's own opinion, or rather it was one of those opinions which, never fully acknowledged by him, recurred to nag him—reaching the surface, so to speak, only at intervals in his work, but present all the time as an unrecognised influence. To trace their continual effect and to consider their implications, never worked out by Orwell himself, are the principal aims of the present essay.

From time to time, in the midst of the political arguments and polemics in which he was engaged, Orwell remarked on their irrelevance to the permanent concerns of mankind; even if all the political aims he espoused should be realised, it would still, he said, leave "all the really important questions unsetttled". Such an attitude must be called religious, and the fact that he was a declared and so to speak a practising agnostic—adopting consistently a markedly hostile attitude to religious belief—does not at all affect the fundamentally religious aspect of his writing. As a writer Orwell began and ended in conscious atheism, but of a peculiar and extraordinarily uncomfortable kind; if it is said that atheism is necessarily comfortless (it is a source of pride for many that it is so) then Orwell is a prime example of that singular unease. He was both unbeliever and religious man, and it is the unrelaxed conflict between the two sides in him that gives all his work its dynamic from beginning to end, and makes him the important witness that he is, in some ways uniquely, for a non-religious, or irreligious time. He is known above all as a witness for the plight of the individual in an age of collectivism; at the same time, and not to be separated from this view of him, he represents the sceptic-religious man who, with "all the important questions unsettled", is trapped into thinking exclusively in political terms.

It is this situation that makes his voice so compelling for us, and the more so perhaps for the generation grown up since his death, whose attitude to "politics" is often one of indifference. It may be urged that the world is already a "post-political" one, that Orwell's successors no longer have the manoeuvres of political life to worry about but the techniques and manipulative applications of sociology; in which case what Orwell has to say is all the more crucial. For of course it is just such a situation that he foresaw and that *1984*, with its prefigurations in his earlier writing, is about : the business of politics, which Orwell found a disagreeable necessity, is transformed in his final vision into a state which has successfully and permanently rendered politics unnecessary.

The "history" of events sketched in *1984* as background for the permanent establishment of "Oceania" and its companion super-States is exactly of such a transcendence of politics by politics, the chaotic political action of "Oceania's" obscure and already largely mythological origins having given way to a stability in which change in a political sense is impossible and all political action therefore quite useless and virtually unthinkable : its place in the story is to be shown up as no more than childish fantasy. The argument that we have now got over the political turmoils and partisanships of Orwell's day, and that his preoccupations in this area are out of date, turns back on itself, therefore, with a vengeance. Indeed we may revert to the "consolation" mentioned at the start—that the symbolic date 1984 will not come, or if it comes we shall not notice it— and see the daunting paradox concealed within the second part of it. For it can be said that, so long as we can talk about *1984* and discuss whether it has come or not, then certainly it has not come : the one thing certain is that when *1984* is actually here and we are living in the kind of world that Orwell described as a warning, we shall be unconscious of it, and the very title of his book which has become a monitory symbol for us will have ceased to have any of its present meaning.

The "meaning" of *1984* is not a single one, but it can be viewed as expressing a single main problem or point of conflict : this can in turn be seen as the main problem with which Orwell contended throughout his work. To examine it the whole of his career as a writer must be looked at, the evidence being both in his life and his work. This is not a biographical study, but it is not possible altogether to separate the writings from the actions and pursuits of the man who produced them and also produced himself: for the writer "George Orwell" was of course himself a product, in a sense to be counted among the creative fictions of the man Eric Blair. To an extent unusual among professional writers Orwell-Blair "lived" his writing. When he said in his apologia, *Why I Write*, that he "always knew I would be a writer" we can glimpse something like a deliberate self-dedication shaping a whole existence. Already, as a child, he tells us there, he had the habit of making a running commentary in his head on everything he did: it was a substitute, or preparation, for writing. When he came actually to start serious writing, he says, the habit ceased. The two impulses apparent in this description, of absorption in the task of expression—for already, we learn, he was searching for "the right words" in which to carry on his interior monologue—and of self-alienation are doubtless common to many writers; but in Orwell it clearly went to an unusual length. He was to an uncommon degree a man of words, one whose sensitivity to language, skill in its use, and sense of its huge importance in human affairs has few equals among English writers, none among his contemporaries. At the same time he was the very opposite of the popular notion of a "literary man", unused to and perhaps aloof from practical occupations: Orwell took pride in being a man of action and made a positively painful cult of practical experience. The expeditions into low life which in various forms and with various degrees of self-abandonment he repeatedly made as a young man are certainly not to be understood merely as looking for "copy". It may be said, in anticipation of the main argument, that there was in these experiments an element at least of compulsive degradation, of search not simply for unfamiliar outward adventure but for satisfaction of a profound inner need. But in any case they were all turned into writing; what he himself recorded of them (at least in the present incomplete state of Orwell's biography) is almost our only evidence about them. What he did in these self-extensions turns up in his work, not only in the direct record of private letters and journals but as the very substance of his books, both his critical writing and his fiction. We know about the events of his life from his work; if, taken together, these have a discernible shape or direction, we can see it there. Such is true more or less of any creative writer, but in Orwell the process is both more obvious than usual, as particular incidents and experiences occur, often many times, as literary material, and of greater significance as personal confession.

The self-awareness of Eric Blair-George Orwell was, as has already been remarked, limited, confined as a rule to the content of conscious introspection. The insights to be found in dreams or subliminal states of mind form a very small part of his material (though they are all the more important, of course, when they do occur). He displayed much of the indifference and even hostility to knowledge of unconscious processes that might be expected in a conventional middle-class Englishman of his time. But despite this, and perhaps it can be said in some way because of it, the combined product, life-and-work, is an unfolding of motives and needs of which the writer seems more or less successfully to have remained unaware. The following essay will seek the meaning of Orwell's life in his work, and will concentrate on that, though it will refer where it seems helpful to what has been independently recorded of his actions and opinions. The most important evidence is in his fiction, for however misleading their factual observations and records may be, in their fictions writers do not lie. What we are looking for is the subjective truth of Orwell's words, and though it can be traced in everything he said, it is most clearly to be seen in his inventions, where it is not disguised nor much contaminated by the accidents of objective fact. Orwell drew the material of his novels from experience, but he only drew what he needed. The dividing line between his fiction and his other writing, in essays, letters, and political-social comment is by no means clear-cut: direct expression of opinion and unassimilated information can enter his novels, and the "facts" of his non-fiction are highly subjective. But like any creative writer Orwell was responsible for his inventions as he could not altogether be for objective communication. If a man tells us as a matter of fact that the effects of destitution or the fear of it work in a particular way, or that the State assumes particular forms of oppression, then he may refer to the objective world as reason for what he says. But if he tells us so in a novel then he is answerable for the assertion in a complete and unqualified way and has so to speak no excuse: no *reason*, that's to say, but its meaning for him.

It is these interior reasons, these meanings, that I wish to examine. It will be objected that they cannot ever be fully elucidated; if dreams, which are the equivalent in ordinary life for the fictions of literature, can be no more than partially investigated by the techniques of psychoanalysis, what prospect of success can there be in subjecting a novel to something like the same examination, when the author is not even there to be questioned? The difference, however, between dreams and published works of fiction is just that the latter are public and have become common property. We do not therefore need to question the author but ourselves: the whole process of literary interpretation is one in which the reader seeks in his own response the meaning of what he reads. He may then refer his discovery to whatever is otherwise known of the author's life and character, but it is always reflected back again where he intended it to rest, in the lives of his readers. It is for this purpose that in producing a work of fiction he has given his subjectivity public and objective existence; we call his work important exactly to the extent to which his subjective fact can be shared and can move us.

Such a process must be applied, of course, to the work as a whole, for although Orwell's novels are in many essentials very much the same, they exhibit a clear sequence, as linked parts of a continuous movement, or journey. Not less than Bunyan (whom he greatly admired) can he be thought of as a traveller, his pilgrimage to be followed through all his books. It leads, appallingly, not to the Delectable Mountains, but to the frightful tower-edifice, in *1984,* of the "Ministry of Love". If we want to see this destination clearly, to understand its importance for us and why it frightens us so much—for if it were merely one man's private fantasy it would hardly do so—we must follow the traveller all the steps of the way, through all the "scenery of his mind". "Miniluv", the most fearful of the four organs of Orwell's all-sufficient, all-powerful State, issued from his imagination replete with personal meanings, but they are personal meanings for us too. Perhaps it would not be claiming too much to say that its towering windowless bulk, in "glittering white concrete" standing high above the metropolis of the future is the dominant object of all our imaginary landscapes. A place of mystery and terror and also of fascination, unapproachable and not to be avoided, by no means to be broken into and the inevitable goal of all endeavour, it presents to us an ambiguous face, apparently quite inscrutable: sanctuary, prison, Chamber of Horrors, journey's end. But if we can understand the journey we may be able a little to understand its conclusion. If we can guess why in his imagination Orwell took the road to Miniluv we may see more clearly what Miniluv is and what—as we have admitted by the fear it inspires in us— there is in store for us there.

II

Loneliness and Loss

ORWELL'S FIRST NOVEL, *Burmese Days*, appeared in 1934, to be followed two years later by *A Clergyman's Daughter*. Before that he had already published *Down and Out in Paris and London*, his first book and the first use of the pen-name George Orwell. This account of his experiences during the preceding six years, when he had returned from Burma and his post with the Indian Imperial Police and was making his first deliberate experiments in poverty, is of importance biographically and as an early expression of many dominant themes and ideas. But, following the rule already formulated, that it is in his fiction that the subjective meaning of his work is chiefly to be sought, the two early novels will be taken as the starting point of our inquiry. Let us look at the story of *Burmese Days* first, and consider its effect on us, dismissing for the moment any knowledge we may have of its origins in Orwell-Blair's own previous career.

The strongest single impression conveyed by *Burmese Days* is of loneliness, a solitude which is the cause of bitter pain and unsatisfied longing, but which is felt in essence to be the subject's own fault. The central character of the novel, Flory, is an English timber merchant in the Burma of British imperial rule, a bachelor in early middle age, seedy and somewhat debauched after years of isolation in a small Burmese town, quite cut off by now from all contacts with family or friends in Britain, and isolated also by temperament from the small community of British officials and others in the place. His introduction is made with calculated effect, and an air of complete detachment; indeed throughout the novel he is described with the same apparent objectivity, almost impersonally, so that although his thoughts and emotions are the substance of the story, his personal life is viewed from outside. Although he is virtually the only person in the book to have an interior life, the narrative presents it from without.

Flory has no first name in the novel; he is always alluded to or addressed by his surname only, in public-school fashion, a trick that establishes and maintains the feeling of being held at arm's length. The name itself was evidently chosen with care. We are told (by Richard Rees, quoted by Peter Stansky and William Abrahams in *The Unknown Orwell*) that the name finally taken as the author's literary persona, "George Orwell", was first thought of for the hero of his first novel. Later on, when already fixed as Flory, he was given a Christian name as well, John : an early draft of the novel contains his epitaph, composed by himself, and running thus :

JOHN FLORY
Born 1890
Died of Drink 1927

Here lie the bones of poor John Flory;
His story is the old, old story.
Money, women, cards and gin
Were the four things that did him in.

He has spent sweat enough to swim in
Making love to stupid women;
He has known misery past thinking
In the dismal art of drinking.

O stranger, as you voyage here
And read this welcome, shed no tear;
But take the single gift I give,
And learn from me how not to live.

It may well be thought that this mordant doggerel was suppressed in the final version of the novel because it rendered Flory's misery, confessed by someone who subscribed his full name, too naked; especially the modulation into first-person appeal in the last verse is an expression of pain and despair too undisguised to be admitted. Detachment is in fact part of the misery, and will not permit such a desperate avowal; although the fact that it was once made should not be forgotten. As it is, another way of showing Flory's plight is found, and used with much skill, from the moment, indeed, of his first entry. A cool and neutral description of outward appearance introduces the "man of about thirty-five, of middle height, not ill made", and under cover of these details a savage surprise is prepared :

> All these were secondary impressions, however. The first thing that one noticed in Flory was a hideous birthmark stretching in a ragged crescent down his left cheek, from the eye to the corner of the mouth. Seen from the left side his face had a battered, woe-begone look, as though the birth-mark had been a bruise—for it was a dark blue in colour. He was quite aware of its hideousness. And at all times, when he was not alone, there was a sidelongness about his movements, as he manoeuvred constantly to keep the birthmark out of sight.

Flory feels himself an outcast, not only because his tastes and opinions cut him off from the other Europeans in the town of Kyauktada—a collection of almost wholly conventional and Philistine men and women upholding the standards of sahibdom that Flory has come to despise—but because he is physically repulsive, or at least believes himself to be so; and it is his birthmark, the ineradicable congenital blot, which is "the first thing one noticed" about him and almost the first thing one is told. Thus straight away is passed a bitter comment on the first hopeful sentence of his description; for if nature did not make Flory ill in general respects, endowing him with all the parts of a man, and all the desires and needs for companionship and love with which a child enters the world, she has deliberately marred her handiwork.

There is something wrong with Flory, and though it is described as a fortuitous exterior blemish, we are made to feel its inevitability in another way, as the outward sign of a more general disability that lies within. The dark mark on his skin sets Flory aside from other men, at once the cause and the symbol of his unacceptableness and exclusion from every close human relationship. He is at ease only with those, like the Indian Dr Veraswami and to a lesser extent his Burmese mistress, Ma Hla May, whose skins are entirely dark, and his intercourse with them, in the circumstances of Imperial rule, is not and cannot be that of equals. (At a later stage he thinks of his affairs with

Burmese women as "dirtying himself".) He himself has no colour prejudice, and his lack of it is one of the things that sets him at odds with his fellow-Europeans, but at the same time he cannot avoid its consequences. He admires the Burmese, but he is a stranger and exile among them; they are described almost as members of another species. The mark of what he has in common with them appears only as an ugly flaw, singling him out immediately from his "own kind" and cutting him off from normal contact. Whenever Flory meets another European, more particularly when it is someone like the girl Elizabeth to whom his affections yearn, he automatically turns "sidelong" and cannot meet the person face to face. The birthmark is the reason why he cannot, but at the same time we are made to feel that he has a birthmark because he cannot. In loneliness and unease he carries his naevus like a leper's bell, keeping others at a distance even as he walks towards them.

He is by no means self-sufficient in his isolation : the story of the novel, which tells of his meeting with the newly arrived English girl, their brief and unsatisfactory friendship, and its catastrophic conclusion, is evidently only the last and most disastrous of failed attempts to break out of his loneliness. He longs desperately, indeed, for closeness to another human being, the sort of intimate mutual sympathy and understanding which is expressed in free and open conversation, but which goes much beyond talking. It is as "talk" that this unattainable intimacy presents itself to him : "To talk, simply to talk! It sounds so little, and yet how much it is! When you have existed to the brink of middle age in bitter loneliness, among people to whom your true opinion on every subject on earth is blasphemy, the need to talk is the greatest of all needs."

Yet clearly it is not simply talk that Flory hungers for : he can talk freely with Dr Veraswami. Nor is it merely physical intimacy : he can have that with Ma Hla May and might indeed have it with Elizabeth. Within the conventions of the narrow code by which she lives she actually looks forward to it. At a crucial point of their always uncertain relationship, when Flory has kissed her for the first and only time, she yields readily to him, ignoring the birthmark (he has directly mentioned it to her, since "he could not kiss her without first asking this question"). They embrace, but it is Flory who withdraws, because his over-powering need, far stronger than physical attraction to the girl, is to explain himself. He begins to talk, and though he is trying, he says, to tell her how much she means to him, it is himself that he talks about. She is waiting for a proposal of marriage in due form, but Flory just continues "talking egoistically on and on", knowing within himself that talk is no use and can neither express nor assuage the longing he feels :

> . . . it was so devilishly difficult to explain. It is devilish to suffer a pain that is all but nameless. Blessed are they who are stricken only with classifiable diseases! Blessed are the poor, the sick, the crossed in love, for at least other people know what is the matter with them and will listen to their belly-achings with sympathy. But who that has not suffered it understands the pain of exile?

It is difficult to believe that "exile" here is merely expatriation—which, however painful, is not impossible to describe and comprehend. What Flory is talking about, and failing to communicate, is an exile from human kind and from himself that is indeed hard to make another understand, for its very nature prevents its expression. A dumb man cannot speak about his dumbness. Flory's isolation is not therefore the less bitter to him, or pathetic to us, but it is truly hopeless, and what happens in the novel, as he meets Elizabeth and makes his bid for understanding and sympathy, and fails, is that he realises fully its hopelessness. There are of course stages to the discovery, and hopes are temporarily roused in Flory for something better which helps to make clear what he really wants, and cannot have. The prologue to the scene just referred to has been a hunting expedition which has turned out an unexpected success—unexpected because we already recognise in Flory a sense of preordained failure. On this occasion things have gone well, Elizabeth has turned out to be a natural shot, the shared pleasure in the strange beauties of the jungle (vividly described) and in the excitements of the hunt brings about an unspoken intimacy between them : when Elizabeth holds in her hand the first thing she has killed (a pigeon) she is "conscious of an extraordinary desire to fling her arms round Flory's neck and kiss him", and their crowning piece of luck, the shooting of a leopard, produces in both, as they walk back together, their shoulders "almost touching", a state of actual bliss :

They did not talk much. They were happy with that inordinate happiness that comes of exhaustion and achievement, and with which nothing else in life—no joy of either the body or the mind—is even able to be compared.

The happiness, which carries with it a promise of closer physical intimacy (as they walk back it is "understood that Flory would ask Elizabeth to marry him") is delusory. Elizabeth is deluded into thinking that she might love a man who can give her the surpassing thrills of shooting and killing (the pathos of their victims, though shown to us, is invisible to her). Flory is deluded into thinking that, because a physical bond is possible between them (although he refrains from kissing her at one moment during the hunt, remembering his birthmark) he may gain what he really longs for. It is very doubtful if what he longs for is love, certainly not the sexual love that Elizabeth, even in her cool English-miss-ish way, is clearly ready for; indeed it is doubtful if he can be said to love Elizabeth himself, though he has tender and protective feelings towards her. His feelings towards her and his demands upon her are of a much more far-reaching, in truth an insatiable kind; for all too clearly when the occasion arises she cannot satisfy them.

We will return to the scene when, with these preliminaries, Elizabeth is expecting a proposal of marriage, and to accept it, and Flory himself is able to "see her answer in her face". Instead of asking her he launches into the attempt at self-explanation already quoted, for the physical communication they have fleetingly achieved is no substitute for what he craves in "understanding" : it is not herself, or even their future together that he is compelled to talk about, but his past. He wants her, but not herself, rather the absolution she can confer on him : "Ah, he must have her, that was certain! Only by marrying her could his life be salvaged." And again, as he tries to make her see what he is asking, and postpones asking the question she is waiting for : "It was so important that she should understand something of what his life in this country had been; that she should grasp the nature of the loneliness that he wanted her to nullify." He cannot explain it, nor can she begin to grasp it, and it is hardly surprising, since what he asks of this ordinary, rather dull young woman, is what the penitent believer,

reviewing his ill-spent, wasted and alienated life, may beg of
God.

It is obvious now that Flory never will ask Elizabeth to be his
wife; when, having finally braced himself to frame the words
"Will you——", he is interrupted by an earth tremor which throws
everyone into confusion, we do not feel that he is baulked of a
real goal by this act of God but rather that it has come in the
nick of time to save him from an impossible situation.

This interview, and Flory's failure either to do what is expected of him or to find the way back from "exile" that he
longs for, is the real crisis of his story. The abortive courtship
of Elizabeth drags on a little longer, interrupted by the arrival
of a young man, Verrall, well-connected, handsome, confident,
and quite without scruple, who easily takes her away from him
and possibly seduces her before decamping; there is a partial
reconciliation, but of a notably lifeless kind, based on expectations which by now neither person believes in. When the last
act is reached and, publicly humiliated by his revengeful
Burmese mistress, Flory is finally rejected by Elizabeth, it is no
more than the foredoomed rounding off of unfinished business.
Elizabeth's shallowness, conventionality, and selfishness are exposed in these last stages of the story with deep bitterness, but
at the same time Flory knows that the real failure is with himself.

It is his ugliness that clinches it. His ex-mistress, cast off by
him, comes to accuse him publicly, during a church service, the
formal pieties of which (together with the ribald comments of
some members of the congregation) make an ironic prologue to
her irruption. Flory has been dreaming of marriage to Elizabeth,
assumed to be settled but clearly by now no more than a dream
of salvation ("Hell was yielding up Eurydice"). When Ma Hla
May bursts in, screaming imprecations, he sits transfixed, "his
face rigid and so bloodless that the birthmark seemed to glow
upon it like a streak of blue paint". Elizabeth looks at him, and
is "almost physically sick"; she is outraged by the scandal, of
course, and all her colour-prejudice rises at the thought that
Flory has been Ma Hla May's lover, which makes her "shudder
in her bones".

But worse than that, worse than anything, was his ugliness at
this moment. His face appalled her, it was so ghastly, rigid,
and old. It was like a skull. Only the birthmark seemed alive
 . .

in it. She hated him now for his birthmark. She had never known till this moment how dishonouring, how unforgiveable a thing it was.

It seems an extraordinary way to think of a congenital blemish, and no doubt part of the purpose of Elizabeth's reaction is to underline the frankly hostile portrait of her as a hard young woman with no compassion and no feeling for weakness. But more strongly and credibly it is a transference to Elizabeth of Flory's feelings about himself : it is he who is convinced of being dishonoured and unforgiveable, and he recognises Elizabeth's treatment of him as natural and in a sense just. She is entirely sincere in her revulsion; bound by convention as she is, she might have married him, under pressure from her mother and in fear of poverty, for good social reasons, but now her instincts rebel. When she tells him, as he makes his last despairing appeal, that she wouldn't marry him if he were the last man on earth, she means it, heart and soul. She does not seriously mind his having kept a mistress : "He might have committed a thousand abominations and she could have forgiven him. But not after that shameful, squalid scene, and the devilish ugliness of his disfigured face in that moment. It was, finally, the birthmark that had damned him." Against all prudential considerations she violently rejects him and runs away :

She knew only that he was dishonoured and less than a man, and that she hated him as she would have hated a leper or a lunatic. The instinct was deeper than reason or even self-interest, and she could no more have disobeyed it than she could have stopped breathing.

This summing up of Flory, though it may still seem extravagant, is in fact the truth about him as he sees himself. And if to think of a man as "dishonoured" by a birthmark is strange, it only makes more obvious the function of Flory's naevus as the sign of a more profound and crippling defect. Beyond remedy divided from himself, Flory is less than a man—and also, we may notice, more than one, being "damned" and "devilish", a most pitiable and downcast Satan. Elizabeth could not hate him more than he hates himself, and when he loses in her his last chance of self-reconciliation he is faced not with any new reason for despair

2—TRTM * *

but one which has been with him all the time and which now comes home with final and deadly force. There is nothing left for him but to shoot himself—after he has first shot his dog, the fawning, "self-pitying" spaniel Flo, who is an image of his own weakness and vulnerability, and who is given a shortened, feminine version of his own name. He shoots himself through the heart, the organ which has tortured him in his loneliness and which he has never been able to lay bare to another person. His face, bearing the sign of his isolation from his fellows, he leaves untouched, and it is interesting to see that his motive is actually vanity—he does not want, when he sees the shattered skull of his dog, to look "like that". When he is dead the birthmark disappears : it "faded immediately, so that it was no more than a faint grey stain". The flawed, "unforgiveable" life is cleansed only in death.

It is apparent now that the epitaph, too openly self-pitying and also self-excusing, would be inappropriate. Clearly it is not women and drink that have killed John Flory, though they may have contributed to his downfall; it cannot even be said that one, unattainable woman is the cause of his death, since it is obviously not for love of Elizabeth that he shoots himself. Yet the last line, with its bitter consolation, that a life lived wrongly may serve as an instructive warning, might very well stand. For the novel, although dealing only with the events of a few months, from April to the onset of the summer rains, and saying scarcely anything about the past—though Flory in the critical scene described talks "on and on" about his past we are not told what he says—draws its strength from a convincing implication of what has gone before. It is highly successful in presenting itself as the last act only of a full-length, though unseen drama, both in the background of imperial history, the establishment and conduct of British rule in Burma with its evil consequences, and, much more important, in the untold story of Flory's life. The title, *Burmese Days*, which seems to announce a general reminiscence rather than a single episode, proves to be justified; we can accept it as the distillation of Orwell's whole Burmese experience—the five years from the age of nineteen that he spent with the Imperial Police—and also, when we look at some of the correspondences between the novel and his other writings, of a great deal more.

Comparison may be made in particular with the account of

his school-days, *Such, Such Were the Joys*, set down by Orwell
towards the end of his life and published only after his death.
This article, a prime source for Orwell's biography, has been
much commented upon by others, and will be referred to again.
The salient point to note with reference to *Burmese Days* is
perhaps the close equivalence of Flory's birthmark to Orwell's
conviction as a boy that he "smelt" and that he was "preter-
naturally ugly". The young boy Eric Blair, as Orwell remembered him—exiled to the painful and incomprehensible world
of prep school—thought of himself as "damned" exactly as
Flory is "damned" and in exactly the same way, by outer circumstances which were nevertheless felt to be his own fault : "I
had no money, I was weak, I was ugly, I was unpopular, I had
a chronic cough, I was cowardly, I smelt." Orwell goes on to
say, turning the screw of memory on himself, that the picture
"was not altogether fanciful", that he was in truth an "unattractive boy" and that the school "soon made me so, even if I had
not been so before". But he emphasises that this rooted belief
in his own unfitness did not need any basis in objective fact, but
was a prior assumption, a childish *post hoc, propter hoc* : "It
was notorious that disagreeable people smelt, and therefore
presumably I did so too." We can detect here the rationalisation
of a phobia which developed indeed into a lifelong obsession
with bad smells and dirt, evidenced in almost everything Orwell
wrote. But we may notice also the peculiar ambiguity, shared
by Flory's disfigurement, as simultaneously cause and effect of
isolation. The deep feeling of inadequacy and alienation, of
being *in the wrong*, finds in unpleasant body-smell or hideous
bodily mark reason and excuse, but one which in no way relieves
the subject of guilt; it simply gives it concrete outward form
which for that very reason is unforgiveable : it may be absurd
to want forgiveness for being ugly or smelly, but if one does want
it, it is also certainly quite hopeless.

This inexorable double bind condemns Flory to failure just as
his author was condemned in childhood and early manhood :

The conviction that it was *not possible* for me to be a success
went deep enough to influence my actions till far into adult
life. Until I was about thirty [Flory, we remember, is "about
thirty-five"] I always planned my life on the assumption not
only that any major undertaking was bound to fail, but that

I could only expect to live a few years longer. (*Such, Such Were the Joys.*)

If Flory is doomed to fail, what is success? It is represented in the novel by Verrall, the callous, rude, and brutal young lieutenant who makes an immediate conquest of Elizabeth and then deserts her. He is the same, in his devotion to sport and physical fitness, as the school football heroes who bullied and humiliated the small Eric Blair; he is also the same, with his "rabbit-like face" and pale, prominent blue eyes which, nevertheless no one can face without flinching, as all the "rabbit-faced" possessors of hereditary wealth and position whose effortless assumption of superiority is furiously resented by Orwell's later heroes and Orwell himself. Verrall, it is true, is not rich, but he is the younger son of a peer, before whom all the intensely class-conscious Europeans of Kyauktada are ready to fall down and worship, and much as Orwell scorns this crude snobbery, it is evident that something in Verrall commands admiration. Entirely selfish, devoted only to horses and clothes, diverting himself with women whom he presently drops, Verrall gets away with everything as by right : he quells the foulest-tempered member of the European Club with one look of his prawn-like eyes, he maltreats Indians and insults whites and always escapes retribution; he does not even have to beckon to Elizabeth for her to throw herself at his head. He is at first completely indifferent to her, till he notices that she is young and fresh-looking, when—she is already blushing with happiness in his presence—"the thought, 'A peach, by Christ!' " passes through his mind and he picks her up as easily as he spears tent pegs. He is not simply like, he is surely the same as Blake's angel, who, after the failure of a blundering mortal, ". . . without one word said/Had a peach from the tree,/And still as a maid/Enjoyed the lady".

He is, visibly, in a state of grace (he dances with Elizabeth, as he rides, with "matchless grace"; on the other hand "the disgraces that ought to have fallen on him never did"). Success, which includes bullying and insulting people, evading responsibility and betraying trust, is the sign of grace; without grace it is impossible to be successful.

In the India of the Empire, observed Orwell in *Burmese Days*, "you are not judged for what you do but for what you *are"*. He used exactly the same phrase later to describe the hierarchical ethos of his prep school, where "success was measured not by what you did but by what you *were*". When he came to write *Such, Such Were the Joys* he claimed to have outgrown such childish acceptance of false values imposed by others, but when we consider the case of "poor John Flory" we wonder how far this can have been true. Or perhaps rather we wonder whether the manifest falseness of the values, now the subject of irony, is not itself a disguise for something that is terribly real. Flory, we may say, is not really condemned for being disfigured by a birthmark, or for falling off his horse while the odious Verrall rides with angelic grace; but that he is condemned for something there is no doubt at all.

Flory is not just damned lonely, he is as lonely as the damned; but if loneliness is the central subject of *Burmese Days*, the special form of isolation which makes a man a Crusoe even in the midst of his fellows, such an apparently irremediable exile is explored to much greater depth in Orwell's next book, *A Clergyman's Daughter* (1935). As much as *Burmese Days*, though under a more complete, if superficial disguise, this novel uses personal experience for its material; the material itself, moreover, the series of events in the story, is seen far more intimately from the inside, with a view of personal thoughts and emotions going far beyond the preceding work in sharpness of perception and candour. In some ways, indeed, *A Clergyman's Daughter* exceeds in perceptiveness anything that Orwell wrote subsequently, and it is a curious comment on his view of himself that it was a book he came particularly to dislike.

Burmese Days may be considered as a quite straightforward novel, using autobiographical material. *A Clergyman's Daughter* is a more venturesome, even a consciously experimental work. It lacks the structural concentration of the earlier story, for although again covering quite a short period of time, it is almost picaresque in form, as the heroine, having left home in a fit of amnesia, suffers a winter of various misfortunes before returning to her starting point. In another way, however, it is highly concentrated, focusing exclusively on the experience of one person, the clergyman's daughter herself, and presenting her viewpoint alone. Why Orwell should have chosen a woman as vehicle for this move into what was to be an increasingly solipsist fiction is a question to be looked into presently.

A Clergyman's Daughter has no obvious literary models, though it may conjecturally owe something to a novel of the previous decade, *The Rector's Daughter*, by Flora Macdonald Mayor (1924), which contains some striking similarities of scene as well as of given situation, that of a young spinster acting as drudge or "unpaid curate" to an elderly father in holy orders. It has also been suggested that Orwell was influenced by D. H. Lawrence's tale *Daughters of the Vicar*, and was trying to do the same thing. In Lawrence's story there is an exchange between the main character, Louisa, and her mother—Louisa, rebelling against her sister's marriage of convenience, declares that she "would beg the streets barefoot first" and, sooner than accept the safety of such a marriage, would "rather be safe in the workhouse"—which might well have provoked Orwell to show what begging the streets and living in the workhouse were really like. The result, however, is so wholly divergent that any possible link seems to be only that of opposites : the fates of Orwell's Dorothy Hare and Lawrence's Louisa Lindley might be designed to show opposing views of human destiny.

While looking for immediate origins of *A Clergyman's Daughter* a passage may be noted in Orwell's first book, *Down and Out in Paris and London* (1933)—a large part of which describes experiences used again by Orwell in the novel—where several tramps, Orwell among them, are lying about on a village green and "a clergyman and his daughter came and stared silently at us for a while, as though we had been aquarium fishes, and then went away again". It seems possible that Orwell, who remarks elsewhere in this book, and not without resentment, the obvious revulsion from tramps and beggars shown by women, may have remembered something of a revengeful desire to put the rudely staring clergyman's daughter in his place and teach her what it is like. In the same paragraph of *Down and Out* he goes on to mention "the first woman tramp I had ever seen"; though she, "a fattish battered, very dirty woman of about 60", is as different as possible from his subsequent creation of Dorothy Hare.

Whatever may be thought of this—as a motive for the novel it does not seem likely to have been more than superficial— Orwell certainly did put a clergyman's daughter in his place,

very literally. Dorothy Hare, in the successive episodes of destitution and near-destitution which make up the greater part of the
story, repeats exactly, though selectively, Orwell-Blair's own
experiences, recorded in *Down and Out* and also in his diaries
and other writings in the early 'thirties. His experimental life "on
the toby", his hop-picking expedition, and, later, the period of
his life when he was earning a meagre living as teacher in a
small suburban school, are all reproduced in the novel, often
described in terms identical with those used in his factual
accounts of the same experiences. There is the apparent difference, of course, that most of these experiences were undergone
by him voluntarily, in a deliberate spirit of experiment; and it
may be remembered, lest it should be supposed that these
adventures in down-and-out-dom were more or less fortuitous,
that their origin went back to Eric Blair's schooldays. A letter
of 1920, when he was just eighteen and still at Eton, recounts an
incident of sleeping rough for a single night which the boy
significantly described as "my *first* adventure as an amateur
tramp" (my italics) : even at that age, evidently, the idea of
subjecting himself to this particular kind of hardship and solitude was not new to him. But if Blair was an "amateur" tramp,
consciously trying it out, and Dorothy Hare becomes one because
she cannot help it, it is a distinction rather than a difference.

The details of Blair's tramp-expeditions—the way that he
acquired old and filthy clothes, privately put on his disguise, and
so forth—are still only sketchily known, and mostly from his own
record in the *Journals* and elsewhere. But clearly they were
repeated many times between 1927 and 1932, and certainly they
were undertaken under a powerful compulsion : the simple
fact of their repetition argues a stronger motive than experimental curiosity. There were real needs that drove him to his
tramp-adventures and also, perhaps, real satisfactions to be
found. In the same way the point that now comes to be considered, why he should present these adventures, when he came
to turn them into fiction, in the person of a young woman, is
hardly to be explained as mere literary experiment.

Some such reasons as those indicated might account for the
introduction of a woman as a secondary character in the novel,
but they are quite inadequate to explain the position of Dorothy
Hare as its central personage, indeed virtually its sole conscious
being. Dorothy's thoughts and feelings are recounted from

within, indeed they form the novel's whole subject-matter :
everyone else is seen only from without, as creatures with exterior
being only and even that, it may be thought, of the most transient and insubstantial kind. The explanation of this oddity, that
in his second work of fiction, and without abandoning the autobiographical material used elsewhere, Orwell should choose to
represent a completely subjective view of this material through
a woman, must go further than the coincidences and possible
associations already touched on.

It will not be found, indeed, on the assumption that Orwell's
motives as author were altogether conscious and calculating,
any more than were Blair's in seeking out first-hand experience
of being down and out. The needs and motives that can be
guessed at lay deeper, and perhaps they were of the same kind
in both cases.

Loneliness and isolation from others were Flory's fate in
Burmese Days; loneliness, from the beginning of her story, is
Dorothy Hare's lot; loneliness, it can be inferred, was Orwell-
Blair's continuing experience, not only while he was in Burma
and not unexpectedly cut off from congenial company, but
after his return to life in lodgings and odd jobs in Paris and
later in Britain. That this life was deliberately chosen makes no
difference : the self-isolation of one who shuts *himself* away is
not therefore less desolating. For Eric Blair the plunge into the
"underworld" of the spike and the high toby was among other
things a move into companionship, undertaken with great
apprehension but bringing an immediate, if limited, reward. In
the many different places in which Orwell described his
"descent"—and it is always thought of in that way, as a plunge
downwards—the fact that it brought him into some degree,
however fleeting, of warm human contact is always emphasised.
Perhaps the most striking account is the description, in the
directly personal part of *The Road to Wigan Pier*, in which the
first venture into a common lodging house basement, made in
great trepidation, expecting either violence or rejection or both,
ends in acceptance : a "hefty" young stevedore, whose drunken
approach is at first taken as threatening, embraces Orwell and
invites him to have a cup of tea; which, when taken, "was a
kind of baptism".

In the same way Dorothy Hare, falling among thieves and
beggars who accept her unquestioningly and share their food

with her (after relieving her of her last vestige of moneyed independence, the half-crown she finds in her pocket), gains
warmth and companionship which last all the time she is "on
the bum". Such human contact is fleeting, it cannot be said to
go very deep in either case, and it certainly does not touch the
underlying causes of isolation, of the author or his fiction, but
it is real so far as it goes, and felt to be so. And, we may surmise,
it is because of the *feeling* to which Orwell's descriptions bear
witness, in the passage from *The Road to Wigan Pier* and many
other places, that when he came to realise these experiences in
fiction he chose to do so in the person of a woman. Dorothy,
we may say, *is* Orwell: almost everything that happens to her
happened to Eric Blair and was recorded by him under his
pseudonym in other places as factual reminiscence; but, cru-
cially, she is, as a woman, just that aspect of Orwell-Blair as a
feeling and suffering being that was most difficult for him to
acknowledge. For Eric Blair, boy and man, tenderness and all
"soft" feeling lay under a taboo, and George Orwell the writer
set down in many places his stern condemnation of "self-pity"
and "softness" ("softness is repulsive", he said in *Wigan Pier*).
A man ought to be hard, clean, and strong like Verrall—for
however odiously Verrall is made to behave, his hardness and
physical self-denial, living "almost as ascetically as a monk", are
a part of his grace, against Flory's disgrace. There is something
of a woman in Flory: his name, at least, is soft and flowery and
his stout, self-indulgent spaniel bitch completes the association
with her pet-name Flo, as already indicated. But this womanish-
ness is fiercely repudiated and in the end actually destroyed. If
it is to reappear it must hide itself in another way. Dorothy,
apparently the most complete disguise Orwell adopted in fiction
—as female impersonation is generally assumed to be the most
effective of all incognitos—in fact allowed him to display, at
least in part, those very feelings that were altogether disowned.

Other commentators have found here evidence for latent
homosexuality in Orwell, and certainly many indications can
be picked up by anyone following this particular trail. The at
times violent repudiation of male homosexuality—when, especially in the last ten years of his life, "pansy" and "nancy-boy"
were among Orwell's favourite words of abuse, generally
applied to pacifists and anti-war campaigners of the Left—may
itself be taken as a sign of temptation furiously warded off. (We

may also remember that "Nancy", being a "nigger's Nancy Boy", is one of the sneers levelled at Flory by the pathologically racialist Ellis.) Earlier and more explicit references to homosexual practices, among tramps and others, are indeed rather more tolerant; but make it equally clear that whatever such tendencies were present in Orwell, he would not, or could not acknowledge them. (A particular example may be found in *Down and Out,* where Orwell recorded how, spending a night in the "spike" in a cell with another man, he found his companion making some homosexual attempts on him—"a nasty experience in a locked, pitch-dark cell". The account goes on to say, however, that Orwell, being stronger than the other man, "a feeble creature", could "manage him easily", and the abortive "attempt" appears to have ended in a quite amicable conversation : "For the rest of the night we stayed awake, smoking and talking", while the man told the story of his life. This does not really sound like the over-emphatic rejection of a hidden invert.)

Granted, however, that hostile remarks about women, preoccupation with bad smells and dung, occasional references to intense rapport with other men, and other such pointers may be found scattered throughout Orwell's writings, the argument that therefore he suffered from a repressed homosexuality, and therefore the sense of being an outcast, seems to me mistaken, or rather back to front. Undoubtedly Orwell felt himself an outcast, not so much perhaps from society as, much more comprehensively, from real life. Undoubtedly a part of this conviction of exile expressed itself in disparagement of women, the embodiments of gross materiality, the flesh and blood which "hard", "ascetic" man fears, envies, longs for, and in defence despises. In Orwell all these reactions can be seen; if he sometimes thinks of women as "stupid", "soft", even "no use" (because, as he is reported as saying, "they can't play games"), he has an equal tendency to be drawn by and even to revere the most obvious physical signs of femininity, especially the maternal feminine, stoutness, "broad hips", "mare-like buttocks". But it was the exile itself, especially the exile from emotional life, from which these symptoms flowed; and this above all applies to the exile from feeling. "

Orwell's detachment was neither a pose nor anything to find satisfaction in (however effective it may have been as defence against pain) but a source of continual disquiet and even itself

a cause of agony. A poem published in 1934, and written presumably at the time he was working on *A Clergyman's
Daughter*, expresses the sense of alienation with great poignancy.
The poem is a key to much of his development, and like certain
dreams, can be taken as a prevision of themes which only emerged
clearly much later; but even at the time there is no mistaking
the desperate tone of the speaker who stands between "warring
worlds" and, unable to choose, declares his "mortal sickness;
how I give/My heart to weak and stuffless ghosts/And with the
living cannot live".

Ghosts have no bodies; they are cut off from the means of
feeling, though not from the longing for it; it is entirely typical
of a man who feels himself to be ghostly, or "dead", that he
should in fantasy try to find a way back to reality and life in a
woman's body, one which is so to speak so much more bodily
than a man's. There is an interesting indication of a passing
surrender to this fantasy in a note by Orwell, writing his weekly
"As I Please" column in *Tribune* in 1944, in which he describes
having answered an advertisement "many years ago" for a cure
for obesity. Very curiously it does not seem to have occurred to
him that such advertisements are practically all addressed to
women, and so he was "surprised" when the advertiser assumed
he was one. Nevertheless he kept up the pretence "for a long
time", while the advertiser sent a succession of letters urging the
supposed fat woman to make a personal visit. This was done
for "fun" and to deceive in turn a fraudulent advertiser. (Orwell
even speculated facetiously that such advertisers, who also
turned out to be men, were "actually engaged in shipping con-
signments of fat women to the harems of Istanbul".) Perhaps a
half-jocular indulgence in the same kind of fantasy was involved
when (as Orwell told a friend in a letter of 1948) he used, in his
riding days to think of adopting a woman's seat : "I sometimes
secretly thought I'd like to try a sidesaddle, because I believe it's
almost impossible to fall off." Being a woman offers a kind of
security; if Flory had ridden sidesaddle he wouldn't have come
his humiliating cropper.

Such impersonations and secret daydreams were, perhaps,
lighthearted enough. The entry into a woman's body in the
person of Dorothy Hare, however, was very far from being a
joke, or undertaken in a spirit of mischief; nor did it afford
security of any kind. Dorothy, exploited, lonely, suffering,

represents above all the passivity of women (at any rate in a man's eyes) and their vulnerability. Dorothy is in no way armoured against fate; she is kicked around, put upon, grossly abused by people and circumstances; in every situation she is the predestined victim. Like Orwell she shuns self-pity, absurdly exhorting herself "come on Dorothy, no slacking", "no funking", but in her misfortunes she certainly excites compassion. Through her Orwell was able to express the helplessness and longing for consolation and comfort that he dared not allow, or despised in himself. He made her naive, innocent, trusting, indeed child-like : "strangers commonly took her to be several years younger than her real age . . . because of the expression of almost childish earnestness in her eyes." Again, it may be supposed that he used her to enter a region of trust and dependence which his knowing, desperately self-sufficient masculine self was excluded from.

He also made her entirely virginal, and the novel has been criticised on the ground that Dorothy, although a woman, is in practice virtually sexless. Orwell explains at some length how she has always recoiled from any kind of sexuality, could not bear the embraces of men, rejecting the very thought of sexual relations as "all that", something she will not even name. This is hardly enough, perhaps, to explain Dorothy's inviolability when she finds herself on the road as a tramp—indeed actually "on the streets"—and, apart from a single attempt, not repeated, immune from molestation by men. It is clear, indeed, that Orwell himself decided to eschew "all that", and its absence is so conspicuous—emphasised by the very words, "tramp", "clergyman's daughter", slang terms for prostitute in American and English—in a situation in which, in fact, most of the people Dorothy encounters assume she is a street-walker, that one must assume it to have been deliberate. But though the verisimilitude of the story may be affected thereby—in realistic terms it is scarcely credible—it seems pointless to complain of it, since Orwell's purposes simply did not encompass sexual experience."

Much as he admired Lawrence's story, *The Daughters of the Vicar*, and may, as already suggested, have taken it as a starting point, he invented and employed his clergyman's daughter for quite other ends than Lawrence's brilliantly realist illustration of contrasting sexual starvation and fulfilment in the Lindley sisters. Of the other man's story he surmised that "probably

Lawrence had watched, somewhere or other, the underfed, downtrodden, organ-playing daughter of a clergyman wearing out her youth, and had a sudden vision of her escaping to the warmer world of the working class, where husbands are plentiful". Whether or not that is a reasonable conjecture about Lawrence (with the interesting comment that, although a good subject for a short story "when drawn out to novel length [in *Lady Chatterley's Lover*] it raises difficulties to which Lawrence was unequal") it states clearly, though without mentioning its existence, the different course taken by his own novel. For Dorothy, although she takes flight from a stultifying existence, does not escape from anything; she cannot even be said to escape from her own sexuality, although her state of fugue is apparently precipitated by a man's unwelcome advances, for truly she has not any to escape from. In her author's view at least, far from escaping to a "warmer world", she moves only from the comfort of illusion to the reality of desolation.

The subject of *A Clergyman's Daughter* is loss of faith, and as such it is an impressive piece of work, showing all of Orwell's capacity, on which he grimly prided himself, for "facing unpleasant facts". For however inadequate may be thought the account in the book of the Christianity by which Dorothy lives at the begining of the story—and part of the point, of course, is precisely the inadequacy of formal, decaying Anglican Christianity—there is no question about its reality for her; nor about the effect of its loss.

Dorothy's religion, even at the beginning, is scarcely orthodox, apart from the observances which she dutifully performs, but it holds meaning for her beyond either these outward rituals or the private and compulsive ones, "punishing" herself masochistically for supposed backslidings which she has invented for herself.

Attending Holy Communion at the outset of the story she runs into a perennial "difficulty", as we are told—and which we know was characteristic of Orwell himself—of extreme disgust at the thought of sharing the cup with an old and, as she described, physically repulsive communicant. She actually finds herself praying that she won't have to take the chalice after this Miss Mayfill, whose mouth, "large, loose and wet", was "not the kind you would like to see drinking out of your cup". Orwell dwells excessively on this disgust, and we remember that it was one he habitually experienced himself, to the point of assuming that it was natural and hardly needing excuse. We may even conjecture that the particular circumstances were a matter of personal experience, since at this time, working in a school, he was going to church regularly, and noted an old woman in the congregation, described (in a letter) in exactly the same terms as "Miss Mayfill". He even expressed some scruples at the time about taking communion as an unbeliever.

But though in his letter he treats the whole business jocularly, as befits an emancipated young man who has seen through all the mumbo-jumbo, in his imaginative reliving of it through Dorothy he does not. She, shrinking from contact with the moribund old woman with her smell of "mothballs and gin", finds herself quite unable to pray : "her lips moved, but there was neither heart nor meaning in her prayers . . . A deadly blankness had descended on her mind. It seemed to her that actually she *could* not pray. She struggled, collected her thoughts, uttered mechanically the opening phrases of a prayer; but they were useless, meaningless, nothing but the dead shells of words." She feels unable therefore to take the sacrament, but is saved by an instantaneous vision of natural beauty. It is worth quoting the passage in full :

Then it happened that she glanced sidelong, through the open south door. A momentary spear of sunlight had pierced the clouds. It struck downwards through the leaves of the limes, and a spray of leaves in the doorway gleamed with a transient, matchless green, greener than jade or emerald or Atlantic waters. It was as though some jewel of unimaginable splendour had flashed for an instant, filling the doorway with green light, and then faded. A flood of joy ran through Dorothy's heart. The flash of living colour had brought back to her, by a process deeper than reason, her peace of mind, her love of God, her power of worship. Somehow, because of the greenness of the leaves, it was again possible to pray. O all ye green things upon the earth, praise ye the Lord ! She began to pray ardently, joyfully, thankfully. The wafer melted upon her tongue. She took the chalice from her father, and tasted without repulsion, even with an added joy in this small act of self-abasement, the wet imprint of Miss Mayfill's lips on its silver rim.

A little later Dorothy experiences a similar emotion, once again
after overcoming her disgusted shrinking from physical human
contact—and once again, with an infirm old woman, Mrs
Pither, whom she has visited in the course of carrying out her
father's neglected pastoral duties. Against her strong inclina-
tion she has forced herself to enter Mrs Pither's depressing,
though pious, home and to treat with ointment the old woman's
"large, grey-veined, flaccid legs". The "self-abasement" this time
gives her no joy, indeed it is relief at leaving Mrs Pither's house
that chiefly lifts up her heart afterwards; nevertheless, in her
happiness, she is taken up by the beauty of the morning and,
presently, transported in a physical ecstacy. She kneels in the
hedgerow, drinking in the scent of flowers and herbage :

> Her heart swelled with sudden joy. It was that mystical joy
> in the beauty of the earth and the very nature of things that
> she recognised, perhaps mistakenly, as the love of God. As
> she knelt there in the heat, the sweet odour and the drowsy
> hum of insects, it seemed to her that she could hear the mighty
> anthem of praise that the earth and all created things send
> up everlastingly to their maker. All vegetation, leaves, flowers,
> grass, shining, vibrating, crying out in their joy. Larks also
> chanting, choirs of larks invisible, dripping music from the sky.
> All the riches of summer, the warmth of the earth, the song
> of birds, the fume of cows, the droning of countless bees,
> mingling and ascending like the smoke of ever-burning altars.
> Therefore with Angels and Archangels ! She began to pray,
> and for a moment she prayed ardently, blissfully, forgetting
> herself in the joy of her worship. Then, less than a minute
> later, she discovered that she was kissing the frond of fennel
> that was still against her face.

The discovery pulls her up short : her father has forbidden
"Nature-worship" and behind his prohibition may be guessed a
half-recognition on Dorothy's part that kissing the fronds of
fennel, likened to "the tails of sea-green horses", is linked with
"all that", the taboo-territory of sexuality. We may indeed
wonder why Dorothy's child-like joy in divine creation should
be thought of as "perhaps *mistakenly*" the love of God. It is
also possible to criticise both these passages on the theological
grounds that Dorothy's love and joy are highly selective : she

doesn't include human beings, and though she surmounts her revulsion from the two chosen specimens of humanity, Miss Mayfill and Mrs Pither, she can hardly be said to be in charity with them; the description of their infirmities as she sees them, with disgust but entirely without compassion, is somewhat revolting in itself. But if something of Dorothy's inadequacies is revealed here, so also is the sincerity and intensity of her religious feelings; there is no mistake about that. Especially in the first passage the transforming effect of a perception of natural beauty is shown with complete conviction. One is reminded of the Ancient Mariner's discovery, when he blesses the water-snakes unaware, that "the self-same moment I could pray"; it seems likely that Orwell, too, had a memory of the same story of a lonely soul rescued by love of living beauty, since one or two phrases, the reference to Atlantic waters and the leaves "greener than emerald", certainly echo the poem.

It is difficult to think that the feeling so vividly expressed here was unknown to Orwell; it seems reasonable rather to assume that, just as the recoil from human bodies was undoubtedly his, with the same obsessed dwelling on mortality and decay, so the joy in other aspects of creation, and therefore the ability to think of them as the creation, living things made by a living God, was known to him also. Sensual life, from which both he and Dorothy shrank, might still catch them unawares with a revelation of reality beyond or within sense, even the treacherous, sexually-linked sense of smell, conveying, through the sweet dizzying odour of fennel, dreams of spice-islands of love. The world Dorothy momentarily regains touch with is a divine world, whatever her father and the conventional, institutional Church may say. Brought up in that church, Orwell was now in full, though possibly uneasy rebellion against it, as the sometimes wild caricature of Anglican fustiness indicates. By the time he was writing *A Clergyman's Daughter* he had, on the evidence of his letters, abandoned any religious belief and had adopted the attitude of conscious and mocking sceptic; but, if only in memory, he was able through Dorothy to say with intense conviction what in one aspect at least it was like. In the same way and with the same conviction he could describe its loss.

For Dorothy the "loss of faith" is devastating and without compensation; there is no question that the mainspring of her

life is removed, although realisation of it is gradual. When she
suffers her episode of amnesia and leaves her tyrannical old
father's home (the "house of faith", cold, comfortless, and nearly
bankrupt, bitterly lampooned) she leaves her formal beliefs
behind too; it is not an emancipation, but neither, to begin
with, is it felt as a deprivation. Only later when, her memory
restored and having made an unsuccessful attempt to get in
touch with her indifferent and absent father, she remembers
how prayer, which "had been the very source and centre of
her life", is so no longer, does she begin to realise what has
happened to her. Even then it is at first no more than a detached
self-observation, "recorded . . . briefly, almost casually, as though
it had been something seen in passing—a flower in the ditch
or a bird crossing the road—something noticed and then dismissed." (It is faith itself here which is like a flower or a bird,
and neither is viewed with the intensity of vision Dorothy was
once capable of; the whole world is becoming "casual". Later
again, when she is teaching in the dreadful little school run by
Mrs Creevy, and attending church in obedience to the latter's
richly cynical requirements—church being a good place wherein
to catch prospective parents—she reflects on the fact that the
observances have become entirely empty for her : she "could
go through them, and utter all the responses at the right time,
in a state of the completest abstraction."

There was never a moment when the power of worship
returned to her. Indeed, the whole concept of worship was
meaningless to her now; her faith had vanished, utterly and
irrevocably. It is a mysterious thing, the loss of faith—as
mysterious as faith itself. Like faith, it is ultimately not rooted
in logic; it is a change in the climate of the mind.

She continues to value her church attendance as providing
"blessed intervals of peace" in her harassed and wretched
existence as Mrs Creevy's teacher-drudge; also because she perceives that "in all that happens in church, however absurd and
cowardly its supposed purpose may be, there is something—
it is hard to define, but something of decency, of spiritual comeliness—that is not easily found in the world outside. It seemed
to her that even though you no longer believe, it is better to go
to Church than not; better to follow in the ancient ways, than

to drift in rootless freedom." What precisely is "cowardly" on
the one hand and "comely" on the other remains unexplained,
but the attitude is recognisable; perhaps not very different from
that of Orwell himself, going to church with his school charges
in the suburban isolation of uttermost Middlesex and finding
in the local curate, "a good fellow", his only friend. Dorothy
is for the time being at slack water : she no longer prays with
meaning, and "knows" that she will never do so again; she
attends church as a habit which has acquired moral value simply
because it is habitual. "Just this much remained to her of the
faith that had once, like the bones of a living frame, held all
her life together."

A less searching writer, less determined to face "unpleasant
facts", might have left it there, where many have left the question of religious belief and observance, as socially and psycho-
logically useful, a false skeleton which nevertheless helps to keep
society going, an expression and enhancement of social cohesion.
Orwell did not; and perhaps it can be said that he understood
the inadequacy of such a definition and defence of religion as
only one can who has at one time lived in faith and known it
as entirely different. Dorothy proceeds to this radical understanding of her loss by gradual degrees; only after she has
returned to her father's house and picked up again the threads
of unmeaning parish routine—perfectly meaningful, however,
as "social cement"—that, being "home", she finds it brought
home to her.

She has already conversed on the subject with Mr Warburton,
the cheerful, eupeptic, promiscuous and kindly atheist, who
saves her, materially speaking, from her desperate state (just
given the sack by Mrs Creevy), helps her along with good
advice, and even—an act which in a confirmed philanderer we
are surely meant to see as an uncommon sacrifice on his part—
offers to marry her. Mr Warburton seems in most ways the
most favourably presented character in the book, worthy of
liking and admiration, moreover, in what might be thought of
as Orwell's own terms : friendly, outgoing, hardheaded and
warm-hearted, ready with practical assistance when needed;
behaving, despite his irrepressible impulse to make a pass at
any woman within reach, with much of the "fundamental
decency" which Orwell was already falling back on, without
definition, as the basis of all real virtue. He is, furthermore,

somebody—large, stout, healthy and well-balanced—who is conspicuously on good terms with life, able to live without faith in God and to get along very well. Yet we cannot think of him as anything but trivial; and his attitude to Dorothy's lapse from religious belief—on which, naturally, he congratulates her— shows a complete want of understanding. That is, indeed, only to be expected, since what Dorothy tries to explain to him of her faith and its disappearance can only be understood from within.

He tells her, no doubt accurately, what sort of life awaits her if she will not marry and chooses instead to return as her father's "unsalaried curate". She will carry on doing "those deadly little jobs that are shoved off on to lonely women" until from super-annuated schoolgirl she becomes undisguised old maid, one of the unhappy band of spinsters who "wither up like aspidistras in back-parlour windows". Later she reflects on his warning, which has remained at the back of her mind "like some in-exorcisable ghost", and which she recognises in outward terms to be true. She does not, however, think in the outward terms that are sufficient for Mr Warburton :

But it didn't matter, it didn't matter ! That was the thing you could never drive into the heads of the Mr Warburtons of this world, not if you talked to them for a thousand years; that mere outward things like poverty and drudgery, and even loneliness, don't matter in themselves. It is the things that happen in your heart that matter. For just a moment— an evil moment—while Mr Warburton was talking to her on the train, she had known the fear of poverty. But she had mastered it; it was not a thing worth worrying about. It was not because of *that* that she had got to stiffen her courage and remake the whole structure of her mind.

No, it was something far more fundamental; it was the deadly emptiness that she had discovered at the heart of things. She thought of how a year ago she had sat in this chair, with these scissors in her hand, doing precisely what she was doing now; and yet it was as though then and now she had been two different beings. Where had she gone, that well-meaning, ridiculous girl who had prayed ecstatically in summer-scented fields and pricked her arm as a punish-ment for sacrilegious thoughts? And where is any of ourselves of even a year ago? And yet after all—and here lay the trouble—she *was* the same girl. Beliefs change, thoughts change, but there is some inner part of the soul that does not change. Faith vanishes but the need for faith remains the same as before.

So she continues to meditate, in deepening despair :

Her mind struggled with the problem, while perceiving that there is no solution. There was, she saw clearly, no possible substitute for faith; no pagan acceptance of life as sufficient to itself, no pantheistic cheer-up stuff, no pseudo-religion of "progress" with visions of glittering Utopias and ant-heaps of steel and concrete. It was all or nothing. Either life on earth is a preparation for something greater and more lasting, or it is meaningless, dark and dreadful.

Dorothy is rescued, at least for the time being, by the very task she is engaged in, a conspicuously absurd one—the preparation for some footling church pageant to raise another small sum of money for that crumbling institution—even by the sort of everyday standards that do not show all human tasks to be absurd. She is reminded by the stench of the boiling glue-pot, and this horrible smell, specifically described as "evil", is represented as the answer to her mechanically repeated prayer, Lord I believe, help thou my unbelief. There is a kind of symmetry in the beginning and end of the novel, which opens with another hostile summons to the uncongenial day's work, when "the alarm clock on the chest of drawers exploded like a horrid little bomb of bell metal", and ends with the even nastier admonition of the glue-pot. Thus, unpleasantly, Dorothy is forced to face "unpleasant facts", and there is a symbolic progress from the first alarm-call to the cold and strenuous, but still devotional morning, and the last, the vile stink of boiled down hoof and horn, the smell of mortality, rubbing Dorothy's nose in a future of unending labour and vexation which she has discovered to be entirely without purpose. It is nevertheless said to be the answer to her need :

The smell of glue was the answer to her prayer. She did not

know this. She did not reflect, consciously, that the solution to her difficulty lay in accepting the fact that there was no solution; that if one gets on with the job that lies to hand, the ultimate purpose of the job fades into insignificance; that faith and no faith are very much the same provided that one is doing what is customary, useful, and acceptable. She could not formulate these thoughts as yet, she could only live them. Much later, perhaps, she would formulate them and draw comfort from them.

It will be late indeed, we feel, before anything reasonably described as comfort can be drawn from this bleak and question-begging "formula". We may suppose, in fact, that the only prop it may eventually offer is the bitter self-esteem of the man who piqued himself on facing the worst and came to think that the worst was all there was to know. In the meantime, however, Dorothy is left alone, with no support or hope, in limbo, simply shelving the question :

The problem of faith and no faith had vanished utterly from her mind. It was beginning to get dark, but, too busy to stop and light the lamp, she worked on, pasting strip after strip of paper in place, with absorbed, with pious concentration, in the penetrating smell of the glue-pot.

The unsatisfactoriness and inadequacy of this end to the novel are obvious, and yet it is acceptable as being true, that is to say as a true reflection of feeling and experience. Once again we may say that Dorothy was the vehicle for an open expression of emotions Orwell could not directly acknowledge in his own person. As has already been pointed out, his outward experience was hers, in close parallel : the knowledge of poverty and destitution—albeit in his case "voluntary"—the schoolteaching, including even the preparation of clothes and properties for a school production. (Letters of this time tell of "suffering untold agonies with glue, brown paper etc.") He goes to church—it is there that he sees the prototype of Miss Mayfill, brutally described in a letter as "a moribund hag who stinks of moth-balls and gin, and has to be more or less carried to and from the altar at communion". He reads the *Church Times* "regularly" ("I do so like to see that there is life in the old dog yet

—I mean in the poor old C of E"), and is also "reading a book called *Belief in God,* by Bishop Gore", who happens, he remarks, to have confirmed him as a boy. He begins to think of taking communion "because my curate friend is bound to think it funny if I always go to Church but never communicate" and, as noted above, has some scruples : "It seems rather mean to go to HC when one doesn't believe, but I have passed myself off for pious and there is nothing for it but to keep up the pretence."

Are these remarks merely the cynical commentary of a man engaged in conscious pretence, a writer putting on disguise in order to get "copy"? Merely to put the question like that is to misunderstand the meaning for Orwell (and, perhaps, of any creative writer who uses such devices) of his self-projections. Even by his own, clearly insufficient explanation, his tramp and beggar-impersonations, although in one sense deliberate masquerades involving changes of clothing and preparation of a cover-story, answered a profound need in himself and were guided by "irrational" feelings (his own word). In just the same way his entry into the person of the clergyman's daughter answered a need, and one that was probably much more difficult for him consciously to admit to than the hope of assuaging his social "guilt" by joining "the lowest of the low". The lightness and schoolboy jocularity with which he described his masquerade of piety doubtless reflected what had by then become a settled habit of mind, and one that was necessary to him; the underlying feeling was only allowed to emerge in fiction.

What Orwell did confess to in these letters was an ordinary loneliness, and indeed there is something exceedingly pathetic in the glimpse here of the awkward, isolated young man, marooned in his dreary suburb ("one of the most godforsaken places I have ever struck") and appealing, with increasing urgency, for companionship and love. His letters to Eleanor Jaques, in which most of these remarks occur, are virtually love-letters, and though at the present stage of Orwell biography no more is recorded of this relationship (Miss Jaques soon after married another of Orwell's acquaintances, Dennis Collings, and went to live abroad, depriving him as he said "of two friends at one stroke") it clearly must have meant a great deal to him. The letters express strong affection (being signed "with love", "with all my love") and, repeatedly, the hope of meeting and talking. They do not voice the desperation with which at a critical point Dorothy writes to her father, receiving no reply; nor quite that of Flory when, having as he realises lost Elizabeth, he finds "everything . . . deadly and meaningless", using exactly the same terms as those that describe Dorothy's loss of faith. In his outer situation at least Orwell was not so wholly abandoned and friendless as she. But that is the point: it was through her that he could give utterance to feelings of utter loss and dereliction that he could not acknowledge in his own person; through her he made the connections between absence of friends and general outward isolation and the inner emptiness and darkness of the loss of God. Through her he directly associated abandonment by a cold, selfish, remote parent, the Rector himself—who never bothers to find out what has happened to her and never answers her letters—and the institutional religion of the decaying church, of no help whatsoever : father at home in Knype Hill and father in heaven are equally distant and unresponsive.

With Dorothy's sense of being a castaway may be compared the attitude of a very different person, presented in *Down and Out* as one whom Orwell actually met, but sharing many attributes with what may be called his own non-Dorothy side, the self-sufficient sceptic and cynic who cares for nobody and cares not that nobody cares for him. This is the "screever" or pavement artist of whom a lengthy account is given at the end of the book : a cripple, thanks to a bad accident, and a man extravagantly unlucky in his life—starting off as the son of a bankrupt, losing his fiancée by an accident and soon after suffering his own crippling fall, eventually completely destitute save for his beggar's rags, his drawing materials, and "a few books"—but ferociously independent and unbeaten. He is "an embittered atheist (the sort of atheist who does not so much disbelieve in God as personally dislike Him)", and is said to take "a sort of pleasure in thinking that human affairs would never improve"; but he feels himself to be free "inside", and declares that while that is the case his beggardom is of no importance. With no obligation either to those who throw him their pennies or to the God who has allowed all his misfortunes to happen, he has "neither fear, nor regret, nor shame, nor self-pity."

"If you've got any education, it doesn't matter to you if
you're on the road for the rest of your life ... You just
got to say to yourself, 'I'm a free man in *here*' "—he tapped
his forehead—"and you're all right."

The contrast between Dorothy, who knows that, given real
religious belief, poverty and drudgery "don't matter", and Bozo
the screever who has found, so it appears, the same independence
of circumstances through disbelief, is very striking; and one
cannot help suspecting that in their opposed prescriptions for
facing and enduring the worst that fate can do they represent
different sides of a debate within Orwell's mind. The screever,
whose past experience tallies at many points with Orwell's
(service in India, life in Paris, casual jobs in London), whose
favourite reading (Shakespeare and *Gulliver's Travels*) is the
same as Orwell's, and some of whose phraseology—notably his
contempt for other, softer beggars as "rabbits"—is Orwell's,
must either, we feel, be a projection of Orwell's own ideas or
else the model he took them from. If in Dorothy he looked back
to the wish for a more secure past, Bozo looks forward to the
future, when Orwell's attitudes had hardened and to be a "free
man" inside one's own skull was to have put on the only reliable
armour against the unpleasant facts of existence. It is not surprising that Orwell, who felt the same about himself, as one
who could not fit comfortably into any niche of life, should sum
up the screever as "a very exceptional man".

At this time the different attitudes co-existed, or possibly
alternated. A poem of this period (published in March 1933
and written perhaps the previous autumn, or in recollection of
it) condenses much of the feeling embodied in *A Clergyman's
Daughter* about the meaninglessness of life that ends in death :

I know, not as in barren thought,
But wordlessly, as the bones know,
What quenching of my brain, what numbness,
Wait in the dark grave where I go.

And I see the people thronging the street,
The death-marked people, they and I
Goalless, rootless, like leaves drifting,
Blind to the earth and to the sky;

Nothing believing, nothing loving,
Not in joy nor in pain, not heeding the stream
Of precious life that flows within us,
But fighting, toiling as in a dream . . .

The poem calls, in Scriptural phrase, on "you who pass" to
remember the inevitability of death, "The crushing stroke, the
dark beyond", and goes on to offer the desperate, not to say
incoherent consolation :

And let us now, as men condemned,
In peace and thrift of time stand still
To learn our world while yet we may,
And shape our souls, however ill;

And we will live, hand, eye and brain,
Piously, outwardly, ever-aware,
Till all our hours burn clear and brave
Like candle-flames in windless air;

So shall we in the rout of life
Some thought, some faith, some meaning save,
And speak it once before we go
In silence to the silent grave.

The muddle of the last stanzas, the remarkable incongruity of
the image suggested by the candle-flame burning in stillness and
peace with the clutching at straws in "outward" awareness,
repeats very closely the "formula" in which at the end Dorothy
finds a desperate reason for carrying on. There is a striking
confusion here, but it is a real one, that's to say it arises, surely,
not simply from carelessness but from motives contradictory at
a deep level, and expressed with painful, even awkward
sincerity.

Nobody is likely to claim it as a good poem; many would
probably deny that *A Clergyman's Daughter* is a good novel.
But the virtue of both lies in part, though paradoxically, in their
very inadequacy, the nakedness with which they expose unresolved fears, unacknowledged longings, problems left standing and
no more than half-understood. Orwell himself was soon expressing strong dislike of the novel; while he was still writing it he said
it made him "spew", and when he had only just finished it and

was sending it to his agent he was, he said, "afraid I have made a muck of it", describing it as "very disconnected as a whole and rather unreal." Later he called it "a bollox", though claiming that he made some "useful experiments" in it : these, perhaps, were just in loosening the bonds of "realism" and allowing the imaginative truth to emerge.

"I did not intend it to be so realistic as people seem to think it is" : the departure from "realism" and the opening of his mind to imaginative possibilities was in part, evidently, deliberate. At one point—the section dealing with Dorothy's night in Trafalgar Square with other down-and-outs—Orwell is clearly embarking on experiment, a conscious attempt to invite the fantasia of the unconscious. It is, indeed, a highly effective piece of nightmare, a vivid descent into a burlesque Hell which is at once successfully comic, as the frozen sleepers-out pile on top of one another in search of warmth, and genuinely horrific, as the gross unfrocked clergyman Mr Tallboys performs his Black Mass and at its climax, when blood runs out of the torn Host, "monstrous shapes of Demons and Archdemons are dimly visible" and "something, beak or claw" closes upon Dorothy's shoulder. The combination of grotesque caricature and physical horror is, one may say, a mark of authenticity, as the Hell-gates and monsters of medieval demonology, the expressions of vivid belief, also have about them something of parody.

The most convincingly hellish aspect of the scene is the double impression of frightful cold and enforced physical intimacy as the street-sleepers try to get a little animal warmth by putting their arms around each other, the women sitting on the men's knees. The jokes and good humour with which this is done do not at all mitigate the effect, at least for Dorothy, through whom the apparently endless miseries of the night are realised : "In this state, enormous ages seem to pass. One sinks into complex, troubling dreams which leave one conscious of one's surroundings and of the bitter cold"; the people "pile themselves into a monstrous shapeless clot, men and women clinging indiscriminately together, like a bunch of toads at spawning time"; there is laughter that is "partly a shudder". In just such cold and such hugger-mugger, with its suggestion of reptilian or batrachian lust, the eternal non-life of the Pit may be imagined, unbearable but enforced : " 'Oh, how can you stand it?' " protests Dorothy ... " 'It's so absurd that one wouldn't believe it if one didn't know it was true. It's impossible.' " Mr Tallboys tells her, "stage curate-wise", in mock-solemnity, " 'With God, all things are possible.' "

One does not have to know that Orwell himself tried to sleep out in Trafalgar Square to recognise the whole episode as authentic experience; and most authentic, perhaps, as a nightmare, an account of dreams that grow progressively "more monstrous, troubling, and undreamlike". The "undreamlike"— i.e. the real—life of fears not permitted conscious existence was not explored by Orwell so far for another decade.

But the novel as a whole was a marked departure from the confines of a realism which, in more than one way, had proved for Orwell a dead end. *Burmese Days* he himself described as one of the "enormous naturalistic novels with unhappy endings" that he originally wanted to write; there is a somewhat hairraising irony in the implication that his other stories end happily. *Burmese Days* ends in suicide; significantly, if we consider the few reasons any of Orwell's characters have for living, the only such finish in his fiction. In realistic terms Flory, having reached the end of his tether, is as it were logically bound to shoot himself : his successors have no less reason at one time or another to hand back their tickets to life, but with one exception, where suicide is made impossible, it hardly occurs to them as a "way out". Instead they plunge down beneath the surface of life in an endeavour to find out both why life is so unendurable and why it must be endured, neither of which questions can be answered in "naturalistic", or surface terms.

Throughout Orwell's life and work we find a tension between a desire to remain on the surface of things (including, in fact most of all, oneself) and the impulse to get underneath it. The surface is safe, it even seems to be the domain of beauty and pleasure : to "love the surface of the earth", which Orwell identified with love of nature and feeling for "the process of life" is an attribute of his most admired authors, such as Shakespeare and D. H. Lawrence, and was claimed also of himself. But there is the simultaneous suspicion that the surface is treacherous, that beauty is indeed no more than skin deep, that every kind of horror lurks below. The desire therefore to go below and see beneath the surface is partly the determination to "face unpleasant facts" in order not to be caught out by them, but more than this, it is a wish for absorption in reality : to have knowledge of the meaning which can never be found above ground.

The compulsive alternation between reassuring surface and depths half recoiled from, half desired, recurs with variations in all Orwell's writings, as we shall see. But at no time before the very end is it invested with so much intimate life and feeling as in *A Clergyman's Daughter*. Dorothy, when she leaves home, loses herself completely in amnesia : she literally doesn't know who she is and only gradually recollects herself in her new and strange surroundings. The expeditions on which Orwell based these parts of her story—his deliberate excursions into the lower depths—were apparently not of this kind; even while he changed his clothes for a tramp's cast-offs, or made himself drunk in order to get arrested and find out what "clink" was like, he remained by his own account conscious of what he was doing and unchanged "inside". But the symbolism of these abandonments of identity is obvious; and in writing a novel making use of them he was able to go much further.

To sum up : Dorothy Hare's fall into darkness, the "black, dreamless sleep" of her first state of fugue, was a plunge for him, too, into the abyss. She is his proxy and, more than that, his soul. Her name (the surname Hare was actually that of Orwell's paternal grandmother) combines the qualities of the most timid of animals, generally seen running swiftly in flight over the surface of the earth (and also known in folk-lore for changing its sex), and that of being the gift of God. As such she could feel and be what neither Eric Blair nor George Orwell dared permit in himself. It is not really surprising that later Orwell-Blair came to dislike her and even to repudiate her, numbering *A Clergyman's Daughter* among the "two or three books which I am ashamed of and have not allowed to be reprinted or translated". By this time, in 1946, he was persuading himself that it was written "simply as an exercise". If it was an exercise it was of that most easily wounded part of the personality which it is indeed risky to expose, but which also is ignored or allowed to become feeble at one's deadly peril.

III

Escaping Underground

ORWELL WROTE TWO more novels between the publication of *A Clergyman's Daughter* and the outbreak of the
Second World War : *Keep the Aspidistra Flying* (begun in
1935, published 1936) and *Coming Up for Air* (written 1938–9,
published just before the war began). During the same years he
produced *The Road to Wigan Pier*, his account of working
class life in the depressed areas, his book on the Spanish Civil
War, *Homage to Catalonia*, and a first collection of essays,
Inside the Whale (published 1940). He also became directly involved in Left-wing politics, fighting in Spain with the later
suppressed contingent of the far-Left P.O.U.M., and becoming
for a short time a member of the British I.L.P.

"Politics", with which most reflective people (and many un-
reflective) were obsessed at this time, while the power of dictatorship in Europe grew week by week, and the full-scale war which
all expected came visibly nearer, left a deep mark on Orwell's
writings, and not only in those obviously concerned with political affairs like *Wigan Pier* and *Homage to Catalonia*. In *Why
I Write* Orwell claimed that all his best writing had "political
purpose" and that without it "I wrote lifeless books and was
betrayed into purple passages, sentences without meaning,
decorative adjectives and humbug generally". Such a self-
judgment must certainly be disputed, and might itself be thought
to contain an element of humbug : an unbiassed comparison of,
say, *Down and Out in Paris and London* with such an example
of explicitly political writing as *The Lion and the Unicorn* or
many parts of *Wigan Pier* would not find the most instances of
sloppy thinking and self-deception in the former.

But it is the contention of the present study, whatever Orwell
may have said, that his writings, and the motives behind them,
were—though full of contradictions—in essence homogeneous
and self-consistent. Where politics began to obtrude they

modified his attitudes here and there, and supplied him with new disguises for old preoccupations, but did not supplant them. Politics are often described in the works of these years as an intrusion, a vile and unlucky interference with man's proper concerns. That they were so thought of did not prevent their contaminating the works in question, not so much in the way implied, of an importunate distraction, as by offering delusive forms of the same objects of pursuit. The confusion in Orwell's mind at the onset of these most "political" years is well shown in the poem of 1936, quoted in *Why I Write* as expressing his "dilemma", but in truth revealing a much more extensive muddle than the lack of an "accurate political orientation". The poem, already referred to, must really be given in full :

A happy vicar I might have been
Two hundred years ago,
To preach upon eternal doom
And watch my walnuts grow;

But born, alas, in an evil time,
I missed that pleasant haven,
For the hair has grown on my upper lip
And the clergy are all clean-shaven.

And later still the times were good,
We were so easy to please,
We rocked our troubled thoughts to sleep
On the bosoms of the trees.

All ignorant we dared to own
The joys we now dissemble;
The greenfinch on the apple bough
Could make my enemies tremble.

But girls' bellies and apricots,
Roach in a shaded stream,
Horses, ducks in flight at dawn,
All these are a dream.

It is forbidden to dream again;
We maim our joys or hide them;
Horses are made of chromium steel
And little fat men shall ride them.

I am the worm that never turned,
The eunuch without a harem;
Between the priest and the commissar
I walk like Eugene Aram;

And the commissar is telling my fortune
While the radio plays,
But the priest has promised an Austin Seven,
For Duggie always pays.

I dreamed I dwelt in marble halls.
And woke to find it true;
I wasn't born for an age like this;
Was Smith? Was Jones? Were you?

The kaleidoscope here of mutually incompatible ideas and wishes is quite remarkable : the clergy disparaged as comfortable hypocrites by the hirsute he-man who presently reappears as a eunuch; the suggestion that the dreams of a former time, or of childhood, were of real, though lost value and at the same time delusions; the lurch, already noted, from one kind of dream to another. But through the confusion, the feeling of helpless resentment, vain regret, and foreboding—looking forward to the time when the speaker, in the merciless grip of the little fat men of technological dictatorship and the pie-in-the-sky merchants, shall be marched away to his doom like the murderer Eugene Aram "with gyves upon his wrist"—makes a sufficiently strong impact. It is the same feeling that dominates the next novel to be considered, *Keep the Aspidistra Flying.*

Gordon Comstock, the hero, is another representative of Orwell himself, or of an aspect of Orwell which is now allowed to dominate. Like his predecessors, he repeats a section of Orwell's personal experience, working in a bookshop and trying to write books himself, as Orwell was doing; in fact, as he was working on this novel at the time he must have been transferring his daily thoughts and observations almost immediately into the story of Comstock. But we must suppose that they were selected, if not distorted : what Gordon is there to express is above all the sense of failure, envy of others' success, bitter resentment of poverty and at the same time determined refusal to escape from it by involvment in "the money system" which certainly had their origin in Orwell's feelings but here completely dominate an entire personality. Gordon is Orwell, but in a different way from that in which the clergyman's daughter stands for her author, as a vicarious sacrifice : Gordon, embodying his hatreds, is an attempt to see them objectively and to deal with them—although the success of this enterprise may be doubted.

Gordon splits off in ludicrously exaggerated form—he is undoubtedly intended as a comic figure—the conviction of defeat and the fancied contempt of the more fortunate that Orwell admitted to elsewhere. His family, members of "the most dismal of all classes, the middle-middle class, the landless gentry", "peculiarly dull, shabby, dead-alive, ineffectual", are not perhaps immediately recognisable from outside as the Blairs; but they illustrate in caricature very much what Orwell says he felt about his social position as a child when, sent at parental sacrifice to a "good" preparatory school and having his family's lack of means constantly dinned into him, he "reached the conclusion that you were no good unless you had £100,000"; that, without this evidence of belonging to the elect, "only a bleak, laborious kind of success was possible", "even if you climbed to the highest niche that was open to you, you could still only be an underling, a hanger-on of the people who really counted". Gordon Comstock's education (although upon it also his family "waste huge sums" at great sacrifice) is only at "third-rate" schools, unlike the "expensive and snobbish" prep school, leading through scholarships to Eton, to which Eric Blair was sent. But it is very much what, according to Orwell in the memoir just quoted (*Such, Such Were the Joys*), he was taught as a child to think that he deserved : even achieving the end for which he was sent to "St Cyprian's" and, getting his Eton scholarship, the confidence and ease with which such an advance should have endowed him, he felt all real success to be out of reach. "Failure, failure, failure—failure behind me, failure ahead of me—that was by far the deepest conviction that I carried away."

Such, Such Were the Joys stops short of Eton, where Eric Blair appears to have been happy and to have gained the esteem of his contemporaries; the novel curiously detaches this more agreeable part of early experience and gives it to another character, Gordon Comstock's friend Ravelston. Ravelston is everything Gordon is not, open, generous, tall and graceful, with, it goes without saying, a "first-class" public school and Oxbridge behind him; also, as the necessary condition of these amiable attributes, very well off. He seems to represent all that, by his own account, Orwell most longed for as child and youth, and felt excluded from; even the more fortunate and happy side of himself, an ego-ideal at the same time admired, rejected as impossible, and somewhat despised. Such a division seems necessary to account for Gordon's vehement attachment to Ravelston, whom he "adores" and, however humiliating to him the contrast, can't keep away from. The attachment is a sort of narcissism, in which the loved and admired reflection is a part of the self believed to be cut off from and quite unattainable by the admiring subject.

The reason why Gordon can never be like Ravelston is said to be want of money, and money, being with or without it, is ostensibly what *Keep the Aspidistra Flying* is all about. In *Such, Such Were the Joys* Orwell describes the delusion imposed on him, a child of comparatively poor family, at "expensive" St Cyprian's : "not only that money and privilege are the things that matter, but that it is better to inherit them than to have to work for them." That at school what mattered was "not only what you did but what you *were*" has already been noted; Orwell emphasises the memory by repetition. In that age before the First World War, he says, "the goodness of money was as unmistakable as the goodness of health and beauty, and a glittering car, a title, or a horde of servants was mixed up in people's minds with the idea of actual moral virtue".

Money in other words is the equivalent of divine grace, narrowed down and made even more brutally concrete than was the state of grace enjoyed in *Burmese Days* by Verrall. The idea merely implied there is now elaborated and codified, with a whole block of religious categories taken over and reproduced deliberately and so to speak of malice aforethought in cash terms. The epigraph of the book is a parody of I Corinthians XIII in which money takes the place of love—"And now abideth faith, hope, money, these three; but the greatest of these is money"— and this "adaptation" is repeated, both in spirit and word for word at different stages throughout the story as the chief article in Gordon Comstock's creed. It appears to be no more than a schoolboy jibe, the kind of facetious blasphemy that can be found, almost a tic, occurring all through Orwell's writing; but there is more to it than that. The idea that "worship of money" actually is a religion is taken quite seriously, and perhaps, considering the ambiguous usage of the word "value", it deserves to be; Orwell was not the first to use "riches" as symbolic of heaven. Now, he says, it is not a question of symbolism but crass fact, money *is* the kingdom of heaven. The ambiguities are by no means elucidated in consequence, rather they are more inextricably confused; but they are given personal life.

They are extended, moreover, well beyond the childhood where, in *Such, Such Were the Joys*, Orwell tried to confine them, as part of "the nonsense you used to believe and the trivialities that made you suffer". Gordon still believes devoutly in "the money God" and all his statutes and ordinances, only his belief has turned inside out in resentment and rebellion, so that he now refuses to obey them. It is by no means a game : his faith in money, negative or positive, is confused with his faith— when as a child he owned to it—in the more common image of divinity : at school, we are told, tormented by consciousness of his family's poverty and the humiliation of their visits, he, "in those days still a believer, used actually to pray that his parents wouldn't come down to school". Money was God, or the sign of God's blessing; at the same time the God of school chapel and Scripture lessons might influence independently the affairs in which possession or non-possession of money was of supreme importance. For Eric Blair at St Cyprian's the same near-identification evidently held good : at this time he also "believed in God and believed that the accounts given of him were true", just as he accepted "the prevailing standards" in general, for "how could the rich, the strong, the elegant, the fashionable, the powerful be in the wrong?" Believing in God, however, did not include loving him : on the contrary, says Orwell, "I hated him, just as I hated Jesus and the Hebrew patriarchs". Conviction of sin and exclusion from grace did not, either in the child Blair or the young Comstock, lead to repentance but rather to a despairing resort to more complete exclusion : Gordon Comstock at school, praying that his own family will not come near him, was, we may say, already embracing that wilful and self-wounding isolation which makes up nine-tenths of his story.

The adult Gordon, "aged twenty-nine and rather moth-eaten already", has of course long given up belief in the God of either the New or the Old Testament, but his attitude towards the God he does believe in, money, is the same. He hates him. Indeed he hates almost everybody and everything, and his history is so imbued with hatred that it is most unpleasant to read. But these multiplied hatreds are all related to his consuming hatred of the false deity in whose power he has implicit faith and against whose commandments he is in conscious rebellion. He hates the rich, because they are rich; he hates even more, and is disgusted by the poor, the "throw-outs of the money-god", "creeping like unclean beetles to the grave"; he hates perhaps most of all women because, as he takes pleasure in telling his girl-friend, they are the servants and priestesses of money: "it's women who worship it." It is women who cultivate aspidistras, the depressing flowerless plant which Gordon selects as the badge of all who surrender to the power of money—not the rich who, living in money's grace, do not have to worry about it or bear its sign aloft, but the struggling, pinching, respectable poor. "Keep the Aspidistra Flying" is a hymn sung originally (to the tune of "Glorious things of Thee are spoken") by the blasphemous Mr Tallboys in *A Clergyman's Daughter*, where aspidistras are also mentioned as the symbol of withering spinsterhood: the aspidistra now enjoys its apotheosis as the burning bush of Orwell's unholy Zion.

Of course this is a joke. Gordon Comstock is a parody of paranoid reactions, and he himself knows how ridiculous he is; but the knowledge only serves to deepen his humiliation and resentment. He even knows, up to a point, that his hatreds have no external justification, that he is "merely objectifying his own inner misery", but it makes no difference, he is "hardly troubled" by the thought, and in no way brought nearer to discovering what his inner misery really springs from. He exemplifies to the point of caricature the kind of self-awareness or self-observation which has nothing to do with self-knowledge, but is rather the splitting off of consciousness from the sources of emotion: self-consciousness, therefore, as a substitute for conscience.

This common phenomenon was apparently carried in Orwell's case to the extreme of a permanent state of mind, at least on the evidence of his explanation of *Why I Write*. The memory of precocious self-observation has already been referred to. He says that from his schooldays onward he was engaged in "the making up of a continuous 'story' about myself, a sort of diary existing only in the mind. As a very small child I used to imagine that I was, say, Robin Hood and picture myself as the hero of thrilling adventures, but quite soon my 'story' ceased to be narcissistic in a crude way and became more and more a mere description of what I was doing and the things I saw". The habit continued, he says, into adult life "right through my non-literary years" but was already composed with careful literary art, involving a search for "the right words" in which to carry on the self-description : "I seemed", he says, "to be making this descriptive effort almost against my will, under a kind of compulsion from outside." Clearly this is a convincing account of one of the common sources of literary effort, and of Orwell's development into a writer in particular : the habit of his "non-literary years" simply transferred itself later into writing. But clearly also it is evidence of more than a literary turn of mind : carried to such length, the splitting of one conscious mind into observer and observed has important psychological consequences. They can be seen very well in Gordon Comstock, who is both the creation of his author's self-consciousness—repeating, in fictitious form, Orwell's thoughts and doings—and enjoys, or suffers the same split himself, so that Gordon knows all the time what he is doing, and very often knows that it is injurious folly, but is quite unable to alter his course. The split is most explicit in the crisis of the story, the idiotic blind on which Gordon embarks, supposedly in celebration of a small literary success which has put £10 in his pocket, actually a mere exercise in waste, insulting and embarrassing to his friends, ending (ineffectively) in a brothel and next morning in a police court. (The later consequences of this abortive orgy reproduce faithfully Orwell's description, in *Clink*, of his deliberate attempt to get sent to prison as "drunk and disorderly".) Throughout this episode Gordon maintains a duologue, magnified by intoxication, between "drunken half" and "sober half", the former wallowing in debauchery, the latter watching "with ice-cold clarity" which, however, in no way modifies his actions.

The accompaniment of such a self-divorce is, naturally, a separation from actual living, loss of the sensation as distinct from the observation of being alive. We may compare Gordon's confession-accusation to his friend, "My poems are dead because I'm dead. You're dead. We're all dead. Dead people in a dead world", with Orwell's poem, already alluded to, in which he laments his "mortal sickness", that he "with the living cannot live". In the poem, giving his heart to "weak and stuffless ghosts" he repeats the very action imagined by Gordon (who is thinking with hatred and revulsion of his own relatives) of "the sort of dingy drabby fornications . . . happening between Egyptian mummies after the museum is closed for the night". The grotesque nastiness of the image is typical of Gordon, who has a strong relish for fantasies of violence and decay, not to say downright necrophilia. The slum-dwellings near his lodging are thought of as places "where families slept five in a bed, and when one of them died slept every night with the corpse until it was buried; alley-ways where girls of fifteen were deflowered by boys of sixteen against leprous plaster walls". The obtrusive fantasies of corpse-copulation, or rather of sexual activity being itself part of physical rotting away, are quite remarkable. Returning to the conversation with Ravelston, we find Gordon denouncing the whole of "this life we live nowadays" in the same terms : "Sometimes I think we're all corpses. Just rotting upright."

From this "death-in-life" and society of "meaningless people" he does however try to escape; the struggle gives the novel whatever it has of movement and life. Gordon is looking for reality, and seeks it characteristically in degradation, a descent into wretchedness much the same at Dorothy Hare's although (here more closely resembling Orwell's own "experiments") undertaken consciously and to a large extent voluntarily.

Gordon undertakes his plunge "down, down, into the mud—down to the streets, the workhouse, and the jail" with his eyes open and also, it is emphasised, of his own free will, if such a term can be used in the context of these compulsions, for he has a "good job" waiting for him all the time, to be had for the asking. The compulsion upon him is not that of economic necessity, the unemployment that drove millions of his contemporaries to the same level, but comes from within. He cannot help himself, certainly, but only because his reasonable self, aware of needs and obligations and the claims upon him of his relatives and friends, is deprived of all force, is in fact ghostly and unreal. This futile, stuffless self is troublesome, but not exigent; Gordon does not really care what it says, and though "at his very centre there was an inner heart that cared because he could not care", this knowledge of emptiness at the kernel of his being is of itself unable to produce change.

Nothing will come of nothing : Gordon can no more than any other mortal lift himself by his bootstraps. Instead, and characteristically, he turns away from his "inner heart" with its terrible demand, that its emptiness should be filled, and seeks to lose himself in the larger vacancy of destitution and complete idleness. He retreats from every claim of affection and loyalty (his girl Rosemary, his long-suffering friend Ravelston), not from any wish to relieve them of a burden but on the contrary to avoid the burden their friendship puts on himself : he wants only to be alone. "Alone, alone ! Free from the nagging consciousness of his failure; free to sink . . . down, down into the quiet worlds where money and effort and moral obligation did not exist." He longs to be where there are "no *duns* of any kind"; perhaps it is not surprising, after the burlesque of St Paul which announces the theme of the story, that "charity" itself is thought of as inescapably evil in its effects : "However delicately it is disguised, charity is still horrible; there is a malaise, almost a secret hatred, between the giver and the receiver." Even Strindberg is not more thorough-going in his definition of all relations between persons as the accumulation and discharge of debts.

That such a freedom from human demands can be found in extreme poverty is hardly realistic; and the moral nihilism which can ignore every kind of "dun" is quite as likely to be found among the rich as among beggars, as Gordon and Orwell behind him had every reason to know. But there is a sense in which destitution frees one from material demands at least simply because one *cannot* meet them : the completely helpless person, like an infant, is not expected to do or give anything in return for the gifts he receives. One cannot help suspecting that it is a return to something like such infantile dependency that Gordon is after, and during his descent "down, down" he does in fact go on taking, from Ravelston, from his former employer (who will not, after his disgrace, give him back his job, but helps him to find another, of the lowest paid kind), and even from the man he then works for, the grotesque dwarfish East End bookseller Cheeseman, who employs him for a pittance, very much as the goblin in a fairy-story will care for a strayed child.

Gordon gives nothing in return, for he has nothing to give. In his sordid lodgings the landlady brings him an aspidistra in a pot to make his dreadful room "more 'ome-like". She—who does this out of the goodness of her heart and because, as a former prostitute, she has "a loving manner towards anything in trousers"—is actually called *Mother* Meakin, described as "a dishevelled, jelly-soft old creature with a figure like a cottage loaf", the embodiment of a half-rejected, half-desired maternal bosom. Gordon, lying on his bed among the bugs, accepts her gift passively, with "a bit of a twinge" but, naturally, without gratitude. When mother is just a mindless dishevelled old tart who needs to be grateful to such a creature for such a gift?

The "peace" Gordon wants and even to some extent finds can hardly last, unless in the permanent passivity of the grave; and though the grave seems to come very near, it is emphasised that Gordon's retreat is not there. The cheap lending library where he now works is, literally, in the midst of mortality, "between a fly-blown ham-and-beef shop and a smartish undertaker"; a notice in the window of the latter causes him to reflect that "you can get underground for as little as two pounds ten nowadays". Yet this underground is not the same as the "under ground, under ground!" of sub-life that he invokes and has deliberately sunk to. He never thinks of dying: as has been remarked, there are no more suicides in Orwell after Flory's, and in Gordon's case the possibility is specifically rejected. Near the beginning of the story he considers the possibilities open to humanity in general: Socialism, which Ravelston the orthodox rich young Marxist hopes for; suicide, and the Catholic Church, the "standing temptation of the intelligentsia". Gordon dismisses all three, Socialism because (with a foreboding look closer than Ravelston is capable of) nobody could want it who could "see what Socialism would really mean", the Church for the contemptuous, though interesting reason that it would be "fairly cosy under Mother Church's wing. A bit insanitary, of course—but you'd feel safe there"; and suicide, "real suicide", actual death, for a more directly personal reason, as "too meek and mild. I'm not going to give up my share of earth to anyone else. I'd want to do in a few of my enemies first".

The idea of death is very close to this man who feels that he and everyone else are rotting corpses, and who longs to bury himself, but it never makes itself felt as a real possibility. The only way Gordon can think of his own death, it appears, is as

of giving up something (his "share of earth", but not the usual
six-foot length) which will then become the property of others.
There is something very odd about this, the significance of
which will not fully emerge till later; in the meantime we may
take Gordon's own explanation at its face value, that he'll have
nothing to do with death for himself because there are so many
people he wants to see die first. The world at large he thinks of
as gripped by a "death-wish", bound for self-destruction and
only feebly pretending otherwise. He looks at a particularly
loathed advertisement of a vapidly grinning "Corner Table"
customer :

> But what is behind the grin? Desolation, emptiness, prophecies
> of doom. For can you not see, if you know how to look, that
> behind that slick self-satisfaction, that tittering fat-bellied
> triviality, there is nothing but a frightful emptiness, a secret
> despair? The great death-wish of the modern world. Suicide
> pacts. Heads stuck in gas-ovens in lonely maisonettes. French
> letters and Amen Pills. And the reverberations of future wars.
> Enemy aeroplanes flying over London; the deep threatening
> hum of the propellers, the shattering thunder of the bombs.
> It is all written in Corner Table's face.

Corner Table's face is surely a reflection of his own. But it is
not taken into his own mind. Death, by suicide or bombs, is for
others, not for him.

Indeed, if death can be conquered by killing, Gordon makes
strenuous efforts in this direction, at least in his imagination.
Though not in deed at all a violent man, his mind is filled with
fantasies of violence and destruction, and he looks forward
eagerly and sincerely to the coming war and "the whole western
world going up in a roar of high explosives". He is described
furthering his destructive day-dreams by imitating, like a small
boy, the noise of the imagined bombing-planes, which he sees
in his mind's eye coming "squadron after squadron, innumer-
able, darkening the sky like a cloud of gnats"—not so much,
perhaps, prescient of the Blitz as looking back to Milton's picture
of the infernal hosts homing in on Pandemonium. He imitates
the buzz as he looks out of the window of his lonely bed-sitter :
"It was a sound", we are told, "which, at that moment, he
ardently desired to hear."

Ravelston disapproves of "our civilisation" in a theoretical Marxist way, and looks forward amiably enough to its destruction and replacement by Socialism, but his opposition to bourgeois society, expressed in wearing worn, though expensive clothes, and in running the left-wing feuilleton *"Antichrist"*, is abstract and free of personal animus—as it is also mockingly shown to be quite ineffective. Gordon's hate, though no more effective (it may be remarked that in political terms it seems more likely to emerge in Fascism than anything else) is virulent and personal, directed not only against any product of our civilisation in sight, from the dirty and disgusting poor to the well-to-do with their "sleek bunny-faces" gliding by in motorcars, "the pink-faced masters of the world", but against his personalised vision of the whole, the sum of everything he loathes, presented to his imagination as "the money-god". He hates "the lord of all, the money-god" with a passionate malevolence far beyond anything parlour-Bolshevik Ravelston dreams of. Furthermore, he has carried his rebellion into practice, refusing to take a "good job" and carrying his "secret" war against money into the open defiance of a voluntary pauperdom.

The rebellion is entirely futile, of course, and the story is of Gordon's defeat and final surrender. It is told however in a peculiar way and with a constantly shifting system of values that renders the result highly ambiguous : the more so since this alone of Orwell's novels has what may be called a happy ending. Gordon, hiding from his friends in "the gutter"—in the squalor and apathy of Mother Meakin's bug-ridden lodging-house—is remorselessly sought out by them; badly as he has treated them, they will not let him go. In "pure magnanimity", a quality rare in this book, his girl Rosemary virtually forces him to make love to her, and consequently finds herself pregnant. Gordon is at last made to face his responsibilities, marries her, accepts the well-paid job in an advertising agency that has been kept for him, and sets up house, installing at his own insistence an aspidistra, as the symbol of his re-entry into human society.

This might, and perhaps is intended to be a positive close, the restoration of hope after the black negativism of Gordon Comstock's preceding history. On the other hand it might be a piece of irony, and again the terms in which Gordon's "rebirth" is described argues some such partial intention. But in

effect it is neither; it is impossible either to believe or disbelieve
in the new course of events, not because they are circumstantially
improbable—such a conclusion to a humdrum and one-sided
love-affair is certainly common enough, and doubtless that was
why it was chosen, an additional sign of Gordon's acceptance
of being like anybody else—but just because the author's inten-
tions are self-cancelling. The irony itself works in both directions
at once, and each negates the other.

What is the aspidistra, that depressing and ugly plant which,
with its seven leaves, like the Seven-fold Light, Gordon at the
end hails as "the tree of life"? What do all the blasphemous-
facetious parodies of religious language signify? It is extremely
hard to say. There is no question but that money, the rule of
the "money-business", is evil, a corruption that reaches from top
to bottom, from the rich and privileged whose very "decency"
depends on it to the poor who are despised for being poor. When
Gordon, drunk, looks at the heart of the money-regulated world,
in the "hideous midnight noon" of Piccadilly Circus, and sees
in the sky-signs "the awful, sinister glitter of a doomed civilisation, like the still blazing lights of a sinking ship" it is a vision
that Orwell shares. But on the other hand the demands of the
money-god are in the end found to be overpowering, not simply
because they are all-powerful—though that is included—but
because they are felt to be *right*.

Gordon's surrender is laudable, not simply because he is
doing "the decent thing" at last—obeying the decency which, as
we have learnt, depends on money—but because money itself,
and in a peculiarly concrete way, represents reality, the "really
real" that Gordon has lost access to. It is the actual feel of
money that seems to matter; when we learn that it is "physically
impossible" for Gordon to make love to his girl with only eight-
pence in his pocket, we remember the singular little detail
recorded of Orwell during a severe illness—that he insisted on
keeping some small change under his pillow where he could feel
them. ("Money is always a fascinating subject", he said, "provided that only small sums are involved."). Mr Cheeseman, the
hobgoblin bookseller, behaves like a traditional miser, keeping his
shop-takings not in the till but in a purse hidden about his
person, which he holds "in a peculiarly secretive way", and
imagined by Gordon counting his gains "in a double-locked
room with the shutters over the windows"; yet the unholy thrill

this dark and spider-like creature feels is transmitted to us. Is he not handling the elements of God?

Gordon's regeneration, or surrender, when at last he gives up the "war" he has declared and makes his peace with the god of money, is brought about by his girl's pregnancy; but not immediately on learning about it. He is brought up short, and characteristically, by the sordid reality of the alternative to marriage, the abortion "for only £5" that Rosemary mentions, and which by its actual price-ticket makes him realise what they are talking about, a "blasphemy" : "It was the squalid detail of the £5 that brought it home." But even then his nose hasn't been sufficiently rubbed in it. Rosemary leaves him free to decide, and he doesn't decide until, on an impulse perhaps sufficiently odd in itself, he looks up an obstetric manual in the public library and looks at the illustrations.

> He came on a print of a nine weeks' foetus. It gave him a shock to see it, for he had not expected it to look in the least like that. It was a deformed, gnomelike thing, a sort of clumsy caricature of a human being . . . a monstrous thing, and yet strangely human . . .
> He turned back a page or two and found a print of a six weeks' foetus. A really dreadful thing this time—a thing he could hardly even bear to look at. Strange that our beginnings and endings are so ugly—the unborn as well as the dead. The thing looked as if it were dead already . . .

Some time before, thinking bitterly of the only success of his "literary career", a single slim volume of poetry, Gordon has pictured them in his mind in much the same way—"Those forty or fifty drab, dead little poems, each like a little abortion in its labelled jar. He had one of those moments of contempt and even horror which every artist has at times when he thinks of his own work." He repeats the image to Ravelston, dismissing the book : "It's dead . . . Dead as a blasted foetus in a bottle." Here again is a baffling confusion of values, or it might be better to say of devaluations. The poems, Gordon's sole creation to date, have been dismissed as abortions, but so in effect is his actual creation in the flesh; it is because of its deformity, suggested by the obstetric illustrations, that he feels his unborn offspring to be real. The two pictures make a deep impression

on him, and it is their *ugliness* that affects him most : it "made
them more credible and therefore more moving". It seems a
strange reason, until we reflect once more that for Orwell "facts
are apt to be unpleasant" and the "facts of life" perhaps most
of all. Very likely some personal shock in boyhood discovery is to
be inferred; but the point concerning the adult, both Gordon
and author, is rather the revelation of a terrible self-disparage-
ment that can only see creation as pitiful and monstrous.

After looking at the midwifery book (under the disapproving
looks of the "intensely disagreeable" woman librarian) he turns
for a moment to glance at some "women's papers", filled with
advertisements, and for a few more paragraphs our noses are
rubbed in their offensive fatuity—most of those quoted, as it
happens, are for deodorants or cures for variously sordid ail-
ments. He recoils again—"To be mixed up in *that* !"—but his
mind is already made up, and in a few rapid pages his story is
rounded up to its enforced happy issue : he gets his job back
with the advertising agency, marries his girl, sets up house in
a small respectable flat furnished on the never-never, with an
aspidistra as an essential part of the household equipment. Before
this he has already destroyed the long, abortive poem he has
been working on, pushing it down the street drain; as it falls,
"with a plop" into the water below he makes his final restitu-
tion : "Vicisti, O aspidistra !" The novel ends on a note of
desperate reassurance : "Things were happening again in the
Comstock family."

The turnabout appears to be complete, and it is noteworthy
that Gordon, once the decision is made and he is "coming back
to the fold, repentant", feels relief : "In some corner of his mind
he had always known that this would happen", and quite apart
from the "precipitating cause" in Rosemary's pregnancy, "it
was what, in his secret heart, he had desired". In his secret heart,
we have already seen, he has known a vacancy which has now
been filled :

He looked back over the last two frightful years. He had
blasphemed against money, rebelled against money, tried to
live like an anchorite outside the money-world; it had brought
him not only misery but also a frightful emptiness, an in-
escapable sense of futility.

He is out of the gutter now and back in real life; and yet was not the descent to the gutter a search for reality? Social reality, indeed, in the shape of money, sought him out even there: through Rosemary he was reminded that by a single step he could return to "the money world", "to effort and decency and slavery. Going to the devil isn't so easy as it sounds. Sometimes your salvation hunts you down like the Hound of Heaven". We must remember that it is the money-god's heaven he is talking about; yet this god behaves exactly like the Lord of the psalmist, finding him out even in the depths and in the darkness. He is, in consequence, "re-born"; there is no question that Rosemary's unborn child, conceived in the cold and filthy garret "without much pleasure, on Mother Meakin's dingy bed", is Gordon himself.

At the end of the book, Rosemary feels the child quicken and Gordon himself experiences "a strange, almost terrible feeling, a sort of warm convulsion" in his own entrails: something is being brought to life in himself. But when we consider how this quickening began, with the shock of "ugliness" and contemplation of a foetus that "looked as if it were dead already"; how the same image has already occurred (applied to "*Mice*", the ironically named poetry book) we must have doubts about this second birth, what life it will lead to and what destiny, in the extreme ambiguity of hopes and desires the story of Gordon Comstock presents, the newborn soul will choose, or have chosen for it.

Before leaving Gordon's story, this may be a convenient place to mention the striking affinities, here and elsewhere, between certain themes in Orwell and in Dostoevsky. These are the more remarkable for being quite unacknowledged; Orwell may be presumed to have read Dostoevsky in translation at one time or another, but never appears to have alluded to it—a passing remark in *Inside the Whale* about the stereotype of Russia represented by "Tolstoy, Dostoevsky, and exiled counts driving taxi-cabs" is the only discoverable reference. Yet it is difficult now to read almost any of their works side by side without coming upon matter which, though the treatment may be very different, could have been suggested by one to the other.

Dostoevsky's *Notes from Underground* and *Keep the Aspidistra Flying* make an obvious example: Dostoevsky's narrator, who introduces himself from "underground"—"I am a sick man . . . I am an angry man. I am an unattractive man"

—might be Gordon Comstock himself, endowed with vastly enhanced powers of self-analysis; and the situation of both in a deliberately chosen sub-world of poverty, idleness and envy is the same, whether the "underground" is thought of principally in terms of their outward circumstances of isolated squalor or of the mental withdrawal that these circumstances reflect. It may even be conjectured that they have arrived there by the same road : the early memory of Dostoevsky's underground man recounted in the poignant and dreadful tale "apropos the falling sleet"—the debauch embarked upon in malice and spite, and the encounter with a prostitute who is treated with self-lacerating cruelty—is only a much more desperate and intense version of Gordon Comstock's night out which ends so humiliatingly in a brothel. It is after this episode, which "marked a period in his life", that he longs to go "down, deep down", into the world "underground" where "decency no longer mattered".

There is no comparison (so it may reasonably be objected) between the penetration of the two authors on this as on other occasions when they seem to be travelling through the same territory. Between Gordon's urge to escape among "the lost people, the underground people, tramps, beggars, criminals, prostitutes", and Dostoevsky's feeling, even through the warped character of the underground man, for the insulted and injured, there is a very large gap of sensibility and self-awareness; but it is the same world they are talking about. Gordon's political cynicism, his mockery of the optimistic progressive in Ravelston and others who do not "see the hook sticking out of the rather stodgy bait" of Socialist orthodoxy, is lightweight stuff beside the underground man's mordant attack on those who propose to build the mathematically certain "Palace of Crystal" and introduce the universal reign of good will and good sense. However much he hates society and wishes to see its destruction, and however sceptical he is of future amelioration, Gordon hardly conjures up the figure of derision and denial foreseen by the underground man, who "springs up suddenly out of nowhere" and consigns all the works of calm rationality to the devil "with one kick". But it is the same doubt that eats both of them.

It is almost as though the earlier writer, out of an understanding far more subtle and profound, were passing comment on the later one. Whether we suppose Orwell to have been directly in Dostoevsky's debt, or—which would make these points of affinity even more curious—we take them as evidence of convergent thinking, he seems often to be standing in Dostoevsky's shadow. In the case of Gordon Comstock especially the voice of Dostoevsky's underground man—speaking as it were from a place far below Gordon's in depths of bitter self-consciousness and knowledge of futility—calls in question the attempt to make a positive end to the story. Upon the news that "once again things were happening in the Comstock family", and the assumption that the movement is in a hopeful direction, the last words of the underground man provide a powerful and sinister gloss:

> ... after all, I have only carried to a logical conclusion in my life what you yourselves didn't dare take more than half-way; and you supposed your cowardice was common sense, and comforted yourselves with the self-deception. So perhaps I turn out to be more alive than you. Look harder! After all, we don't even know where "real life" is lived nowadays, or what it is, what name it goes by. Leave us to ourselves, without our books, and at once we get into a muddle and lose our way—we don't know whose side to be on or where to give our allegiance, what to love and what to hate, what to respect and what to despise. We even find it difficult to be human beings, men with real flesh and blood of our own; we are ashamed of it, we think it a disgrace, and are always striving to be some unprecedented kind of generalised human being. We are born dead and moreover we have long ceased to be the sons of living fathers; and we become more and more contented with our condition. We are acquiring the taste for it. Soon we shall invent a method of being born from an idea. But that's enough; I shall write no more from the underground ...

We need only remember that it was not in fact (as Dostoevsky rounds it off) the last word of "this paradoxical writer", for "he could not help going on". There is much more to be learnt underground than Gordon Comstock allowed himself to discover.

One of the signs of Gordon Comstock's regeneration is a change in his feelings about the coming war, which formerly he had eagerly looked forward to as agent of his destructive wishes—the "curious thought" strikes him at the end of the book that he no longer wants it to happen. That it was going to happen all the same had become even more obvious by the time of its publication in 1936 and, in the years immediately following, its approaching shadow dominated Orwell's thoughts more and more. It looms very close in his next novel, *Coming Up For Air*, written 1938-9, and published in fact less than three months before the war broke out; his first piece of fiction since his marriage, his experiences during the Spanish Civil War and his commitment, by his own account, to "politics", but reflecting these only in a negative way, being quite non-political, even anti-political in implication.

Coming Up For Air is the only novel of Orwell's told in the first person, and in view of what he said later about this mode (comparing it, we remember, with a "stimulating but very deleterious and habit forming drug") we may suppose that on this occasion he gave way to the "temptation", as he called it, for particular reasons. In his remarks "for and against novels in the first person", entered in a note-book near the end of his life, he reckoned as "advantages" that "in the first person one can always get the book actually written" and that "*anything* can be made to sound credible" because "you can daydream about *yourself* doing no matter what, whereas third-person adventures have to be comparatively probable". Against were the considerations that "the narrator is never really separate from the author", that there can be only one centre of consciousness in the story, and that "range of feeling [is] much narrowed, as there are many kinds of appeal you can make on behalf of others but not for yourself".

Such reflections make curious reading in the light of his own novels, in which it can be said that, with one exception, there is never any real separation between narrator and chief character, and that the latter is virtually always the sole conscious person, within whose individual thoughts and "range of feeling" the story is confined, however it may be told. If it be the case that "an 'I' novel is simply the story of one person—a three-dimensional figure among caricatures—and therefore cannot be a true novel", then none of Orwell's is a true one. It seems, indeed, that there is an element of disguised self-criticism in these notes; Orwell did of course confess his feeling that he was "not a real novelist anyway". This was said (in a letter of 1948 to Julian Symons) with direct reference to *Coming Up For Air*, in which he had, he said, given way to the "vice" of writing a novel in the first person, "which one should never do". His reasons for doing so can be guessed at if we remember his account in *Why I Write* of his habit, "as a very small child", of picturing himself as "the hero of thrilling adventures", given up at an early age in favour of a detached self-commentary on his actions, told in the third person. It may well be thought that this switch from first person fantasy to third person self-description marked a crucial point in the development of his consciousness and his moral-emotional perception of himself and other people. The immediate inference, however, seems to be that the first person story of *Coming Up For Air* was a return to the fantasy-habit of small childhood, thought of as a self-indulgence. The fate of such fantasising is, in fact, the theme of the novel.

Bearing these later observations in mind we may turn to the story told of himself by George Bowling, the "I" in question. Orwell tried hard to "separate himself" from his creation, making this other George as different as possible from his outward self. He owned, indeed, in the letter to Symons, that he had been unsuccessful in this respect, and that "my own character is constantly intruding on that of the narrator"; but George Bowling, the suburban insurance-agent, eupeptic, full of bounce and bonhomie, with "fat red face, false teeth, and vulgar clothes", "incapable of looking like a gentleman", is certainly a very heavy disguise for Orwell-Blair. Bowling's obesity, gone into in detail in the novel's first pages, is a particular point of contrast, so much so—especially in view of the disgust frequently expressed by Orwell at fat men and women—that one may suspect something of the affinity frequently inherent in such reversals. George Bowling, with his "pudgy arms" and "tendency to be barrel-shaped", is described—not, indeed in realistic terms so much as like the fat-men caricatures of the comic postcards— in nearly the same words as are used for Flaxman, the travelling salesman of *Keep the Aspidistra Flying*, "really horribly fat", filling his clothes of "startling vulgarity" "as though he had been melted and then poured into them", who excites revulsion and contempt in Gordon Comstock. It is almost as though Orwell were trying to make up for an injustice: the "fair hearing", in fact, that he demanded, in the essay on *The Art of Donald*

McGill, for "the Sancho Panza view of life". Sancho Panza and Don Quixote, he says there, are both to be found in most people, and he makes a strong plea for Sancho Panza to be given a fair deal :

> He is your unofficial self, the voice of the belly protesting against the soul. His tastes lie towards safety, soft beds, no work, pots of beer and women with "voluptuous" figures. He it is who punctures your fine attitudes and urges you to look after Number One, to be unfaithful to your wife, to bilk your debts, and so on and so forth. Whether you allow yourself to be influenced by him is a different question. But it is simply a lie to say that he is not part of you, just as it is a lie to say that Don Quixote is not part of you either, though most of what is said and written consists of one lie or the other, usually the first.

How much success Orwell achieved in redressing the balance we shall see; in the meantime credit must be given to the attempted demonstration, not only in the usual way that (as George Bowling says of himself) "there's a thin man inside every fat man, just as they say there's a statue inside every block of stone", but (against this essentially Manichaean view of the flesh) the less commonly acknowledged fact that a thin man may feel he really ought to be fat.

It seems, however, that George Bowling is more a refuge and hiding-place than a fully recognised component of the whole personality; and perhaps it could hardly be otherwise in a story which is all about hiding and taking flight, and of which the very mode was later thought of as escapist. *Coming Up For Air* is quite explicitly an "escapist" book in subject, if not in effect, and it is interesting to find Orwell two years later, when the war George Bowling dreaded was in full swing, and Orwell's political attitude towards it had markedly changed, writing in answer to a question put by *Partisan Review* : "I don't see any tendency to escapism in current literature, but I believe that if any major work were now produced it *would* be escapist, or at any rate subjective. I infer this from looking in my own mind. If I could get the time and the mental peace to write a novel now, I should write about the past, the pre-1914 period, which I suppose comes under the heading of 'escapism'."

Coming Up For Air is the story of just such an attempt to construct a refuge, from the ghastliness of life in the 'thirties and the looming threat of war at the end of them, in "the pre-1914 period". It presents a highly sentimentalised view of that time, with an open appeal to nostalgia for the mythological good old days : "I tell you," says George Bowling, "it was a good world to live in. I belong to it. So do you." It may very much be doubted if that was true of many, even in 1939—nor could Orwell himself, born in 1903, be said in any ordinary sense to "belong" to the pre-1914 era. (He made George Bowling just ten years older.) In one sense, however, everyone may belong to the past he is recollecting and yearning for : not the historical past but the past of childhood which all share, though not all may remember with pleasure. George Bowling goes back, first in memory and later in person, to Lower Binfield, the small country town of his birth and upbringing; his purpose is to recapture the safe world of his childhood, and what he recalls, even before the inevitable disillusion of his physical return to the place, is a curious mixture, reflecting in an interesting way on Orwell's view of his own childhood.

In outer detail Bowling's upbringing and circumstances are, like his adult figure, as different as possible from Orwell-Blair's —he is the son of a small shopkeeper, educated as a day-boy at the local grammar school, and put at once into "trade" when he leaves. Inwardly, perhaps, it was in some respects the childhood Orwell wished to have had. The most prominent point made about it is the feeling of tradition, regularity, and security —"ours was one of those houses where everything goes like clockwork" or (George Bowling quickly corrects himself, disliking the mechanical associations of clockwork) "like some kind of natural process". (And what, one would like to ask, is any family life but some kind of natural process?) A procession of "enormous meals" is remembered, served up by a fat, large, reliable mother and "always ready on the tick", just the sort of substantial food, "good solid tommy" recalled with longing by one of Orwell's tramp-acquaintances. It is a *Schlaraffenland* of boiled beef and dumplings, roast beef and Yorkshire, pig's head, etc. etc.; it is also a golden age of security and confidence, of the small child's delight in the world : "It always seems to be summer when I look back. I can feel the grass round me as tall as myself, and the heat coming out of the earth. And the dust in the lane and the warm greeny light coming through the hazel boughs." The Bowling family is conventional, narrow, ignorant, but life in it seems, at any rate to the small George, absolutely safe and ordered; even the disobedient adventurousness of the small boy is contained within understood standards and parental authority, especially that of his stout mother who leathers him when he gets home.

Much is made of these adventures, and in the adult George Bowling's recollection of them one begins to feel that perhaps his early years were not altogether idyllic. Like other small boys George was often violent and cruel, and the "strong, rank" boyhood feeling of "knowing everything and fearing nothing ... all bound up with breaking rules and killing things" is remembered by middle-aged George with a particular emphasis on the natural savagery of the age and the pleasure taken in killing and torturing small animals. Such may be common enough, but when we note that it seems to be almost the boy's sole emotion, counterbalanced by nothing else, we begin to feel that despite the security something seems to have gone wrong with this childhood. There is no warmth in the Bowling family, nor any word of affection. George is distant from his parents, speaks of his father throughout as of a stranger seen from outside, and lets him drop into dust—the father dies while George is in France during the Great War—without apparently any feeling whatever. His mother, though seen in memory as a "great splendid protecting kind of creature, a bit like a ship's figurehead and a bit like a broody hen", has also faded. He has some momentary emotion at her funeral, when "they chucked some earth on to the coffin and I suddenly realised what it means for your mother to be lying with seven feet of earth on top of her", but the feeling is deliberately belittled: he is careful to point out that at the same time he was thinking of his new officer's kneebreeches. That, again, may be common enough; it is not so much the way George's mind wanders at his mother's graveside that strikes one as the fact that he never acknowledges her as an object of love at all. When looked at a little more closely, it becomes evident that little George, who returns in memory chiefly doing things by himself or in the care of a neighbour's child—his parents remembered as by a detached observer, "fixed in some ... characteristic attitude", his older brother an object only of fear and dislike—must have

been a lonely child. Despite the different home he was provided
with, he was not, perhaps, so different from the boy Orwell
remembered himself as : "I do not believe that I ever felt love
for any mature person, except my mother, and even her I did
not trust, in the sense that shyness made me conceal most of
my real feelings from her."

Another point at which George Bowling's memories may sup-
plement those Orwell owned to in his own person is, in fact,
their starting point, the stimulus of his Proustian recollection.
It is a smell ("some chance sight or sound or smell, especially
smell, sets you going, and the past doesn't merely come back to
you, you're actually *in* the past") which is presently identified
as the smell of church :

> You know the smell churches have, a peculiar, dank, dusty,
> decaying, sweetish sort of smell. There's a touch of candle-
> grease in it, and perhaps a whiff of incense and a suspicion
> of mice, and on Sunday mornings it's a bit overlaid by yellow
> soap and serge dresses, but predominantly it's that sweet,
> dusty, musty smell that's like the smell of death and life mixed
> up together. It's powdered corpses, really.

Life and death are mingled in the atmosphere : so they are also
in the next memory, of two men in the choir of the parish
church, one of them thin and the other fat. One was "a great,
gaunt powerful old devil of about sixty, with a face like a death's
head", "exactly like a skeleton", who "looked as though he'd
live to be a hundred and make coffins for everyone in the church
before he'd finished"—he was in fact the local undertaker. The
other had "a very pink, smooth face" and, when singing, "a
kind of desperate agonised bellow, as though someone had a
knife at his throat and he was letting out his last yell for help".
The church thus contained both the Grim Reaper in person
and his victim, and young George "used to imagine they were
deadly enemies and trying to shout one another down"; but
"you always knew which of the two was the master".

Death has the victory, but in George Bowling's memory was
still enclosed within a continuity. The idea of the Church—
"that peculiar feeling—it was only a feeling, you can't describe
it as an activity—that we used to call 'Church' " returns, as a
compound of incomprehensible rigmarole and outlandish

doings, "sacrificing burnt offerings, walking about in fiery fur-
naces, getting nailed on crosses, getting swallowed by whales",
but also as a feeling of safety and certainty, especially associated
with "the sweet graveyard smell". "I could smell the corpse-
smell", says George: "In a manner of speaking I can smell it
now. I'm back in Lower Binfield, and the year's 1900", and
there follows a catalogue of apparently changeless things in the
small world of the country town as he remembers it, and the
larger world, indeed the universe outside:

> Vicky's at Windsor, God's in heaven, Christ's on the cross,
> Jonah's in the whale, Shadrach, Meshach, and Abednego are
> in the fiery furnace, and Sihon king of the Amorites and Og
> the king of Bashan are sitting on their thrones looking at one
> another—not doing anything exactly, just existing, keeping
> their appointed places, like a couple of fire-dogs, or the Lion
> and the Unicorn.

This is the world that "was good to live in" and, it seems, good
to die in. Later, thinking about the church again, Bowling
reflects how, though he "never met anyone who gave me the
impression of really believing in a future life", it did not then
matter:

> . . . it's precisely in a settled period, a period when civilisa-
> tion seems to stand on its four legs like an elephant, that such
> things as a future life don't matter. It's easy enough to die
> if the things you care about are going to survive. You've had
> your life, you're getting tired, it's time to go underground—
> that's how people used to see it. Individually they were
> finished, but their way of life would continue. Their good and
> evil would remain good and evil. They didn't feel the ground
> shifting under their feet.

There are some strange assumptions here, the most curious of
which is the implication that a moral indifferentism—good *and*
evil being equal and opposite, and apparently equally desirable
—is a part of the feeling of security. But the idea of a safe
harbour predominates; it isn't perhaps so surprising that Orwell
insisted in his will on being buried in a country churchyard.
    To the Church, therefore, as an institution of nonsensical but

comforting changelessness George Bowling returns when he embarks on his holiday from the present, the skive which a gift from providence or the devil—a chance win on a racehorse— makes possible. Like Gordon Comstock, he is looking for a refuge underground, where in this case the past is buried; like him, but more bitterly, he finds out his mistake. He visits the parish church, smells again "the same dusty, sweetish corpse-smell", and for a moment thinks that nothing has altered; but now there are no people. They are either outside in the church-yard, "full to the brim", where his parents lie, or he is outside them, having lost all contact with the living of Lower Binfield. The vicar, the same vicar as twenty years ago, speaks to him but doesn't recognise him, and George doesn't remind him because, as he carefully explains, the sight of a man not, in the terms of middle age, so very much older than himself makes him realise how old *he* is, and therefore excluded from the land of the living. This may seem an odd way of reasoning, but it suffices George, who meets a girl outside and notes the look she gives him, "not frightened, not hostile" but "like a wild animal when you catch its eye" : because his memories must be mean-ingless to her she is "living in a different world ... like an animal". He walks the streets of the town unrecognised and feels "invisible", a "ghost", but again makes no attempt to bridge the gap. In particular, when he comes across the woman who was the sweetheart of his young manhood he doesn't greet her; there follows a strange and blood-chilling episode which in fact reverses without altering his reaction to the sight of the elderly, but well-preserved vicar.

We are first introduced to this woman, Elsie, when she and George are lovers in Lower Binfield before 1914; it is her with whom he has his first sexual experience and, he then says in recollection, "I'm grateful to Elsie, because she was the first person who taught me to care about a woman". No such feelings return to him now, when he notices something familiar about her back and, following her "cautiously", presently catches sight of her face : "And Jesus Christ! It was Elsie ... That fat hag!" He continues to follow her, fascinated by the change into a fat, middle-aged woman which he, a fat, middle-aged man, describes in detail and with loathing, reflecting brutally on "the things that twenty-four years can do for a woman ... It made me downright glad I'm a man. No man ever goes to pieces quite so completely as that". He even goes into the small shop she now keeps and pretends to buy something in order to have a closer look, careful to remain unrecognised, thinking of "the July nights under the chestnut trees" of the Elsie of his youth, and finding no spark of former feeling in himself :

> Here was I and there was she, our bodies might be a yard apart, and we were just as much strangers as though we'd never met. As for her, she didn't even recognise me. If I told her who I was, very likely she wouldn't even remember. And if she did remember, what would she feel? Just nothing.

He does not, however, take the risk of reminding her.

So callous an attitude seems to require more explanation than the fact that people and places change, and that the process is often painful to discover. George Bowling himself, or Orwell on his behalf, is well enough aware, as he confesses to getting "a kind of scientific kick" out of studying the physical decay of his former mistress, that there is something horrible about such behaviour. To understand it we must look for more urgent pressures upon George Bowling in his return to Lower Binfield than a fit of sentimental sight-seeing, and a more bitter disappointment than regret for old, familiar faces. In the opening sentence of the novel he contemplates his "new false teeth", seen a few sentences later "magnified by the water in the tumbler ... grinning at me like the teeth in a skull", a much more frightening *memento mori* than the skull-faced undertaker in the church choir. But though thus brought face to face with his forty-five years it is not simply in an attempt to escape from middle age and to recover lost youth that he sets off to revisit the past. Rather is he looking for something he never had; he doesn't even know what it is, but it is far more precious than memory. There is an inkling of it before he even makes his disillusioning trip, though it is then that the "wonderful idea" occurs to him.

Driving through the country on business the previous March he stops his car on impulse and looks over a spring field where "a tramp or somebody had left the remains of a fire. A little pile of white embers and a wisp of smoke still oozing out of them". He gazes at the scene, "alone, quite alone", but in a frame of mind very different from the "scientific detachment" with which he had protected himself from contact with the decayed Elsie, although expressed in much the same words. Now, though alone, he has an apprehension of shared being, almost of mutual recognition : "I was looking at the field, and the field was looking at me." He thinks about the dying fire, and finds in it a message no more than half grasped, but of high importance :

> You know the look of a wood fire on a still day. The sticks that have gone all to white ash and still keep the shape of sticks, and under the ash the kind of vivid red that you can see into. It's curious that a red ember looks more alive, gives you more of a feeling of life, than any living thing. There's something about it, a kind of intensity, a vibration—I can't think of the exact words. But it lets you know you're alive yourself.

This, though couched in ordinarily realistic description, is an attempt to describe the reality within or beyond appearance, of which the embers still glowing in their cerements of ash become a momentary symbol. They are a symbol of unseen life; also, because when the wind blows such a fire can spring into flames again, of resurrection. Within George Bowling their import works for a little while with profound effect. He thinks of himself and the badges of his dull existence—"wife, two kids and a house in the suburbs written all over me"—and even, to complete the picture, takes out his false teeth and looks at them, seeing for an instant that *"it doesn't matter*. Even false teeth don't matter" : that the sordid and repulsive, the meanness and wretchedness, the horror of mortality dissolve like smoke in the presence of reality itself. "It's a feeling inside you, a kind of peaceful feeling, and yet it's like a flame."

It does not last, of course. George Bowling's grasp upon the insight that has given him a glimpse of "happiness", as he calls it, actually of eternal life—"I felt that though I shan't live for ever I'd be quite ready to"—is terribly precarious, as is shown by the next thing that happens. In his solitary but not lonely pleasure and sensation of peace he has picked a bunch of primroses and is smelling them when he hears a car approaching; in immediate panic at being caught out—"A fat man in a bowler hat holding a bunch of primroses!"—he throws the flowers away and "as the car went past I pretended to be doing up a fly-button". The conviction that circumstances don't matter and can't touch the feeling which is like a flame has not in fact survived the first return of self-consciousness, and is laughed off with a ribald reversal of the usual euphemism about plucking a rose. "Fat men mustn't pick primroses, at any rate in public" : it is not doing up one's trousers but the exposure of emotions that is obscene.

At the beginning, speaking about his status as a fat man and the supposed character it imposes on him, George Bowling has tried to imagine himself behaving like the hero of a romance and breaking down "in a paroxysm of weeping", concluding : "You couldn't, with a figure like mine. It would be downright obscene." This is so absurd, unless George Bowling is indeed a Donald McGill caricature and no more, that one looks for more meaning in it than appears. What is obscene is the display of emotion itself, and especially of emotion connected with love and loss (the imagined occasion being the infidelity of Bowling's wife, "suppose I did care"). What makes it more obscene in a fat man is that his very fatness renders the emotion, in the traditional understanding of the passions, more real, more of the flesh. We can see how little the thin man taking Bowling's bulk as a disguise has entered him in spirit : he can hide behind a swag-belly and allow his outward man to be pudgy and soft, but to be possessed by the tender bowels of feeling is too dangerous to be admitted.

Yet it is clear to Orwell-Bowling that an essential part of human capacity has been wasted, or cut away, and that without it we are lost. After throwing away the wild flowers and covering up his brief interlude of feeling, Bowling begins to think again of the dark future, "the next slump and the next war" and all that they will bring : "And you can't face that kind of thing unless you've got the right feeling inside you. There's something that's gone out of us in the twenty years since the war. It's a kind of vital juice that we've squirted away till there's nothing left." He has tried to explain it already as "a feeling of security, even when they weren't secure" among people before 1914; but that could hardly supply the right feeling which might enable them to face a dire future in which all security and continuity will have been broken. What the vital juice is he doesn't say, but Orwell provides an association at least in a metaphor used more than once, most fully elaborated in a note of a year or two later. Discussing in 1940 Malcolm Muggeridge's "brilliant but depressing" book *The Thirties* he is reminded "of a rather cruel trick I once played on a wasp. He was sucking jam on my plate, and I cut him in half. He paid no attention, merely went on with his meal, while a tiny stream of jam trickled out of his severed oesophagus. Only when he tried to fly away did he grasp the dreadful thing that had happened to him. It is the same with modern man. The thing that has been cut away is his soul, and there was a period—twenty years perhaps—during which he did not notice it".

The relation of this memory to George Bowling's fleeting perception is obvious, and so perhaps is that of the next sentence, "It was absolutely necessary that the soul should be cut away", to Bowling's self-mutilation. The obscene bowels of passion and compassion must be ruthlessly excised, with immediate consequences on any attempt to flee the wrath to come. Back in his car, Bowling thinks again of the "bad time coming", and the want of any vital juice to fortify those who will have to face it. He thinks of mankind's distraction by outer circumstances : "All this rushing to and fro ! Everlasting din of buses, bombs, radios, telephone bells. Nerves worn all to bits, empty places in our bones where the marrow ought to be." The next sentence is, "I shoved my foot down on the accelerator", and one can't be sure whether or not the irony is intentional.

It is in this frame of mind that he resolves to go back to Lower Binfield. It is evidently an enterprise of vital importance, in the exact sense of the word; just as evidently it is bound to fail. He hopes there to climb out of the "dustbin" of modern times, and dwells obsessively on the dustbin's contents, a catalogue of the hateful things jostling in his mind, machine-guns and rubber truncheons, aspirins, the cinema and radio, the terror of the sack and of the looming concentration camp. The same list, with variations, occurs over and over again in Orwell's other writings. To Gordon Comstock's itemisation of horrors are now added all the things made clearer in the last years of the 'thirties and learned by Orwell at first hand in industrial England and in Spain. He was now intensely conscious of political hopes and even more of fears, his "accurate political orientation" giving him at least a fairly accurate idea of what political upheaval

may involve. His exploration of the depressed areas and his encounter with civil war, recorded in *The Road to Wigan Pier*
and *Homage to Catalonia* was highly personal, and the amplifi-
cation they lent to his nightmare vision took idiosyncratic
forms even there. In *Coming Up For Air* they become the
nightmare of someone who is not supposed to know anything
about them : at the beginning of his story George Bowling
observes that there's not much news in the paper, "down in
Spain and over in China they were murdering each other as
usual", and we are intended to accept this as the extent of his
interest. Later on, as preface to his Spring resolve to revisit the
home of his childhood, he has a further contact with contemporary politics through the somewhat improbable device (considering the character that has been sketched for him) of a Left
Book Club meeting to which he is dragged by his wife.

It produces a characteristic and (as may well be thought)
wildly distorted view of an "anti-Fascist" lecture of the time, in
which Bowling sees nothing but an expression of hate, a general
outburst of fear and hatred concentrated in the image (one to
which Orwell always seemed to turn when thinking of violence)
of "smashing people's faces in". That it is his own hatred is
made very clear when, feeling that the lecturer had "got inside"
his skull, he "turns the tables" and gets inside the other man's :
not, however, so much by empathy as projection. "For about a
second I was inside him, you might almost say I *was* him";
and thus is enabled to see and describe with something very near
to relish the vision of face-smashing. ("Smash! Right in the
middle! The bones cave in like an eggshell and what was a
face a minute ago is just a great blob of strawberry jam.")
The idea leads George Bowling back naturally to the fear of
war always in the hinterland of his mind and to the "after-war"
which frightens him more, described in terms looking forward
to a world elaborated later :

The world we're going down into, the kind of hate-world,
slogan-world. The coloured shirts, the barbed wire, the
rubber truncheons. The secret cells where the electric light
burns night and day, and the detectives watching you while
you sleep. And the processions and the posters with enormous
faces, and the crowds of a million people all cheering for the
Leader till they deafen themselves into thinking that they

really worship him, and all the time, underneath, they hate him so that they want to puke. It's all going to happen.

George Bowling's mingled fascination and horror at his own prevision ("so terrified of the future", as he says himself, "that we're jumping straight into it like a rabbit diving down a boa-constrictor's throat") is simply Orwell's own, and it is important to remember that in his case it had corroboration at least in actual experience. When he was about to start on *Coming Up For Air* Orwell wrote to a friend that he would probably "have to finish it in a concentration camp"; in fact he finished it in Morocco, on a convalescent holiday; but in the conditions of the time it was not a very unreasonable expectation. When, in his record of the fighting in Barcelona and the politics behind it, Orwell said (again, in a characteristic image) "it is a horrible thing to have to enter into the details of inter-party polemics; it is like diving into a cesspool," he must be owned to know what he was talking about. George Bowling, however improbable the knowledge in the ordinary, apolitical man he is supposed to be, must be allowed the benefit of his author's experience: "Wherever we're going, we're going downwards. Into the grave or into the cesspool—no knowing." It is that prospect that can't be faced without "the right feeling inside".

The outward justification for Bowling's fears should be remembered just in order to appreciate their inner meaning: everything he sees and dreads in his world may be true, and yet is related to events within himself. As he walks about the streets of Lower Binfield unrecognised, outraged by the changes he sees on every hand, it seems to him that the war has already begun. His town, either rebuilt or disguised with fakery—his very birthplace turned into an arty tea-shop where the waitress receives him with a sour look—has suffered an "enemy invasion"; the people, predominantly young, who crowd the streets, are "bloody aliens"; everyone regards him either with hostility or indifference. The new inhabitants of the town are hardly to be distinguished from the "huge army" of accusing persons that he has imagined pursuing him when he takes the "forbidden" turning to Lower Binfield and immediately thinks *"they"* are after him. "They", all the people who would try to prevent his escape into the past, include as he says, almost everybody, from his wife and children to "the Home Secretary,

Scotland Yard, the Temperance League, the Bank of England, Lord Beaverbrook, Hitler and Stalin on a tandem bicycle, the bench of Bishops, Mussolini, the Pope" the "people whom you've never seen but who rule your destiny all the same". With this throng after him his journey backwards is already a panic flight; the accusing crowd without and within continually reflect each other.

The most extreme effect of this naked paranoia shows later when he resolves that "if I'm a ghost I'll *be* a ghost" of a malevolent kind, haunting the old places and maybe working "a bit of black magic on some of these bastards who've stolen my home town from me". In this spirit he encounters a party of schoolchildren at ARP drill, marching up the street in columns of four with a banner, "BRITONS PREPARE", and regards them with dislike while noting a couple of the bombing planes from a nearby airfield flying over another part of the town. The past is inaccessible, the present unbearable, what's coming is an unthinkable future; and the future actually arrives before its time, so to speak, when a bomb is dropped on the town accidentally. He now sees the schoolchildren again, running in panic down the street and dutifully wearing their gas masks, so that they seem to him a herd of galloping pigs, "a sort of huge flood of pig-faces". It should be noted that he feels no sympathy with the children whatever: transformed to Gadarene swine they are thought of only with disgust and contempt, "bolting for some cellar where they'd been told to take cover". He himself has reacted to the explosion with fright but also with exhilaration: "Even in the echo of that awful, deafening crash . . . I had time to think that there's something grand about the bursting of a big projectile." When with other curious persons he reaches the place where the bomb has fallen, killing three people, he is able to take a detached interest in the scene, including the appearance of a severed leg "with the trouser still on it and a black boot with a Wood-Milne rubber-heel". He learns later that an Air Ministry official reporting on the accident has described the effects of the bomb as "disappointing". The heavy irony makes its point, of course; but considering his first reaction, and how much of Gordon Comstock continues in George Bowling, one may wonder whose is the real disappointment. Indeed he recognises, though without any sense of remorse, that the bomb has fallen in response to his own wish: disillusioned and having discovered that the refuge of his secret imagination "didn't exist", he has taken violent revenge :

I'd chucked a pine-apple into my dreams, and lest there should be any mistake the Royal Air Force had followed up with five hundred pounds of T.N.T.

The final disillusion, the climax of the whole story of a failed search, has come just before, when he revisits a boyhood haunt outside the town, a deep pool once hidden in the woods. The significance of this place, and his bitter rage at finding it changed like the rest of the town, must be looked at more closely. It is the true object of his return, and his approach to it, with the progressive disappointment of his hopes, is gradual. First he learns that in the general transformation of the neighbourhood to ignominious or sinister uses the private mansion in whose grounds the water lay has been turned into a lunatic asylum. Then, when he gets to the spot, he finds the lake still there but surrounded by new houses and turned into a children's boating pond, the water now "dead". On its edge he meets an "oldish" man of a "type" that has in many other places roused the fear and hostility of Orwell's spokesmen, or directly of Orwell himself (notably in *The Road to Wigan Pier*): a "crank", with "something vaguely queer about his appearance", wearing shorts and sandals, with twinkling blue eyes behind his spectacles and "a benevolent old chuckle and a way of wrinkling his face up, like a rabbit"; "one of those old men who've never grown up". He proudly tells Bowling about the "Woodland City" the place has now become, a colony of sham half-timbering and nudist parties, inhabited by vegetarians, lady novelists and psychical research workers; a scrap of the original woodland has been preserved as "the Pixy Glen".

This grotesque cartoon-figure of elderly simple-lifing produces an extreme repugnance in Bowling as he is shown round the estate ("some of the houses made me wish I'd got a hand-grenade in my pocket"), cited by some commentators as an instance of violent recoil from unacknowledged homosexuality. The "queer" old man, of the sort who are "always either health-food cranks or else they have something to do with the Boy Scouts" does indeed suggest something of the kind. But what he certainly also is, is a reflection of Bowling's own failure in trying to recapture his own boyhood, the emptiness of trying to get back to Nature when the emotionally grasped essence of nature has departed; the childhood he had tried to reconstruct is indeed a hollow shell of sham-Tudor beams and false buttresses "that don't buttress anything". Being so flimsy a refuge it can only be destroyed in what, truly, is childish rage at childish weakness.

The elderly pixie appropriately has the worst news for George Bowling : the small, secret pool that once lay beyond the lake and that he has thought of as peculiarly his own has been filled in, used as the "Woodland City's" rubbish dump. He goes to see. The water has been drained off and all that is left is "a great round hole, like an enormous well, twenty or thirty feet deep. Already it was half full of tin cans". Bowling goes away cursing, "finished with this notion of getting back into the past". "Coming up for air! But there isn't any air. The dustbin that we're in reaches up to the stratosphere."

He tells himself that he doesn't really care, and perhaps it is true, since like Gordon Comstock he has lost the part that would be able to care. But his rage is left, and the bomb that falls on Lower Binfield the next day is a revenge for his loss.

What is this pool, obscure and hidden, yet at the heart of the story? Once, we are told, it was connected with the larger and shallower lake, and then had been cut off—"the stream had dried up and the woods had closed round the small pool and it had just been forgotten", so that the fish in it were left to grow enormous. Despite the assurance that "it's a thing that happens occasionally" it does not seem a very probable natural occurrence. But it is a powerful symbol of an interior event, a picture of the deep source of feeling within, the connection to which has dried up so that it is forgotten or denied, but which remains hidden below consciousness with living things in it of "monstrous sizes". When George Bowling comes upon it as a boy—the consequence, as in a fairy tale, of a "good turn" done to a gnome-like old man who is caretaker of the grounds where lake and pool are secluded—it is hardly like anything in a physical landscape but something seen in a dream, intensely real but not in terms of waking life. It is of "very clear water and immensely deep", so that although the boy can see far into it nobody can actually see the bottom. Having seen it once, George resolves to return but never does, and when he comes back after thirty years it has nothing in it but rubbish.

The dream-pool is not only a reservoir of deep and pure water, it contains fish; it is in the hope of catching one of the "monsters" there that George Bowling goes back to look for it. There is a great deal about fishing in the novel—it was in fact a favourite pastime of Orwell's youth, but here it has become something more than one of the remembered pleasures of boyhood. The whole book swarms with references to fish and fishing, not only as the most prized activity of George Bowling as a boy but as recurrent metaphor and simile, with the striking ambiguity of effect which is now becoming familiar. The very idea embodied in the title is derived from the thought of sea-creatures coming up to breathe, and yet it is down beneath the surface, to what Orwell elsewhere (in *Such, Such Were the Joys*) called "the alien under-water world" of childhood that George Bowling seeks to go. Between the underwater world as place of heart's desire and of "alien" life George Bowling's feelings continually swing to and fro. When he is walking like a ghost about the transformed streets of Lower Binfield he thinks of himself as in two places at once, like the character of an H. G. Wells story which he remembers, suffering "a kind of hallucination that he was at the bottom of the sea", with "the great crabs and cuttlefish reaching out to get him". At the same time he is getting ready to go fishing again and, if he can, bring something up out of the strange waters. In hysterical rage and fear he sees the time soon coming when "everything you've ever known is going down, down, into the muck", "into the cesspool"; at the same time it is strongly suggested that the real air, the life-giving oxygen the soul requires, is to be found only in the depths.

Jonah, the recalcitrant prophet who was swallowed by a great fish, appears many times, and always inside the whale, which is regarded as the proper place for him to be—only at the end, and in despair, Bowling reflects that "there's no way back . . . you can't put Jonah back into the whale". A relationship can be traced at many points between *Coming Up For Air* and the essay Orwell wrote soon afterwards, *Inside the Whale* : there he is quite clear that "being inside a whale is a very comfortable, cosy, homelike thought . . . . The whale's belly is simply a womb big enough for an adult. There you are, in the dark cushioned space that exactly fits you, with yards of blubber between yourself and reality, able to keep up an attitude of complete indifference, no matter *what* happens".

George Bowling obviously feels strongly the attractions of such a situation, and so we may infer did Orwell, though in his case with an intermixture of moral doubt. The essay (written at the time the war broke out, and published in 1940) arrives at the idea from which it takes its title by the most roundabout way— Orwell, commenting on Henry Miller among other contemporary authors, seizes on a discussion by Miller of Anais Nin, and thence upon Miller's reference to yet another writer, Aldous Huxley, from whom eventually is taken the image of being "inside the whale". Such a tortuous process suggests that Orwell meant to get there anyway; and in fact the story of Jonah and the whale is at the centre of the essay's moral debate between advocacy of politically active writing, what is now called "committed", and of the kind of passivity, not to say indifferentism, that Orwell found in Miller. Orwell, though it is obvious that he more than half envies Miller's attitude, left the argument unresolved and even, it may be thought, in a state of confusion, which must be further examined later.

The novel's use of the same metaphor, or complex of metaphors is not, perhaps, less confused, but at a different level: what in the essay is regarded as a symbol of choice between political or non-political positions is for George Bowling (who cares as little as Miller for political controversy, and is as full of foreboding of the political future as Orwell) an image of personal, or ontological significance; whether to be inside or outside the whale is a question of modes of being. For Bowling the idea of Jonah safe within the whale's belly continually returns to join the uneasy alternation between the wish to be wholly contained—to return in fact not merely to childhood but the womb—and to have within oneself something worth containing. Perhaps, especially if one is large-bellied and blubbery, like a woman, one should be one's own whale and swallow oneself?—and indeed at one point, during a spell of voracious reading in a backwater of the First World War, Bowling imagines himself tearing into the books "like a whale that's got in among a shoal of shrimps".

During the war, while still in France, Bowling and a like-minded fellow-soldier make plans (which are frustrated) to go fishing behind the front; he remarks, recalling this, that "fishing is the opposite of war". Even when connected as it is there with the idea of escaping from "the noise and the stink" of army life, it seems an extravagant claim. But when we read it, or in another place how, having long given up angling, Bowling watches a man catch a large sea-fish and feels that "something kind of moved inside me"; or how as a boy he would gaze at the fish in the river with a "kind of passion," we can see that it is not hyperbole. Fishing is the opposite of war not because it is a tranquil occupation—on the contrary, as described by Bowling it is full of frantic excitement—but because unlike the incomprehensible horrors of modern warfare, the "enormous machine that had got hold of you", it has personal meaning. One can perhaps say—and anyone who has ever pulled a fish up from the depths and felt it moving on the line, alive though not yet visible, may be able to agree—that, "sport" apart, it actually represents the discovery or recovery of meaning: a living shape rising and taking on definition through the waters of existence. Hook and line are not only the hunter's cruel device but the means of making a personal connection. George Bowling remembers catching his first fish : "Christ, that feeling! The line jerking and straining, and a fish on the other end of it!" Later he associates it with other savage feelings of boyhood, "breaking rules and killing things", with the comment "thank God I'm a man, because no woman ever has that feeling". A woman, it may be thought, does not have to hunt for living meaning with such predatory hunger, for she already contains it.

These meanings converge and have their most intense, though also their most mysterious expression in the "monstrous", still uncaught and perhaps uncatchable fish that swim in the deep pool hidden in the woods. The first glimpse of one of them has an extraordinary effect on fourteen-year-old George Bowling : it "almost made me jump out of my skin"; it glides across the pool, "deep under water", becomes a shadow and disappears into shadow, and "I felt as if a sword had gone through me". He watches for a while and leaves with plans to return with all the tackle to haul one of the great fish to the surface, but he never returns and never sees them again.

The carp—though he is not sure if they are carp or what they are—remain George Bowling's secret, "stored away in my mind". He thinks of them as *his,* but something or other always prevents him making his claim good. While courting his Elsie he goes once with her to the large and shallow lake and thinks to go further; but, being dressed in his Sunday best and also because "I wanted Elsie very badly"—reasons given in that order—he turns back and, finding her pliable and inviting, has with her his first experience of sexual intercourse. "So that was that. The big carp faded out my mind again. . . ." If fish and fishing have an obvious association with sexuality, here it is a very ambiguous one. And if the carp, the first sight of which went through young Bowling "like a sword", seems to present him with the possibility of alternative sexual experience, that of a woman, that neither limits nor exhausts the potentiality of meaning within it.

The pool and what is in it fade from his conscious thoughts in all the intervening, irrelevant years of growing up, going to war, getting married and earning a living : "When I look back I realise that my active life, if I ever had one, ended when I was sixteen." They return to him in his last, middle-aged attempt to rediscover what he has lost, and we have already seen what happens then; but before this final disintegration of hope into hatred and rubbish, he remembers the pool "in the dark place among the trees, waiting for me all those years. And the huge fish still gliding round it. Jesus!"

Perhaps the exclamation is no more than a casual profanity, to which George Bowling is prone. Perhaps on the previous occasion, when he turns aside from the pool for the charms, coolly taken and coolly felt, of the complaisant Elsie, there is no conscious association with the man who, making his excuse, had married a wife and therefore could not come—although we know that Orwell used this scrap of parable in facetious reference to his own marriage in 1936. It seems possible, however, to take the whole story of the fish as Orwell's own parable : of the great, mysterious, and moving treasure waiting like truth in the deep well, of its severance from the ordinary affairs of life, including a discovery of sex chiefly remarkable for shallowness and impermanence; of the contrast between the traditional Church where the chief activity is of the dead burying their dead, and the living Christ, the Self, uncaught, whose word is like a sword; of the devastating effects of denial and separation. But neither George Bowling nor Orwell was able to interpret it.

IV

The Moral Pigsty

"MOST OF THE good memories of my childhood and up to the age of about twenty", said Orwell (in *Such, Such Were the Joys*), "are in some way connected with animals." He did not enlarge on the confession at the time, merely dropping it in, so it seems, to emphasise by contrast the bad memories he had connected with human beings. It fits well enough into the picture supplied from other sources of a boy largely brought up (despite belonging to the "landless gentry") in the country and with much holiday time devoted to fishing and shooting. Close and accurate observation of animals is scattered throughout his writings, from the boyhood memories incorporated in *Coming Up for Air* (George Bowling, for instance, reading penny dreadfuls in the privacy of his father's grain-loft with a mouse for company, "I'm watching the mouse and the mouse is watching me") to the grievous empathy with an animal victim so powerfully shown in *Shooting an Elephant*. It may be remarked that Orwell evidently shared the sensitive, though unsentimental appreciation of their quarry found in many sportsmen : the shooting expedition in *Burmese Days*, culminating in killing a leopard—conveying at the same time the excitements of the hunt, the grace and beauty of the hunted, and the pathos of its appearance in death, "like a dead kitten"—is as good as anything in the literature of "big game". The "good memories" may have been largely bound up, as in George Bowling's case, with "killing things", but there were pets as well, and also no doubt the fantasies by which children enter animal lives; we are told at least that Orwell was especially fond as a boy of Beatrix Potter's *Tale of Pigling Bland*.

Such is the background of *Animal Farm*, Orwell's penultimate work of fiction, and in several ways his most successful. It may be inferred that he took a particular pleasure in writing it, and certainly he prized it highly, fighting doggedly against a succession of setbacks and obstructions to get it published and even considering at one time publishing it himself as a privately printed pamphlet. His persistence had a political motive, of course, just as the obstruction was political in origin : publishers, obediently self-censoring, were unwilling to touch so bitter an attack on the Soviet regime while the USSR was an ally of Britain, and Orwell was the more determined that such expedient reasons should be ignored. Yet both determination and reluctance were connected with a quality in a sense independent of political considerations : it is because *Animal Farm* is so good a story that its attack is so devastating. The full effectiveness of the satire is hardly to be separated from its referents, and perhaps it is impossible to distinguish means and meanings : as Orwell said, it was "the first book in which I tried, with full consciousness of what I was doing, to fuse political purpose and artistic purpose into one whole" and the fusing, we may say, was complete. It is worth remembering, however, that right from the beginning *Animal Farm* has been taken by some, and not all of them children, simply as an "animal story".

The writing of it was however clearly a political act, and not only as expression of Orwell's views on the USSR, which he had voiced frequently and vehemently ever since his experience of Stalinism in action in Spain, but as summing up of his feelings about political life as such. In this sense it can be taken as the culmination of his personal involvement in politics through the preceding decade, as the foreboding 'thirties passed into the catastrophic 'forties and public events pressed more and more closely upon him. These were the years in which he became as he said "a sort of pamphleteer" : the characteristically divided feelings about politics appear in the context of this confession, in *Why I Write*.

Having listed what he reckoned as a writer's chief motives— "sheer egoism", "aesthetic enthusiasm", and "historical impulse", with "political purpose" last—he said that "by nature— taking your 'nature' to be the state you have attained when you are first adult—I am a person in whom the first three motives would outweigh the fourth". In a more "peaceful age"—the sort of age when presumably he might have been "a happy vicar"— he might, he said, "have written ornate or merely descriptive books and might have remained almost unaware of my political loyalties". There is a double assumption here, on the one hand of a "nature" fundamentally non-political, without any strong "desire to push the world in a certain direction", and on the other of loyalties also felt to be part of his nature, in the sense that they can exist, at any rate as a predisposition, before he himself is conscious of them. The division is the ostensible subject at least of the poem Orwell then went on to quote; and no doubt both assumptions were true, that political activity was naturally uncongenial to him, and also that elements in his nature inexorably drew him into it. Probably they are true of most people in whom opinions about public affairs, the "accurate political orientation" that Orwell went on to claim for himself, crystallise gradually through time and circumstance.

The evolution of his opinions is amply recorded in the succession of books from *The Road to Wigan Pier* and *Homage to Catalonia* to *The Lion and the Unicorn*, the wartime booklet written for the Ministry of Information and its later version *The English People*; letters and other writings, notably the weekly commentary he contributed to *Tribune* from 1943 to 1945, and his wartime reports to *Partisan Review*, fill in the picture. The changes and contradictions in his views, and especially his abrupt about-face which he made, in common with many others at the time, in his attitude to the war itself, have been much commented on. (Having opposed British war-preparations from, roughly, a Left-wing Socialist standpoint he became an active supporter of the war-effort in 1940, heaping approbrium on pacifists and other opponents of the war with energy and venom.)

The opinions themselves and the way Orwell altered them are outside the scope of the present study, though some of their implications are not; perhaps all that need be said here is that he changed his mind quite often on political matters, which is usual, and, what is less common, generally had the honesty to admit it. The point is rather to see in *Animal Farm* the mature fruit of this evolution and of the two strands within it, the urge to political action and at the same time his profound disillusion with the "world of politics", the world of man as political animal.

Orwell himself seems to have felt about *Animal Farm* in something of this way, both as the nearest approach to "what I have most wanted to do throughout the past ten years . . . to make political writing into an art", and also as the goal of his personal development. In the preface which he provided to the Ukrainian translation he devoted what may well seem disproportionate space to an account of himself and his life, amounting to a potted autobiography. It is introduced almost wilfully, as by one forcibly buttonholing his readers : "they will", he says, "most likely expect me to say something of how *Animal Farm* originated, but first I would like to say something about myself and the experiences by which I arrived at my political position." There follows a condensed but quite comprehensive sketch of family background, Eton education, and the events of his adult life from Burma to Spain. Hardly anything is said in fact about the "origin" of the story beyond description of an incident when Orwell watched a large horse being driven by a small boy and subsequently reflected that "men exploit animals in much the same way as the rich exploit the proletariat."

Evidently he felt that the origins of the story were more personal than this more or less fortuitous episode, and that, especially for readers who could not be expected to know anything about him beforehand, the important thing was to understand something about the author. And in truth this apologia does not strike us as irrelevant, just because everything personal is excluded from the work itself. *Animal Farm* can be recognised readily enough as the expression of Orwell's opinions, but alone of his works it is one from which he is entirely absent as subject. A stranger reading it would know nothing about the way these opinions had been arrived at, and Orwell felt that he should. Upon the work itself he had no wish to comment : "if it does not speak for itself, it is a failure." But for himself he wished to speak, and could only do so outside.

Within the world of *Animal Farm* there is no subjective life at all. The beasts have feelings and are endowed with thought, of a simple, "animal" kind; the two carthorses, Boxer and Clover, who share something like the heroic role, reflect upon events with dim unease as the Revolution is betrayed, pondering but not understanding what is happening—Boxer, of course, has been introduced to us as "not of first-class intelligence". The animals who on the other hand are supposed to be the most intelligent, or cunning—the cat, Moses the raven, the pigs themselves, the "cleverest" of all—have no interior life. We are never told what they think or feel, except by inference from what they do. Benjamin, the sceptical and worldly-wise (and also literate) donkey, who clearly represents an Orwellian view from inside the story, is described like the others from outside, and in any case stands on the fringe of events, a marginal observer.

All this seems to us perfectly natural, and such laborious "analysis" of the animals' personalities, or lack of them, must be a ponderous absurdity. We recognise the classic mode of telling "animal stories", from Aesop to Beatrix Potter, and note with relief the absence of subjective thought which when attributed to "animal heroes" is usually so embarrassing. Nevertheless, when *Animal Farm* is considered in relation to Orwell's other writings, both fiction and non-fiction, the way in which self-consciousness has been eliminated is very striking. It is in fact unique among Orwell's works in this respect; yet in it, in the dry, clear, almost flat tone of the narrative, and the progress of the story with the absolute, impersonal conviction of a true fairy-tale, we also recognise what we take to be the characteristic Orwellian style. *Animal Farm* exemplifies completely what he reckoned the mark of good writing, the effacement of the writer's "own personality" which nevertheless allows what he wants to say to show the more clearly and, indeed, to be most unmistakably *his*. The paradox is that style, the distinguishing mark of the author as individual, is most plainly recognisable—is most fully realised for us in his writing—when he himself has vanished from our minds. "Good prose", Orwell said, "is like a window pane." And when he said it he must have had in mind the work from which the "subjectivity" he deplored had for once been erased. To erase it is itself a subjective act, and conclusions about the writer may be drawn therefrom. But first his success must be acknowledged, that here as nowhere else did he contrive to give an account of "his" world from which he himself was absent. The window pane of his prose is beautifully transparent, unclouded by personal reflection; the author, having stepped out of the way, leaves the view, which is his view, quite unobstructed.

It is a view at once restricted and comprehensive. In political terms it goes far beyond the immediate purpose of satirising the Russian Revolution and its consequences and of exposing, as

Orwell put it in his preface, "the Soviet myth". It should not be necessary to point out, but it is often ignored, that the assumptions of *Animal Farm* are no more favourable to the political systems of "Western democracy" than they are to Soviet tyranny or to Nazism. The animals who take over Manor Farm are the victims in the end not only of their own rulers but of "Frederick" and "Pilkington" on either side of them, and finally it is all the "neighbouring farmers", the great and powerful of all the earth meeting to divide and squabble over its spoils, whose condition is contrasted with their own. No "anti-communist" politico should take comfort from the fable, which is an attack on politics as such : it shows political activity of any kind and in pursuit of any ostensible aim as ridiculous, base in motive, and of disastrous consequence. It represents strictly, even literally, a view of man's life as nasty, brutish and short, but is precisely the reverse of Hobbesian in implication : the despotic power set up over the lives of all, whether by immemorial tradition (the ordinary farms where animals accept their exploitation as the natural order) or by revolutionary innovation, is not a reconciling and serviceable one but destructive and self-seeking; if there is any such thing as a covenant or contract between rulers and ruled it is simply a fraud. Tyranny may be necessary in the sense that it is inevitable, but it is not good : Leviathan may be an imitation of the work of God, but it is evil.

If we say that the device of the story is literally to show man as "political animal" we must not forget the division between those who practice politics and those who are the victims of them. The real political animals of *Animal Farm* are the pigs, a selection which, however dubious in terms of actual animal capabilities (one might rather think of dogs as the ones to take over and run a farm), seems absolutely right in the scheme presented. Orwell did not like pigs, though perhaps he had a certain grudging respect for them (late in his life and after *Animal Farm* had been published, he had a hand in keeping a pig on the farm of Barnhill, on Jura, and wrote to a friend, "they really are disgusting brutes, and we are all longing for the day when he goes to the butcher" : it was almost as though justifying his use or abuse of pig-nature in the story).

Pigs stink, and (however unjustly, as pig-lovers tell us) have long symbolised greed and filth. Political life is a "cesspool", as Orwell said many times; when we get down to political

"realism" all parties and nations live in a "moral pigsty".
(Though it is worth remembering that when Orwell said that,
in 1943, while in the midst of writing *Animal Farm*, the context
was a declaration of disbelief in the efficacy of "realism" : the
"first step" out of the pigsty is "probably to grasp that realism
does not pay", that *realpolitik* is not in the long run realistic.)
In *Animal Farm* it doesn't pay either, the "realists" all betray
each other, Frederick pays for stolen goods with forged bank-
notes, Pilkington and Napoleon simultaneously play the ace of
spades. But neither does anything else pay; neither the self-
sacrificing loyalty of Boxer the proletarian carthorse nor the
sceptical understanding of Benjamin the donkey avails against
the treachery of their rulers.

In political terms, and those are its terms, *Animal Farm* is
an expression of despair; that it is full of humour and even
playfulness in no way softens the conclusion of a profound
pessimism about men and affairs. The view, detached but not
aloof, is strictly tragic : Orwell's "little squib", as he called it,
has all the elements of irony, of inexorable momentum, of the
feeling of helplessness before the working out of destiny, or
history, that belong to classic tragedy. It permits a close sympathy with its creatures both as beasts and as representatives of
men, so that we feel each animal to be true to its nature and
at the same time find the hopes and aspirations which belong
to men genuinely embodied in the "short animal lives". There
is a strict justice which, even while dividing mankind into types,
allows each type its due (with the exception perhaps of Moses
the raven, representing religion and not more than a caricature
of a caricature); where men are identifiable as individuals the
lampooning, though savage, is also fair. In the case of Stalin
himself, so devastatingly exhibited, and with such complete
conviction, as the black boar Napoleon, Orwell was careful to
keep the record straight. The only recorded alteration he made
to the story after it was finished was to say that when the invad-
ing men blow up the animals' windmill "all . . . except Napoleon
flung themselves flat on their bellies" : the exception was inserted
when it was pointed out to him that at the most disastrous stage
of the German invasion of the USSR Stalin had not left
Moscow.

A lesser satirist, or one still entangled in the partisanship of
Left and Right, might have depicted the seizure of "Manor

Farm" and its transformation into "Animal Farm"—"the only farm in the whole county—in all England!—owned and operated by animals"—merely as a plot of the pigs. Orwell gave it far greater significance; it is precisely his success in transmitting the feeling that the hopes exploited by the pigs are just, and that the overthrow of Farmer Jones is in itself a joyful liberation, that gives the tale its moral momentum. (It was also the reason, we are told, why it offended so deeply conservative a critic as T. S. Eliot; when other publishers were fighting shy of *Animal Farm* as inconveniently rude to the USSR, Eliot is said to have rejected it for Faber because it was too sympathetic to revolution; the hierarchy of men over animals ought not to be disturbed.) In Orwell's narrative it is the warmth and sympathy with which "the Rebellion" is treated at the beginning that conditions the effect of the end. The aims and desires of men as social beings are transposed into animal terms without losing their force, indeed with actual enhancement, since the idea of innocence is immediately acceptable in animal terms; consequently the betrayal of innocence and the disappointment of hope is as bitter as possible.

The key device, which does not simply turn men into animals but shows a relationship between them, becomes thus a dynamic instrument : the Country of the Houyhnhnms is a static society, in which the satirical reversal overthrows man and exhibits him as an object of abhorrence, but irremovably so and without any possibility of change in the relations of horses and men. The more powerful and subtle way of turning things upside down in *Animal Farm* makes the same point, with a different emphasis, that man in the animals' eyes is disgusting and hateful, but proceeds step by step to bring back the "old order" in a new guise. The principles of "Animalism", the seven clauses of the "unalterable law" by which Animal Farm shall be guided, are conceived in relation to men : the first are merely descriptive of men, as beings that go upon two legs, wear clothes, sleep in beds, drink alcohol, all of which are forbidden; the last two, which are the really important ones, deal with the consequences of being human, that they are the ones who kill and oppress their fellow creatures. By not being human, animals shall be clean of inequality and murder. Thus the scene is set in which one by one the laws of Animalism are overthrown (always, of course, by stealth) and the laws which govern human behaviour are restored.

Everything in the story moves towards the denouement when the animals, "the creatures outside"—all the poor and oppressed, the wretched of the earth, those excluded from warmth and light—look through the farmhouse windows "from pig to man, and from man to pig, and from pig to man again; but already it was impossible to say which was which". The double vision so adroitly maintained throughout, as men are seen in animal terms and as the pigs progressively undermine the difference, comes to a sharp focus, appallingly combining both images; showing simultaneously that men who use the human ideals of freedom and justice to impose a tyranny over their fellows are no better than swine, and also that swine, in their natural state of merely animal greed and squalor, cannot possibly be so bad as men.

The end reflects exactly the feelings that so many who hoped for most from the Russian Revolution—investing in it all the Paradisal expectations of a long millenniary tradition—have come to share. But more than that, it presents with the directness, homeliness and simplicity of an authentic fairy-tale the tragic condition of humanity in general, the apparently unalterable process of corruption by which all the best efforts of men come to nothing, and decency, kindness and trust are always left out in the cold. The animals, enslaved at the beginning, have endeavoured to return to a "state of nature", naked, innocent and free, and end in a worse slavery than before. But they, who retain their animal character, suffer no moral change; only as they come to resemble men, walking on their hind legs, aspiring to consciousness and self-determination, are animals corrupted. Evil belongs to mankind.

That this dark picture is also brilliantly comic in no way lightens the effect, nor is it inconsistent with Orwell's conscious aims. Humour according to him (in the essay *Funny But Not Vulgar* published in 1944, shortly after finishing *Animal Farm*) is "the debunking of humanity", and that is the purpose of showing men in animal form: "Animals ... are only funny because they are caricatures of ourselves." Every kind of humour, even pure fantasy, says Orwell, has the fundamental aim of bringing mankind "down with a bump", "not to degrade the human being but to remind him that he is already degraded". Such debunking requires detachment; even if laughter is not solely the Hobbesian sudden glory of enjoying a supposed superiority it can only be fully effective when the debunker stands outside his object. A comparison with *Gulliver's Travels* is again instructive. Throughout his travels Gulliver is always present as subjective consciousness, a man among men, and however much they are distorted by caricature, there follows a certain intermittency and inconsistency in satirical point, as Orwell himself pointed out. The land visited by Gulliver in his last voyage is a society at least distantly comparable with that of *Animal Farm*—an Animal Farm, that is, wholly successful and static, in which mankind, the Joneses, Pilkingtons, and Fredericks have been retained as slaves. But in *Gulliver*, Orwell observed, the assault upon humanity is radically weakened by giving the entire narration over to a Yahoo who is disgusted by Yahoos. "Swift", says Orwell, "has overreached himself in his fury and is shouting at his fellow-creatures 'You are filthier than you are'."

So far as the sentiment is concerned—recoil from the stench and dirt, physical and moral, of mortal humanity—we may reflect that here, as so often in Orwell's remarks about Swift (chiefly set out in the essay on *Politics vs Literature*, 1946), what he says is true also of himself. We may take it a little further and suppose that just as, according to Orwell, Swift chose the horse as his "ideal being" because it was "an animal whose excrement was not offensive", so Orwell may have chosen pigs as morally the worst of animals, enslavers of the clean and loyal horses, for exactly the same reason, that men find pig dung peculiarly offensive, being somewhat like their own.

There are subtle shifts to be seen here in the relationship of both authors, as men, to what their fables say about man. It is undeniable that Gulliver's status as a Yahoo, ashamed of his Yahoodom but nevertheless tolerated by the Houyhnhnms as "gentle", makes a logical anomaly in the story which is aggravated by his function as its conscious centre. As Orwell points out, he finds the Yahoos disgusting at first sight, and before he has had a chance to make comparisons with the clean and noble Houyhnhnms; yet he is a Yahoo himself, and has never before noticed how revolting he is. But there is real psychological penetration in the contradiction, making clear a self-division in Gulliver (or Swift) which Orwell was, perhaps, unwilling to admit; at any rate, by making the narrator of *Animal Farm* neither a man nor an animal but an impartial and omniscient observer, the detached and timeless story-teller of once-upon-a-time, he was able to avoid it. He was also able to add pity to the irony with which, not much less ferociously than Swift, he savages mankind. If Swift's intention was to take the lord of creation, ruler and enslaver of all other creatures, and roll him in his own dirt, Orwell found an even more uncompromising way of saying, You, who think yourselves above the brutes, are more brutal than they are, and your only excuse is that, like them, you cannot help yourselves.

This conclusion, so beautifully and economically expressed in *Animal Farm*, marks the final stage of one whole side of Orwell's development, not merely as the bitter fruit of his political education but of his attitudes to people and ways of imagining them which go back earlier, before he began to feel that politics and writing are inseparable. He was always apt to see men and women as animals. Even while condemning "the assumption that human beings can be classified like insects" he had often done the same thing, thinking of some human groups as black beetles or rabbits. His description of individuals abounds with animal similes, from George Bowling's wife Hilda, "just like a hare" (and a sister evidently of Dorothy Hare the clergyman's daughter) back to the account of Charlie, the wallower in evil of *Down and Out in Paris and London*. In the latter case the comparison is the more striking just because it is not explicit but visible through hindsight, an animal model waiting to show forth :

Picture him very pink and young, with the fresh cheeks and soft brown hair of a nice little boy, and lips excessively wet and red, like cherries. His feet are tiny, and his arms abnormally short, his hand dimpled like a baby's. He has a way of dancing and capering while he talks, as though he were too happy and too full of life to keep still for an instant. . . . He declaims like an orator on the barricades, rolling the words on his tongue and gesticulating with his short arms. His small, rather piggy eyes glitter with enthusiasm. He is, somehow, profoundly disgusting to see.

Look forward fifteen years or so to Squealer, the propagandist pig of *Animal Farm*, of whose eloquence the others said that he "could turn black into white", and who in his highly adaptable literacy, and as the first to appear on hind legs, is the forerunner in the horrible transformation of pigs into men. With the addition only of a tail, "which was somehow very persuasive", Squealer is the same creature as Charlie; and we have in him an elegant example of the way an impression can sleep in an author's mind and emerge, as mature imago, to serve a slowly perfected purpose.

Such is the perfection with which this purpose is realised, the unique "fusion" in *Animal Farm* of political and aesthetic aim, that one may be inclined to call it Orwell's "masterpiece" and leave it at that, as the work by which he became famous and for which he may possibly be longest remembered. So flawless a piece seems almost outside the scope of the present study, since it is from the flaws and unresolved contradictions in Orwell's writing —so I wish to argue—that most can be learned. From this point of view, *Animal Farm* is a digression; but, before leaving it, there is a feature of the story, apparent when it is looked at in its own terms, which deserves remark.

Such is Orwell's success in making a complete world of *Animal Farm*—representing, along with the neighbouring farms, the whole of modern civilisation—that we do not notice how much, in its own scheme of equivalents, has been excluded. It is, first of all, a most peculiar place where breeding, the chief activity of stock-farming, hardly seems to take place at all. After their take-over the animals multiply, so that there are "many more mouths to feed"; the dogs have puppies, to be taken away and trained for the secret police, Napoleon's sows produce large litters to swell the membership of the Party, the hens lay eggs and stage their brief revolt (the resistance of the Russian peasants to collectivisation, here shown as a kind of infanticide) against their collection and sale to the hostile outside world. But how this all takes place is outside the picture. With the exception of Napoleon himself, as literally the Father of his People, none of the principal animal characters has any sexual life at all. The animals have feelings for each other, but—fear and suspicion apart—these are almost wholly of a social, comradely, or maternal kind. Clover, the large, stout "motherly" mare, appears to be past foaling, and Boxer, the magnificent shire horse who stands for all Orwell most admired in the working class, is her

mate evidently in name only; perhaps in fact, like Squealer the
fat porker and type of literary lackey, he is a gelding. (When
new horses are needed for the work of Animal Farm they are
brought in from outside.) The other mare, Mollie, whose flirta-
tious nature makes an amusing marginal decoration to the story
—the pampered servant of the old regime who follows her
"master" into exile, seduced by vanity and lump-sugar—seems
at first to be a real filly with the appropriate nature of her sex,
until we remember that her seduction, when she runs away, is
not by a stallion but a man.

Such objections seem absurd : it is a fairy-story, not an
account of animal husbandry. But they point (apart from the
possible light they cast on Orwell's sexual inhibitions) to the
absence of an important element in the story as a fable of
revolution. It becomes clearer if we consider another anomaly
in the economy of Animal Farm, that the cows continue to give
milk (which is all taken by the pigs for themselves) but there is
no mention of calves or of a bull. Where could a bull fit into the
fable? Perhaps a place for him would have been possible if he
had been thought of only as one of the "harmless law-abiding
brutes that only wanted to get to their stalls in peace" remembered by George Bowling as being driven to slaughter through
the streets of his boyhood town. But there is more to a bull than
a lump of meat; is it possible to imagine that huge unthinking
passionate force loosed in *Animal Farm*, the ring no longer in
his nose, without throwing the whole pattern of parallels into
disorder? Such an element certainly could be accommodated
within a story of animals in revolt, and indeed it needs to be if
a full account of a revolutionary movement is to be given in
those fabulous terms. The Rebellion which first ejects Farmer
Jones is really too gentle an affair even to represent the February
Revolution, let alone October; Boxer, who sheds tears over the
stable-boy whom he thinks he has killed in Jones's attempted
come-back, is quite unable to suggest the realities of the Civil
War and Intervention. A bull, savage after years of being
chained in his yard, perhaps might do so, and without at all
affecting the moral balance of the story as a parable of social
injustice and social revolution. But the introduction of a power
in rebellion which, though roused by the violence of tyranny,
is itself violent and destructive, would have turned *Animal Farm*
upside down in a way Orwell was clearly unwilling to handle. It

was not something he was altogether unaware of; but in the picture of mankind his tale so persuasively suggests—a picture fundamentally of innocence and harmlessness except for the self-seeking pigs—it must always have been unassimilable.

It is hardly noticeable at first but, again, once remarked cannot be forgotten, that all the animals who play any significant part in the affairs of Animal Farm are domestic. It seems natural enough, perhaps; after all, the beasts one chiefly sees on a farm, the farmer's slaves and property, are so by definition. But they are bound to represent men only in a one-sided way. There are, it is true, some others, very much on the periphery; there is the abortive campaign to convert the "Wild Comrades", providing some shrewd comedy in the case of the cat, eager to "re-educate" the sparrows. But the very mention of them reminds us that none of the more formidable wild creatures, even those to be found in rural England—figures in many other fables—is ever heard of.

Such a limitation accords well with Orwell's scattered but copious animal similes elsewhere, especially when applied to the working class. The proletariat are likened to sheep or cattle, the footprints of the clog-wearing Lancashire mill-workers are like the marks of cattle's hooves, the gas-masked schoolchildren in *Coming Up For Air* are like a herd of pigs; when Orwell is feeling particularly gloomy about the passivity of the workers and the possibility that they may be permanently reconciled to oppression they are "a breed of hornless cows". In *Keep the Aspidistra Flying* we meet a police constable (who gives helpful advice to Gordon Comstock, run in as drunk and disorderly, and who was perhaps originally encountered by Orwell himself in "clink") "with a kind face, white eyebrows, and a tremendous chest" which "reminded Gordon of the chest of a carthorse"; the prototype possibly of Boxer himself, or it may be rather of one of the horses who, too stupid to know what they are doing, are harnessed to the knacker's cart which takes Boxer to his death.

Oppressed mankind is tamed; tyranny is able to impose its will by using the tame against the tame. Tyranny itself is domesticated. U Po Kyin, the calculating manipulator of Europeans and his fellow-Burmans in *Burmese Days*, is a crocodile to Flory and Dr Veraswami, but by the time of *Animal Farm* his vastly more powerful and tyrannical successor,

Napoleon-Stalin himself, is a black Berkshire. With rare exceptions it seems to be the rule that when Orwell thought of men as animals, which he did fairly often, he thought of them as tame, with everything that implies not only of docility but limitation of possibility : people know, or think they know, how domestic beasts will behave in all circumstances; of wild creatures they are not so sure.

There is at least one place, however, where Orwell uses a hackneyed but for him an unusual animal metaphor borrowed from the wild bestiary. In *The Road to Wigan Pier*, discussing bourgeois fears of revolution, especially the fears that "turn an ardent Socialist at twenty-five" into "a sniffish Conservative at thirty-five", he says :

> In a way his recoil is natural enough—at any rate one can see how his thoughts run. Perhaps a classless society *doesn't* mean a beatific state of affairs in which we shall all go on behaving exactly as before except that there will be no class-hatred and no snobbishness; perhaps it means a bleak world in which all our ideals, our codes, our tastes—our "ideology", in fact —will have no meaning. Perhaps this class-breaking isn't so simple as it looked. On the contrary, it is a wild ride into darkness, and it may be that at the end of it the smile will be on the face of the tiger.

Here is a distant glimpse of *1984*; but it should be noted that in 1936, however ambiguously—at thirty-three himself he might be partially identified with the former "ardent Socialist" turned Conservative at thirty-five—Orwell regarded the ride of revolution and "class-breaking" as something desirable, its wildness not altogether a deterrent.

For in truth the domestic parallels do not really apply to the nature of man—who, in so far as he is an animal, is the most successful of all wild species, and may soon be the only one surviving upon earth. And though the commonest corollary of such a realisation is that man is a wolf to man, that does not exhaust the associations and images that will occur to anyone who thinks of man's future as a "wild" ride, a ride not along the packhorse paths of domesticity, but actually in the wilderness. There are many wild beasts in man. There are tigers, crocodiles, wild horses, lions, bulls, eagles of the spirit, and it is in them that "the energy that actually shapes the world" will be found, as Orwell knew. It can be shaped for evil or for good, but the choice does not lie with the domesticated. "At present," said Orwell in *The Prevention of Literature*, "we know only that the imagination, like certain wild animals, will not breed in captivity." In *Animal Farm*, the most finished product of his own imagination, there is no place for it.

V

Clean and Decent

ANIMAL FARM I have called a digression, a kind of brief holiday before the final steps of Orwell's journey. It may be taken as such, despite the obvious continuity of political theme, since it is not this theme we are pursuing, but rather the subjective meaning of Orwell's political preoccupations. From this point of view *Animal Farm* is a detour, almost an evasion, since the form of animal fable itself and the "objectivity" it permitted him to achieve also allowed him to avoid subjective reflections altogether; as has been remarked, the animals have virtually no inner life at all. The way within must presently be resumed, but before doing so this may be a convenient point at which to pause and inquire into a matter of equal importance for the subjective individual in Orwell's writings and for his changing ideas of social action and social needs : the point to be considered indeed seems to offer a bridge between the individual and society, the point at which personal good and the good of the group might be reconciled.

This is Orwell's notion of "decency", almost the only term he used for whatever is morally desirable in man or group. He never defined it, indeed he probably regarded definition as unnecessary, since any decent person would know what decency means, "common decency" ought to be common enough to be immediately understood. Nevertheless, as the principal, almost the sole normative standard of a man deeply concerned with how men ought to behave it needs to be examined; although, as quickly appears, that is an extremely difficult thing to do. Decency and decent are words occurring with great frequency through all Orwell's works, in a bewildering variety of contexts and with an almost equal variety of implication.

In *Burmese Days* we find Elizabeth, the cold, formal and conventional girl who finally destroys Flory, thinking longingly in her poverty-stricken exile of "the decent world" represented by society snapshots in the *Tatler*, people "with their horses and their cars and their husbands in the cavalry"; probably that was and is the commonest use of the word, meaning at bottom simply money, or the amenities that money can buy. (It need not of course necessarily mean riches : in the tentative social recommendations at the end of *Down and Out in Paris and London* Orwell proposed for the inmates in casual wards at the least "a scheme which fed them decently", and here again he was obviously following common usage.) The same usage doubtless embraces whatever is not indecent, taking again the common sense of the word as indicating something obscene, indecorous, or sordid. Remembering Orwell's extreme dislike of dirt and bad smells, his strong recoil from anything of supposed obscenity, we may imagine that decency for him originally meant not only the undifferentiated schoolboy approval of "jolly decent" but also something not far removed from the cant "clean and decent" of schoolmasters, undertakers, and inspectors of institutions. Such a decency, it may be noted, is a standard imposed by authority and rule.

When we come on to *Keep the Aspidistra Flying*, in which money is both devil and saviour, decency still has an intimate connection with the possession of it : as Gordon Comstock sinks "underground" he thinks with perverse satisfaction that he is going "down into the shadow world where shame, effort, decency do not exist"; once there and visited by his friend Ravelston, who urges him to get a "decent place to live" he replies that he doesn't want one—" 'I want an indecent place' ". Cleanliness, moral effort, and group responsibility (in Comstock's case, as Ravelston sees it, to his status as a "gentleman") are inextricably confused, and all are connected with money : Ravelston, a thoroughly decent chap, can afford to be : as Gordon reflects, with bitter envy, "money buys decency".

There is more to it than that, however; and the modulation of meaning attached to decency in *Keep the Aspidistra Flying* reflects very closely, indeed one may say it actually *is* the moral struggle going on through the novel. Decency is a matter of a decent income, decent clothes, a decent place to live, and though once acquired through an expensive upbringing it may be a permanent part of one's character—for Ravelston's decency is "fundamental"—there is no doubt, to begin with, of its belonging to him along with £1,000 a year. But later on there is a change : for Gordon, deliberately sunk in the indecent sub-world where, he believes, the money-god can't reach him, finds that he is pursued even there, and precisely through decency : "The money-god is so cunning. If he only baited his traps with yachts and race-horses, tarts and champagne, how easy it would be to dodge him. It is when he gets at you through your sense of decency that he finds you helpless." Decency, then, can survive the abandonment of money; and can make one wish, against one's principles, to make money again. In the end, surrendering to this claim, agreeing to take a "good" job (a decent one) with the odious advertising agency, marrying his girl and buying his aspidistra Gordon feels "nothing but relief that now at last he had finished with dirt, cold, hunger, and loneliness and could get back to decent, fully human life".

An extraordinary confusion begins to show here, arising from Gordon's entire want of insight (despite his "conversion") into his motives. While from the conventional point of view, the system of external standards which he affects to despise, dirt, cold and hunger are indecent, that is not the reason why he embraced them, nor are their exterior effects in discomfort the reason why he changes his mind. Hatred, including a profound self-hatred and with it a total self-absorption, put him "in the gutter"; what brings him out is not recoil from its degradation but the first glimmer of an acknowledgment that other human beings exist and that he has responsibilities towards them. Even then, this first embryonic stirring of real feeling is only brought about in him by something in the gutter itself, the peculiar "ugliness" of concrete detail—the £5 abortion, the "monstrous" foetus—which are for him a contact with reality. Thus he is trapped by decency, which means the first minimal regard for others, but the agent—the feeling itself, since the pathetic ugly foetus is clearly representative of something within himself—is a part of that indecent, sordid reality where the decent conventions observed by servants of the money-god no longer rule.

"The gutter" and indeed the whole of Gordon Comstock's "war against the money-god" are symbolic, as it is perhaps needless to insist : it is a war within his own mind that he is engaged in. But as he does not fully understand that, neither it seems does his author. The absurd spasms of his "inner misery", as he lashes out, savaging himself and anyone near him, and his eventual relinquishment of them remain as exterior events, their meaning never properly reflected upon; they can be considered a species of "acting out" whether thought of as actual event within the life of the novel, or as Orwell's fiction, his act as a writer. The consequent confusion is compounded when, through Gordon's thoughts, Orwell turns again to consider general issues; for Gordon's personal sickness is always related to "the sickness of society". Feeling somewhat better, he reflects upon the petty-bourgeois "puppets" of money whose small lives have been the special object of his hatred and contempt : he now comes to think there may be something to be said for them, since although "they lived by the money-code . . . yet they contrived to keep their decency".

True enough, one may say, and about time Gordon Comstock should see it; but also puzzling, if the money-code is credited with the all-pervasive power he attributes to it. In the same passage an astonishing formula is evolved to account for this troublesome fact, that common virtue can survive, and be thought of as common, in adverse circumstances : "Our civilisation is founded on greed and fear, but in the lives of common men the greed and fear are mysteriously transmuted into something nobler." Mysterious indeed : for in his attempt to account for the fact that humanity can still live in the midst of greed and fear (themselves human) he slips into exchanging a *despite of* which, while still mysterious, makes sense—that good lives in despite of evil—for a *because*—that evil qualities, thought of as all-powerful, are the cause in themselves of their opposite; which is absurd. It may be that Orwell was faintly brushed here by the constructions of Marxist dialectic : if quantity can become quality, the evil consequences of living by the evil money-code may turn into something different. Clearly he did not mean that as greed and fear are the raw material of "something nobler" the more we have of them the better; it is a pity that, in his anxiety to find a visible source for what he could not explain he seemed to say so.

There is another word for the quality that counters greed and fear, and Orwell might have avoided this muddle, had he been able to use it. But in *Keep the Aspidistra Flying* he does so only to pour elaborate scorn on it, in the burlesque of the Epistle to the Corinithians and in every reference to *charity* throughout the book. ("There is a malaise, almost a secret hatred, between giver and receiver.") Unless translated into such terms, of giving and receiving between unequals, with all the consequent tangle of obligation and dependency which he so vehemently repudiated, it was a word he could not bear to have in his mouth; just as he could not bear the symbolic gesture of charity, or love, in the sharing of a cup. In *A Clergyman's Daughter* (where there is in fact very little talk of whatever is decent or indecent) it was still possible for Orwell to think both of the symbol and of what it symbolised as having good in it, even if only the good of tradition. At the end of the story, when Dorothy Hare is reflecting upon the loss of her faith, she perceives (as noted before) "that in all that happens in church, however absurd and cowardly its supposed purpose may be, there is something —it is hard to define, but something of decency, of spiritual comeliness—that is not easily found in the world outside". But Orwell's next mouthpiece, Gordon Comstock, entirely in "the world outside", has got beyond that : it is decency only, not charity, that abides, and we can begin to see indeed that the parody of Paul's words is not altogether a parody, for decency, however hard Gordon tries to keep it separate, keeps on renewing its connection with money.

Advancing through Orwell's work and watching his attitudes harden and become more extreme, we can observe "decency" becoming a conscious device, deliberately undefined, an escape from all the things he wouldn't say as well as those he didn't know how to. (The two were perhaps practically the same.) We can also observe it becoming less and less adequate to bear the moral burden put upon it.

The process coincides with Orwell's closer contact with and involvement in Left-wing politics : it was this perhaps that forced him to think more closely about human conduct and at the same time made him shy away from any really searching analysis of it. He repudiated with angry scorn and the most abusive language he could summon the shibboleths of the orthodox Left, rotten with hypocrisy and deceit as he found it to be, especially in Spain, where lies were backed by murder. Yet however many he offended, and however violently he seemed to be cutting away any basis for his generalised, provocatively non-partisan "Socialism", he remained doggedly loyal to it. Many who were outraged by the polemics in the second half of *The Road to Wigan Pier,* where Orwell flaunted his prejudices —the locus classicus, among other things, of his obsession with the idea that "the lower classes smell"—expected him to take what might appear the logical next step to Fascism : in fact he had no sooner finished writing that book than he went to fight the Fascists in Spain. This is not the place to discuss Orwell's political adventures and allegiances; if it is said that in all their vagaries and contradictions they were honourable and *decent,* that is enough for the present purpose, although it begs the present question. Nor do I wish here to investigate the unconscious motives which, despite much that would obviously have predisposed him to support the extreme Right, guaranteed that in almost any conflict he would show that, as he said at a late stage in the story of his opinions, "I belong to the Left". Perhaps it can be left for the moment with his own explanation, that he would always be "on the side of the weak against the strong". It still remains to discover, beyond the dividing lines of political loyalties, what "decency" may mean and whether in practice it can serve as a sufficient normative principle, politically and otherwise.

By this time Orwell was quite evidently using the term to block ethical argument. In Spain, he said (in *Homage to Catalonia*) he was fighting for "common decency", and though he had not been there long before finding how very indecent, in his own or anyone's understanding, was much in that dreadful conflict, he continued to be struck by the "essential decency" of the Catalan workers with whom he mixed; and at the end, deeply disillusioned by the "cesspool" of Spanish politics and the revelation of what a civil war is like, he was left with "not less but more belief in the decency of human beings". But he refused to say what decency was, using it, undefined, to define other abstract qualities : the English, he said in his patriotic essay on *The English People* (written in 1944), have been characterised by opposing modern political theories not by more theorising but by "a moral quality which must be vaguely described as decency". Decency recurs at almost every point where Orwell feels he should say why the English are so worthy of admiration; the essay (admittedly one of Orwell's poorest) amounts virtually to saying that it's decent to be English because the English are so decent. At the same time he was extending application of the word as far as possible, discovering both the "natural decency" of people met during his tours of industrial England, the personal decency of a poet (Kipling) as a man, the "fundamental decency" of another poet's (Byron's) writing together with the indecency of some of his personal behaviour, and the fact that in another case, Ezra Pound's ("one has the right to expect ordinary decency even of a poet") indecent behaviour made it impossible for a contemporary to judge his poetry dispassionately; even the possession in a philosopher (Bertrand Russell) of "an essentially *decent* intellect". It appears that decency had come to mean no more than something Orwell approved of; though that still does not tell us why he approved in such terms and whether he found the idea a sufficient basis on which to construct his moral discourse.

It is clear that as time went on he did not : decency was not enough to counterbalance the fears which more and more oppressed him. He came to see that what he and people of his class and upbringing generally learnt to call decent was largely governed by their background. He did not by any means disparage it on that account, and was even ready to bring together, if he could, the "warm, decent, deeply human" attributes he found in working-class homes and what others called "bourgeois morality"—"in moral matters it is the proletarians who are bourgeois". He believed, and clung to the idea that the untheoretical decency of "the English common people", which he considered as an historical relic of Christianity (Christian ethics without Christian doctrine or belief) somehow separated them both from other less fortunate nations and from other classes, especially from the Europeanised British intelligentsia. But less and less could he persuade himself, for all his attachment to these homely qualities—they tended very much to become the domestic virtues—that they were adequate to stand the moral strains as he saw them of the present age, let alone those of the future. The decency he saw and praised was relative, historical, with no guarantee of survival; above all, it proved on close examination to be founded most precariously on externals.

The difficulty can be seen very clearly if we compare the description of a working-class family fireside (in *The Road to Wigan Pier*) with one in a summary-parody of Dickens. First, the home life of the ideal "manual worker" :

I have often been struck by the peculiar easy completeness, the perfect symmetry as it were, of a working class interior at its best. Especially on winter evenings after tea, when the fire glows in the open range and dances mirrored in the steel fender, when Father, in shirt-sleeves, sits on the rocking-chair at one side of the fire reading the racing finals, and Mother sits on the other side with her sewing, and the children are happy with a pennorth of mint humbugs, and the dog lolls roasting himself on the rag mat—it is a good place to be in, provided that you can be not only in it but sufficiently *of* it to be taken for granted.

Now the caricature (quite a moderate one) of a typical Dickensian happy ending, sketched in the essay first published in 1940 :

> The ideal is to be striven after, then, appears to be something like this : a hundred thousand pounds, a quaint old house with plenty of ivy on it, a sweetly womanly wife, a horde of children, and no work. Everything is safe, soft, peaceful, and above all, domestic. In the moss-grown churchyard down the road are the graves of the loved ones who passed away before the happy ending happened. The servants are comic and feudal, the children prattle round your feet, the old friends sit at your fireside, talking of past days, there is the endless succession of enormous meals, the cold punch and sherry negus, the feather beds and warming pans, the Christmas parties with charades and blind man's buff; but nothing ever happens, except the yearly childbirth. The curious thing is that it is a genuinely happy picture, or so Dickens is able to make it appear. The thought of that kind of existence is satisfying to him. This alone would be enough to tell one that more than a hundred years have passed since Dickens's first book was written. No modern man could combine such purposelessness with such vitality.

The two pictures are, with the difference of income and the Dickensian frills, exactly the same : each is of a "warm, decent, deeply human" family, each breathes an atmosphere of domestic security and cosiness that is, at least for certain moods, extremely attractive; certainly it must have been so for Orwell, whose own childhood possibly included few of such scenes. There is a strong resemblance, even down to the feeling of solidarity with the decently buried dead, between the early nineteenth-century

mock-up and the fantasy boyhood Orwell constructed for George
Bowling in compensation, as has been conjectured, for things
wanting in his own. There is much pathos in his proviso concerning the working-class scene, that one must be not only in
it but of it : was Orwell, we wonder, *of* such a family circle
anywhere?

The difference between the two that in one case the pater-
familias is a working man and in the other a wealthy idler
affects the essentials of the "genuinely happy scene" in no way,
for it is family relations, not source of income or outside occupation, that is important to both; if it is sentimental to suppose
so, the sentimentality belongs as much to one as to the other.
For although it is immaterial whether they are purchased on the
lavish scale of an inherited fortune or by a weekly wage, the
externals of each situation, and their assumed permanence, are
the real standard set up. That the Dickensian world is completely static is also, in absence of any indication to the contrary,
true of the other; and it is equally true of both that here they
reveal their incompleteness, not to say their unreality. For
when something "happens"—when, in the context of Victorian
bourgeois life, Father goes bankrupt or Mother dies in child-
birth, or the destructive passions that Dickens knew all about
threaten the family from within; when, in twentieth-century
Wigan or Sheffield, Father is on the dole or is killed down the pit
or equally catastrophically wins the pools; when war breaks out
and the bombs fall or, looking a little forward, the secret police
knock on the door—how well will these domestic circles survive?
Quite well, it may be said, if there have been love and respect
within the family already, but Orwell says nothing about that :
it is the externals, the material props of the scene, which can
be destroyed in a moment, that he dwells on. In the case of
Dickens, moreover, he sees quite clearly how inadequate the
ideal of the soft domestic nest and Cheeryble morality is to deal
with the real problems of humanity. Even if, as he says, the
Dickensian proposition that " 'if men would behave decently the
world would be decent' is not such a platitude as it sounds",
it is still a tautology, and the question of the power of decency
in an indecent world is still unsolved. And when Orwell frames
a proposition of his own (in *The Road to Wigan Pier*), that
"economic injustice will stop the moment we want it to stop",
that may also be not altogether a platitude, despite the scorn

cast upon it; but the question of motive, why people should ever want to stop injustice, since according to this formula they obviously don't want to yet, remains not only unanswered, but unasked.

Orwell, in short, was not able to deceive himself. Out of greed and fear he had once persuaded himself would grow something nobler, but it was not long before he saw all too well that out of greed and fear grow only greed and fear. George Bowling could look back longingly to the "decent, God-fearing" security of his boyhood, but knew that it was "finished for ever". Reflecting upon the character of his gentlemanly-scholarly friend Porteous, who deals with rumours of the coming war by reading Keats, he comes to the conclusion, *"He's dead.* He's a ghost. All the people like that are dead", and "it's a ghastly thing that all the decent people, the people who *don't* want to go round smashing faces in with spanners, are like that. They're decent, but their minds have stopped. . . . All the decent people are paralysed. Dead men and live gorillas. Doesn't seem to be anything in between". As for poetry and "the eternal verities", they are only there, with Porteous as their amiable, but dusty and unreal champion, to be shown up by the realities of power : "what use would that be against machine guns?" Poetry, which is evidently purposeless and usually harmless, has no vitality either; it is inconceivable to "modern man" that anything without purpose directed to some visible end should have any place in real life whatever.

Poets, furthermore, are as we know frequently most indecent; it is perhaps impossible that they should not be, since they must share the "sheer egoism" which Orwell put at the top of his list of reasons for writing at all. Writers, indeed, are worse than most :

> The great mass of human beings are not acutely selfish. After the age of about thirty they abandon individual human ambition—in many cases, indeed, they almost abandon the sense of being individuals at all—and live chiefly for others, or are simply smothered under drudgery. But there is also the minority of gifted, wilful people who are determined to live their own lives, and writers belong to this class.

In the mass, anonymously, and in favourable circumstances,

people can still be called decent. But at other times, and especially when you get close to them, it only needs enough pressure (in this particular instance bombardment by flying bombs, with everyone hoping the doodle-bug will fall on someone else) to reveal "the bottomless selfishness of the individual". And it may be even worse when the individual is not motivated by fear alone, but by greed as well; perhaps that is why it is only people in the mass who look comparatively decent :

> The mass of the people never get the chance to bring their innate decency into the control of affairs, so that one is almost driven to the cynical thought that men are only decent when they are powerless.

One may think it a pity that Orwell was not driven all the way to this thought, which he calls cynical, but which might then have caused him to examine more closely what decency meant to him, and, even more, what it must mean in such a context to speak of it as innate. It is less cynical in implication than the declaration, in *The Road to Wigan Pier*, that "all my notions of good and evil . . . are essentially middle-class notions". That, perhaps was said more in provocative bravado than in conscious attachment to moral relativism. But it was doubtless true enough, and he believed it enough, to make him yearn for some moral underpinning which was not just that of his social group and background. We have seen how he tried to extend the basis of "bourgeois values" by claiming that they were also, and more truly, the values of the working class; that it was the proletariat, and not the bourgeoisie, which really upheld them. But, proletarian or bourgeois, these boiled down presently to decency; and decency simply will not do, not just because it remains utterly vague but rather because there is a generally accepted collection of meanings associated with it, and all of them are concerned with outward forms, the visible fruits but not the springs of an inward condition. By their decencies you may know them, perhaps; but how to *be* decent, what beyond the impulse of conformity can even make a man want to be decent has still to be discovered.

We can see here, paradoxically—for everything about Orwell enters back to front—one of the reasons for his attachment not simply to Left-wing but to active and even extreme revolutionary causes. Though deeply and increasingly suspicious of "the ideals of the Left", in which he detected for the most part either meaningless jargon and slogan-mongering or an excuse for the most atrocious acts, he remained strongly attracted to an element in them. Liberty and Justice have little share in the programme of any modern Socialist party, not solely because such high aims have come to be abandoned—though that, as Orwell and others have concluded, is doubtless partly true—but also because they are too abstract to have much use even among the promises made to be broken. But it was precisely their abstraction, their removal from "practical politics", that drew Orwell to them, because they seemed thus to be removed from contamination by the indecencies of political life. If only they could be restored they might show a way out of the cesspool; they would provide some value incorruptible by greed and fear and beyond class and the unhappily relative and mutable standards of decency. Thus he ended *The Road to Wigan Pier*, after lambasting every existing Socialist party, group and tendency in sight, and asserting that the aims of Socialism were mostly either delusory or pernicious, by declaring roundly for the two which, as the world goes, have probably been as rich a source of delusion and false hopes as any in all the ideological property of the Left, and which have proverbially been the excuse for some of its worst actions :

> The only thing *for* which we can combine is the underlying ideal of Socialism; justice and liberty. But it is hardly strong enough to call this ideal "underlying". It is almost completely forgotten. It has been buried beneath layer after layer of doctrinaire priggishness, party squabbles, and half-baked "progressivism" until it is like a diamond hidden under a mountain of dung. The job of the Socialist is to get it out again.

Before too quickly dismissing such a plea as impossible naivety, we should remember again what Orwell was looking for. He was not talking (although he may have thought he was) in terms of political programme or social-economic scheme : he was searching for something extra-political, even anti-political, but at the same time powerful enough to stand when decency dissolves. Ten years later we find some remarks which belong

to the same train of thought and take it further : in *Tribune*
(January 11, 1946) he was discussing some proposal for "the
pleasure resort of the future", and was naturally drawn back
to a persistent strand in his critique of Left-wing ideology, the
inadequacy of hedonism as motive or guide. He describes the
proposed palace of pleasure (incidentally not at all unlike those
now supplied in many places of mass resort) as one from which,
among other things, all contact with "Nature" is excluded; and
goes on to define the essence of what is valuable in such contact :
"the whole notion of admiring Nature, and feeling a sort of
religious awe in the presence of glaciers, deserts or waterfalls,
is bound up with the sense of man's littleness and weakness
against the power of the universe. The moon is beautiful partly
because we cannot reach it, the sea is impressive because one
can never be sure of crossing it safely."

There is an idea here of the greatest importance, which must
be followed further if we are to understand the direction of
Orwell's search; although he did not himself follow where it
eventually leads. The association of inaccessibility and beauty he
accounted for by calling in "the sense of mystery", which is of
course a quite usual way of explaining the link; no doubt it
is true if by mystery is meant not the effect of mere ignorance
but "a sort of religious awe". Orwell indeed recognised this,
pointing out in the same passage that even "a botanist who
knows all there is to be known about the flower" he contemplates can still feel the mystery and take pleasure in it—the
pleasure being therefore of a different kind from that to be
found in "pleasure resorts". He also saw that the danger to
the mystery lay not in scientific knowledge but the possibility
of control which it confers, "man's power over Nature" which
by domination and appropriation brings more and more of
the natural world within the dominion ruled by greed and fear.
He did not, however, take the argument on to the point at
which it becomes clear not so much that the moon is beautiful
because it is inaccessible, but it is inaccessible because it is
beautiful : the very idea of beauty, as an absolute quality of the
kind that inspires awe, is dependent on detachment. Beauty
itself is the awful mystery; the moon is mysterious because it
is beautiful, and its beauty can be known because, by the mere
accident of distance, it cannot be possessed. If now, with astro-
nauts planting flags on its surface, it seems to have lost beauty

and mystery at once, that is because it is now in process of being acquired as man's property; and beauty cannot be possessed or controlled.

To see this clearly we may turn to another writer, Simone Weil : "Distance is the soul of the beautiful." Here as at many other points the affinity between Orwell's and Simone Weil's thinking shows up; an affinity, remarked by several commentators, which is the more striking since there is no record or even likelihood that Orwell ever heard of her or her writing. Her thought, however, does not simply resemble his, it develops it : that is to say her reflections, pursued with an intellectual rigour and passion much greater than his, show where it was tending : where attitudes, qualities and obsessions recognisably kin to hers might have led.

Much of Simone Weil's religious writing deals with the distance or "absence" of God, and insists on the need for such a conception of the divine in order that it be not corrupted or exchanged for idolatrous illusions. Devotion, or the love of God, must be directed to a point wholly beyond human reach, "an unchangeable purity placed beyond all possible attack" : "To love purely is to consent to distance, it is to adore the distance between ourselves and that which we love." Perhaps the clearest expression of this conviction in Simone Weil is in her notes on the Lord's Prayer, where she finds an essential element of the petition that it is addressed to our Father "who art *in Heaven*" : "We must be happy in the knowledge that he is infinitely beyond our reach. Thus we can be certain that the evil in us, even if it overwhelms our whole being, in no way sullies the divine purity, bliss and perfection." Such a way of speaking seems entirely alien to Orwell, and we may be sure it would have been repudiated by him; in fact, as already indicated, it takes a certain step or leap apparently beyond his capacity. How close was the starting point, however, may be seen if we turn from the language of religion to politics, where Simone Weil's loyalties and even her experience were remarkably like Orwell's. In Spain, a volunteer six months before Orwell went there, she also came in contact with the anarcho-syndicalists and, though revolted by their ferocity, found much to admire in them, especially their "impractical idealism"; it was precisely in its impracticality that she found its value. A note from a later period makes the reason clear :

A future which is completely impossible, like the ideal of the Spanish anarchists, degrades us far less and differs far less from the eternal than a possible future. It does not even degrade us at all, except through the illusion of its possibility. If it is conceived of as impossible, it transports us into the eternal.

In the same way Orwell can be seen looking for a political aim high enough to be in effect impracticable, though at the same time—this was the test, as he realised—one upon which people could be found to stake their lives. Like Simone Weil he thought that he caught a glimpse of it in Spain, where he went to fight for "common decency" but where he found a quality transcending it, or defining it in a new way, the lofty abstractions of liberty and justice made, not more accessible, but real, in flesh and blood. The Spanish Civil War was a profoundly disillusioning experience for Orwell as it was for many, but it also provided him with some other revelations of human possibility which were new and quite different: he treasured them long afterwards. These were in particular his experiences with the POUM militia at the Aragon front, a period of a few months which, he said, "formed a kind of interregnum in my life, quite different from anything that had gone before and perhaps from anything that is to come, and they taught me things that I could not have learned in any other way".

These things were evidently in part—perhaps chiefly—the lessons of loyalty and mutual respect of men under fire that have been learned in many wars, regardless of "war aims". But with the then fanatically egalitarian militia Orwell learned more, for to the comradeship of the front was added the feeling that Liberty, Justice, Equality were now acquiring substance, not in institutions, but in the actuality of men's lives being risked for them. For Orwell, whatever the political parties were doing back in Barcelona and Madrid, where the Communists were preparing to suppress their rivals, it was a "foretaste of Socialism", the "microcosm of a classless society" which, far from disillusioning, "deeply attracted" him:

The ordinary class-division of society had disappeared to an extent that is almost unthinkable in the money-tainted air of England; there was no one there except the peasants and ourselves, and no one owned anyone else as his master. Of course such a state of affairs could not last. It was simply a temporary and local phase in an enormous game that is being played over the whole surface of the earth. But it lasted long enough to have its effect upon anyone who experienced it. However much one cursed at the time, one realised afterwards that one had been in contact with something strange and valuable.

Perhaps it is possible to see what this something was; at least to guess at what this brief and doomed interval of time in which men, in equal danger, treated each other as of equal value, meant for the man who had always doubted whether he was of any value at all. If it partook of what can be felt in more common circumstances in which men share danger—down a coal-mine, for example—there was also an element in it more powerful—and, in a spiritual sense, more dangerous. Others have borne witness to the extraordinary excitement and hope of those early days of the Civil War, and of similar stages in other revolutions, in which the perception of worth and expanding human possibility among people long denied them bursts out with violent but exhilarating force, and for a time may offer a vision for which decency is an altogether inadequate term. It is an "impossible" vision in terms of practical politics, and perhaps as Simone Weil suggested, it remains pure just so far as it is impossible. If it is intoxicating, exciting men and women to extraordinary deeds of heroism and self-forgetfulness, it may induce less admirable effects of drunkenness, and lead to appalling political hangovers. Perhaps such evil consequences are inevitable whenever an attempt is made to possess the vision by force, as the violent seek to bear away the Kingdom. So many who have felt its power have come in time to believe, and Orwell would in the end probably be among them. But even in the knowledge of these consequences he retained, at least for a while, the memory of "something strange and valuable", something which survived in the face of fear and disillusion; perhaps not unlike the idea expressed in that most strange of revolutionary utterances, Alexander Blok's poem *The Twelve*.

For Orwell it concentrated itself in the memory of a single incident, the starting-point of *Homage to Catalonia*. There he records an encounter with a fellow-militiaman, an Italian volunteer; presumably an anarchist, though Orwell did not speak with him long enough to find out, and could only guess at such political details later, imagining his "probable end" either at the hands of the Fascists or the GPU. The meeting was brief, scarcely more than momentary—as Orwell describes it the two men exchanged no more than half a dozen words in broken Spanish and shook hands—and even at the time, it seems, he wished to keep it so: "I ... knew that to retain my first impression of him I must not see him again." This remark, not missed by various commentators, may well be thought to reflect an unusually remote view of human relationships. But it may also be supposed that the "something" Orwell saw in the Italian's face, which "deeply moved" him, was of a kind that would not be visible through ordinary sublunary time; a realisation, rather, beyond the accidents of time and personal history : "It was as though his spirit and mine had momentarily succeeded in bridging the gulf of language and tradition and meeting in utter intimacy."

We should remember the high value Orwell placed upon both language and tradition, both closely connected with the notion of "decency"; and what he saw in "the face of a man who would commit murder and throw away his life for a friend" can hardly have come within the meaning of decency, even stretching the word to its utmost. Perhaps (it has been suggested) what drew Orwell to the "tough-looking youth" had an element in it of homosexual attraction. If so, it does not affect the essential experience of seeing, momentarily, an essence in another human being transcending considerations of social cause and effect, of material circumstances, of time itself. Such an insight may well be called visionary, but it is not therefore unreal.

Later on, in *Looking Back on the Spanish War*, Orwell tried to tease out more explicitly the meaning for himself of this casual, unforgotten meeting. In the essay itself it boiled down once more to "decency", the right of "people like that Italian soldier" to lead "the decent, fully human life which is now technically available". He was entangled again in the vague orthodoxies of Socialist utopianism, the same dogma that a "fully human life", otherwise undefined, is dependent upon technical resource, which he had already found quite inadequate. He even forced himself bravely to put a time limit on the achievement—"I want it to be sooner and not later—some time within the next hundred years, say, and not some time within the next ten thousand years"—like a hopeful Kruschev announcing the advent of "full communism" by 1980. But in the poem which ends the essay (written, he tells us, some time after he had been in Spain and "when the war was visibly lost") he put it in a different way.

There is no need here, perhaps, to give the whole of this much-quoted poem; or to speculate further on the reasons why Orwell should find the Italian soldier's "battered face" "purer than any woman's" : the possible homosexual element in the meeting has already been mentioned. It is more important that in the poem the clasp of "The strong hand and the subtle hand" —the hand of the soldier, simple, child-like, pure of heart, and the hand of the man deeply divided in self-consciousness and self-doubt—brings about a realisation of value. In the man himself the "impossible", "unrealistic", "meaningless" seem to be, for a moment, incarnate :

> For the flyblown words that make me spew
> Still in his ears were holy,
> And he was born knowing what I had learned
> Out of books and slowly.

Miraculously, deception itself is seen to have been deceived, it is no longer necessary to think that truth will always turn out to be dirty and unpleasant—"my gold brick was made of gold—/Oh! who ever would have thought it?" The revelation is of a treasure present in the flesh but outside time and circumstance. The Italian soldier is certainly dead, along with his comrades, and his memory, so far as the world goes, is defiled by politics, "the lie that slew you is buried/Under a deeper lie". Violence, bad faith and disillusion have their way, but do not touch the intangible discovery :

> But the thing that I saw in your face
> No power can disinherit :
> No bomb that ever burst
> Shatters the crystal spirit.

This inviolable crystal, we may be sure, is the same as the

"diamond" which (in *The Road to Wigan Pier*) was "hidden under a mountain of dung", identified there as the ideals of liberty and justice. Now, although it is doubtless still connected with those ideals, which are genuinely believed in by the Italian soldier, it is itself undefined, indefinable, indeed : but not like decency inherently vague. On the contrary, its realisation recorded in the poem, is piercingly clear; it is something real, beyond the discredited abstract ideals, which nevertheless seems to justify them.

So, in 1942 and in the middle of a bigger and more dreadful war than he saw in Spain, Orwell was still able to believe, even if rather desperately. We have now to see what happened to this belief in the last years of his life.

VI

The Iron Haven

IN APRIL 1934 the *Adelphi* published a poem by Orwell (under the name of Eric Blair; he had not yet adopted his pseudonym for all purposes) to which reference has already been made. It is appropriate now to give the whole of this short piece, "On a Ruined Farm near the His Master's Voice Gramophone Factory":

> As I stand at the lichened gate
> With warring worlds on either hand—
> To left the black and budless trees,
> The empty sties, the barns that stand
>
> Like tumbling skeletons—and to right
> The factory-towers, white and clear
> Like distant, glittering cities seen
> From a ship's rail—as I stand here,
>
> I feel, and with a sharper pang,
> My mortal sickness; how I give
> My heart to weak and stuffless ghosts
> And with the living cannot live.
>
> The acid smoke has soured the fields,
> And browned the few and windworn flowers;
> But there, where steel and concrete soar
> In dizzy, geometric towers—
>
> There, where the tapering cranes sweep round,
> And great wheels turn, and trains roar by
> Like strong, low-headed brutes of steel—
> There is my world, my home; yet why
>
> So alien still? For I can neither
> Dwell in that world, nor turn again

To scythe and spade, but only loiter
Among the trees the smoke has slain.

Yet when the trees were young, men still
Could choose their path—the wingèd soul,
Not cursed with double doubts, could fly
Arrow-like to a foreseen goal;

And they who planned those soaring towers,
They too have set their spirit free;
To them their glittering world can bring
Faith, and accepted destiny;

But none to me as I stand here
Between two countries, both-ways torn,
And moveless still, like Buridan's donkey
Between the water and the corn.

The landscape of this desolate utterance is at once familiar, at
least to all who in the past quarter-century have been haunted
by the images in Orwell's last work; and we can say, conversely,
that he himself had been haunted by them for more than ten
years before he began to write it. The poem sets down in shorthand the essentials of *1984*, both the setting and the programme.
We recognise immediately the "dizzy geometric towers" of steel
and concrete rising in the distance, just as the four Ministerial
headquarters, white and sinister, dominate the view from
Winston Smith's flat; we can perhaps add the point of resemblance that one of the buildings in the poem—so it is implied
by the title—is the home of His Master's Voice, a place where
voices are manufactured, as the Ministry of Truth manufactures
the lies which are the voice of Big Brother.

We can see Winston himself in the lonely speaker standing in
unhappy division of mind, neither in one world nor the other;
ruin and decay on one side, alien power on the other, himself
conscious only of his unreality. The difference is that the watcher
in the poem is as yet only a watcher, outside both worlds; yet it
is clear to us that, as Buridan's donkey will starve until a decision
is made, so the speaker is bound to turn one way or the other,
sooner or later. It is also clear which way he will go, since he
recognises the world where he belongs; although he recoils from
its manifestations of mechanised power he calls it home. *1984* is

the story of Winston Smith's homecoming; but in fact we can see that his destination was decided long before, and that the journey had been going on in Orwell's writings since the beginning.

Looking back through these writings, one can find every separate element of *1984* foreshadowed, often many times over. The first recorded piece published by Orwell in adult life (a short article in *G.K.'s Weekly* dated 1928, describing a "Farthing Newspaper" in Paris) contains the germ at least of that later prospect when the dissemination of news, under cover of championing liberty and truth, shall be nothing but propaganda, aimed at the suppression of all other communication. Point by point in the intervening twenty years Orwell can be seen taking up, elaborating, and in many cases obsessively returning to every idea in his last book. Many of these ideas were of course common currency at the time, but the form he gave them he evolved for himself. Thus fears of a "machine civilisation" uniform throughout the world have been (and remain) general enough to be called universal, with many different expressions in literature, but the way they show in Orwell, from the localised landscape dominated by "strong brutes of steel" to the triple tyranny sharing the entire earth of *1984*, is wholly personal. If he was influenced by other men's fears it was chiefly (as no doubt is usually the case) because they reinforced his own, and the shape they assumed for him remained characteristic of himself.

The idea of a modern slave-state, stable and self-perpetuating, he might have taken principally from such anti-Utopias as H. G. Wells's *The Sleeper Awakes* and Aldous Huxley's *Brave New World*, familiar to him no doubt from an earlier date but recalled at the time (1946) when *1984* was taking shape in his mind. He recalled them, however—especially in the case of Huxley—chiefly to point to inadequacies in the prediction : Huxley's satire depicted a society without motive or aim, neither compelling nor compelled : "There is no power hunger, no sadism, nor hardness of any kind." Such a society, he thought, would be too "pointless" to last; and already before the war he found a different way to account for the "entirely unprecedented" nature of "the modern dictatorships", and the possibility therefore of their lasting indefinitely. It was the permanency of tyranny that was his particular preoccupation.

Early in 1939, for instance (in a review of one of "the 'anti' class of books on the USSR"), he casts doubt on the author's hopes of revival of "the thirst for liberty", reflecting that a combination of terror, modern techniques of propaganda, and mass passivity threatened an unprecedented and dreadful possibility of endurance :

> In the past every tyranny was sooner or later overthrown, or at least resisted, because of "human nature", which as a matter of course desired liberty. But we cannot be at all certain that "human nature" is constant. It may be just as possible to produce a breed of men who do not wish for liberty as to produce a breed of hornless cows. The Inquisition failed, but then the Inquisition had not the resources of the modern state. The radio, press-censorship, standardised education and the secret police have altered everything. Mass-suggestion is a science of the last twenty years, and we do not yet know how successful it will be.

The idea of eugenics used to produce contented slaves may be taken from Huxley, but the allusion here is not so much to "breeding" as to conditioning; it is not the geneticist but the modern Inquisitor, equipped with the most sophisticated techniques of persuasion and terror, who presents the stronger threat. Indeed, considering Orwell's tendency to see men as domestic animals, we may suspect that he thought the breed of hornless cows was already in existence. Men were already behaving like obedient cattle or sheep; the passage quoted can be said to foreshadow *Animal Farm* as well as *1984*.

The consequence of tyrannical power over men's minds, that a fully effective Inquisition will be able not merely to repress but to control thought and make men believe whatever is desired by their rulers, was further elaborated in *Looking Back on the Spanish War*. There we find a fully worked out theory of the way a dictatorship, denying the existence of any such thing as "the truth", can make anything true that it wishes. Already the idea has assumed its characteristic symbolic form : a society so ruled is "a nightmare world in which the Leader, or some ruling clique, controls not only the future but *the past*. If the Leader says of such an event, 'It never happened'—well, it never happened. If he says that two and two are five—well, two and two are five."

When writing this in 1942 Orwell already found—having had some experience of both kinds of assault—that the prospect of such thought-control "frightens me much more than bombs". But the same anxiety turns up earlier, and though in a literary rather than a political context, perhaps for that reason showing its origins more clearly. In 1936, reviewing Henry Miller's *Black Spring*, he paid particular attention to Miller's surrealist style at the time, quoting a full passage to show "how something that is or might be a description of ordinary reality slides away into pure dream". Such an effect, he says, may work in "a Mickey Mouse film", but in words must fail—"The truth is that the written word loses its power if it departs too far, or rather it stays away too long, from the ordinary world where two and two make four." We should remember that the written word was of paramount importance for Orwell, his principal hold on the reassuring nature of "ordinary reality". He is sufficiently sure of what is real at this point ("There is no need to get bogged up in metaphysical discussions about the meaning of 'reality' ") to think of Miller's use or misuse of words as damaging, not to the ordinary world, or the ordinary man's perception of it, but merely to Miller's description as a piece of literature. Reality, which is two and two making four, is assumed to be unassailable. But in another situation what is here no more than an objectionable literary device can assume the most terrifying aspect. What if, one's conviction of personal reality being already uncertain—as it must be if one's heart is given to weak and stuffless ghosts—the anchor of reality in the ordinary world outside oneself is forcibly loosened: if one should be persuaded by terror or suggestion or some physical insult to the brain that two and two no longer make four? Everything then will "slide into dream" : the entire world will collapse.

Such a foreboding is always in the background; such, perhaps, had a share in Orwell's knowledge, which he had accepted as he said ever since 1931, that "the future must be catastrophic". The catastrophes of which (writing in the catastrophic month of June 1940) he claimed to have had foreknowledge were of course thought of in political terms, the "wars and revolutions" he was sure were coming, so that although he was not sure when and where they would arrive, "they never surprised me when they come". It may be thought that as a political forecaster he never had much more than the ordinary bystander's perception of the way things were going. It can certainly be said that the particular dictatorships he was talking about in January 1939 proved less lasting than he feared. But the accuracy and farsightedness of his prediction in particular terms is not the point. The prevision is general, enjoying the licence of art; *because* it is offered in artistic terms it can be taken, personally, as deadly accurate, and *because* it is accurate in personal terms it reflects again on the political. The point is that *1984* is implied, in almost all its details, by the already-existing tendencies of Orwell's thought, not by other people's political forecasting; it is his thought, the way he tried to define himself in his world, that is the present matter in hand.

Animal Farm, I have argued, is the most "objective" of Orwell's works and therefore the most purely political in a narrow sense : the only one in which he looked at a political issue as something outside himself. Not that he was indifferent to its consequences, of course; just that by using the method of fable he set it at distance. What it feels like to be an animal on Animal Farm isn't examined, or examined only in those appropriately animal terms, without self-consciousness, which exclude the greater part of subjective experience. But what it feels like to live on Airstrip One in the year 1984 is not just included in the view, it monopolises it : the whole description of life in that imagined world—not excluding the "academic" account interpolated in the book of the supposed heretic Goldstein—is presented in personal terms, as direct experience. (It is just because of this, clearly, that certain matter had to be included in an appendix : whatever, like the principles of "Newspeak", could not readily be accommodated within Winston Smith's experience, could not be brought into the story at all, but had to be tacked on outside.) Subjectivity thus returns with a vengeance, both in the sense that the centre of consciousness in the story, the mind of Winston Smith, is wholly inside the situation, is indeed trapped in it, and in the implication that private motives are not different from and cannot in the end be kept apart from those that rule public life. Winston longs for privacy, and a large part of the uniform wretchedness in which he lives is the fact that private life has been destroyed, and yet the totalitarian claim that "everything is political" is tacitly admitted.

Winston's "private" acts are directly related to the State which forbids them; they are secretly engaged in not for their own sake but because they are a means of rebellion. The book is "about politics" in that all its significant action is brought into the area of public concern, and that it was written with what at least seemed clear political purpose. It is also intensely personal, and the personal combines with the political, not only in showing how the political demands of absolute tyranny invade every corner of life, but as politics seen in the most literal sense "from inside", as the reflection of a state of mind. That does not by any means imply that only personal significance can be found in it and that political meanings can be ignored; it shows rather that there cannot be any such separation. Politics do indeed reflect the state of people's minds; a man's way of thinking affects, not just his view of political events, but the events themselves. What can be seen in Orwell's case is a way of thinking from which certain political consequences flow : from the direction in which it points, as mental process, political predictions can be made. Thus Orwell, knowing—or rather feeling—what was happening within could foretell what was going to happen without not merely as a shrewd student of public affairs but as a man guided by internal evidence. Prediction can be described as projection, but it would be unwise to dismiss it for that reason. The catastrophe foreseen with such certainty is primarily a personal one, but its realisation touches more than one person.

The process is described by George Bowling at the end of *Coming Up for Air* :

> It's all going to happen. All the things you've got at the back of your mind, the things you're terrified of, the things you tell yourself are just a nightmare or only happen in foreign countries. . . . It's all going to happen. . . . There's no escape. . . . It's just something that's got to happen.

Because the events are already present at the back of George Bowling's mind their emergence into external reality is certain; it may be said further that the ambiguity of his imperative, that "it's got to happen", carries with it at least the strong suggestion that it ought to happen. Here, indeed, in the implied questioning of what is willed and what is fated, and whether or not an inevitable fate is to be embraced, we touch the centre of Orwell's problem in *1984*, and the argument must not be anticipated. Parenthetically, however, it may be observed that the feeling of inevitability so strongly expressed here, not to mention other similar indications before and after, casts doubt on the plea sometimes advanced, that *1984* was written by a sick man, latterly a dying one, and that its horrors are therefore to be discounted. Orwell himself thought it might have been "better" if he had not been ill while writing it, but it seems likely that he was talking about possible technical improvements, and not amelioration of what he had to say. Considering how much of his spiritual history it gathers together, one can hardly suppose that *1984* would have been greatly different had Orwell written it in more favourable circumstances. It could only have been different if Orwell had been a different man, and the question, how it might have been different, is as absurd as doubtless it always is when asked of a work of art; only because we so badly want it to be different do we ask it.

Yet it may have a more substantial justification in that the book asks it of itself. *1984*, written at the end of its author's life, sums up that life as a moral entity and questions it; if the answer seems to us unacceptable, in a double sense profoundly *wrong*, we must look both at the object of his self-questioning, and its mode : what is the life that is under this terrible self-inquisition, how are the questions framed?

1984, it may be objected, is not alone among Orwell's novels in showing such a process. John Flory, Dorothy Hare, Gordon Comstock, George Bowling all undergo experiences which call their lives in question; each of them, however inadequately, is engaged in an inquest on his or her past self. They are shown at a point where change is demanded of them, or more accurately where change is somehow in the air, to be more or less successfully, more or less consciously resisted. It is literally in the air as a change of season, the approach of the rainy season in *Burmese Days*, in England typically the onset of spring. Spring, at any rate in the urban surroundings with which it makes so jarring a contrast, is an uncomfortable time in all these stories. It is in April, "a bright blowy day, too cold to stand about in, with the sky as blue as a hedge-sparrow's egg, and one of those spiteful spring winds that come tearing along the pavement in sudden gusts and blow dry, stinging dust into your face", that

Dorothy Hare finds herself on the street, with no job and no idea what to do with herself. Gordon Comstock, though finding most of the seasons in London drearily the same, notices how in spring the streets are swept by "vile dusty winds", the sky is patched with "harsh blue"; his aspidistra, that minatory plant, puts out new shoots at the same time. George Bowling also knows "the kind of beastly weather that people call 'bright' weather, when the sky's a cold hard blue and the wind scrapes you like a blunt razor-blade"; it is only in the country, during his brief transitory communion with field and tree, that "the first day of spring" and the putting forth of buds and flowers is balmy and benevolent.

In his own person, though he spoke with longing of the spring and the feeling towards the end of his life that "each winter I find it harder and harder to believe that spring will actually come", Orwell greeted its arrival (in April 1946) in ominous phrase : "not even the narrow and gloomy streets round the Bank of England are quite able to exclude it. It comes seeping in everywhere, like one of those new poison gases which pass through all filters." That of course was a joke, a simile chosen for its incongruity; Orwell went on (in a piece in *Tribune*, "Some Thoughts on the Common Toad") to describe the irresistible advent of a London spring with charming lyricism. He reflected with pleasure on the fact that spring comes whatever evil is brewed by mankind : "So long as you are not actually ill, hungry, frightened or immured in a prison or a holiday camp, spring is still spring. The atom bombs are piling up in the factories, the police are prowling through the cities, the lies are streaming from the loudspeakers, but the earth is still going round the sun, and neither the dictators nor the bureaucrats, deeply as they disapprove of the process, are able to prevent it."

We shall see presently what becomes of this brave though frail consolation; in the meantime, and at the risk of seeming to make too much of a light-hearted passage, note may be taken of the ambiguities within it, and the way spring alters its associations. By the end of his remarks it had become for Orwell a reassuring sign of continuity, of the natural order which persists no matter what men may do; and it might be said that the coming of any season, autumn or winter as much as spring, would be a warrant that "the earth is still going round the sun". If spring is different it is because it is thought of above all as the time of renewal, of the unexpected and even the unhoped-for : and it is when these thoughts are uppermost that it is likened to a deadly enemy, "seeping in like poison gas". It is hostile, it is ineluctable; it is also something the soul yearns for.

In any case, by the time we come to *1984* and its arresting first sentence, it is clear that April is the cruellest month. The whole situation, both in its sameness and its crucial difference, is brilliantly summed up in fourteen words : "It was a bright cold day in April, and the clocks were striking thirteen." For Winston Smith coming in from the street out of the "vile wind", pursued by a "swirl of gritty dust", the day and weather are the same. The street outside is much the same as the one Gordon Comstock looked out upon with jaundiced eye at the beginning of *Keep the Aspidistra Flying*; if the general outlook has altered it is only to conform with the townscape of an immediately post-war London, the "vista of rotting nineteenth-century houses . . . the bombed sites where the plaster dust swirled in the air and the willow-herb straggled over the heaps of rubble; and the places where the bombs had cleared a larger patch and there had sprung up sordid colonies of wooden dwellings like chicken-houses".

That things have not changed—or at least that the ugliest aspects of London in 1948 have remained the same—is deliberately rubbed in, partly as a swipe in the eye to those who expect all such disagreeable sights to be cleared up in the future, but much more to show in the clearest possible light just how the case is altered. The clocks strike thirteen, instead of, for Gordon, two-thirty; the torn poster flapping in the wind that caught Gordon's eye now reveals, not the patent name of QT Sauce but the ominous word INGSOC, the vehicle in the background is not a tram but a police helicopter. Within doors, away from the searching winds of spring, it is worse : the same smell of "boiled cabbage and old rag mats" that pervaded Gordon's comfortless lodgings, but now on every landing the huge poster waiting with the caption "BIG BROTHER IS WATCHING YOU". A little later Winston has a "vision of London, vast and ruinous, city of a million dustbins, and mixed up with it was a picture of Mrs Parsons [Winston's neighbour] a woman with lined face and wispy hair, fiddling helplessly with a blocked waste-pipe" : exactly what Orwell saw in the industrial slums of the North of England, including the detail of the woman trying to clear a drainpipe which, in *The Road to Wigan Pier*, he recorded having observed from a train. There is a significant difference even in this detail, however. In *The Road to Wigan Pier* Orwell has been saying that those who do not have to live in them share a responsibility for the slums, "it is a kind of duty to see and smell such places now and again", and the woman slum-dweller whose image stayed with him for a decade is viewed with compassion but from outside, through the window of a passing train. In her face he perceived not only "the most desolate, hopeless expression I have ever seen", but consciousness of her condition, "not the ignorant suffering of an animal". The nameless woman "understood as well as I did how dreadful a destiny it was to be kneeling there in the bitter cold, on the slimy stones of a slum backyard, poking a stick up a foul drainpipe". But Winston Smith is himself right inside the slum, Mrs Parsons is not glimpsed momentarily but is his known and named neighbour; and she fills him, not with a vestige of pity but only with disgust.

Winston Smith is in this world and cannot escape from it. He is ill and hungry, and permanently frightened; though technically as yet at liberty, he knows the whole world only as a prison. It is no good telling him that "spring is still spring", not because he doesn't notice it—on the contrary—but because spring itself has become a menace. The view from the window of Victory Mansions is dreary and squalid as his predecessors found the urban scene, but now it is fearsome as well, the new element made visible in the four great new buildings which dominate the entire townscape : the enormous pyramidal sky-scrapers of "glittering white concrete, soaring up, terrace after terrace, 300 metres into the air" which house the Ministries of Truth, Peace, Plenty, and Love. All are appalling to see, but it is the last which is "the really frightening one", the centre of Winston's thoughts and the outward form of the threat that terrifies him from the start.

Fear and hatred have alternated in many of Orwell's characters. Dorothy Hare is frightened by living so much that she forgets herself; Gordon Comstock on the other hand hates it too much to know when he is afraid. George Bowling, who sees fear as the universal element, in which we all "swim" like the fish he tries to catch, swings between panic and thoughts of revenge, visions of an army of people chasing after him and of party zealots smashing in faces with spanners giving way to fantasies of doing some smashing himself. But Winston Smith is dominated by fear from the first, and the hatred which is his only recourse against it proves quite inadequate : though fear and hatred beget each other, it appears that fear is the stronger and the older of the two. Returning, the cruel and unrelenting spring revives and concentrates an old terror, something he has "always known" was going to happen. "Nothing", he is told at last, "has happened to you that you did not foresee"—and was not foreseen, in fact, by his fellow-characters of Orwell's fiction before him. But in him the fear which has been held at arm's length, or postponed, catches up. The dreaded future arrives and, having arrived, becomes an everlasting present.

Much emphasis is laid in *1984* on the fact that the dictatorship which has everything in its grip—the "huge evil intelligence brooding over the town" that Orwell sensed in the "nightmare atmosphere" of Barcelona after the Stalinist takeover; the "world of rabbits ruled by stoats" that he foresaw in *The Road to Wigan Pier*—is permanent and unchanging; it will neither alter nor depart, it is in truth eternal. "History has stopped", Winston reflects. "Nothing exists except an endless present in which the Party is always right." It may be remarked in passing that this is not only a quite unreal expectation in terms of actual human affairs and institutions, but the exact opposite of the Marxist expectation that with the establishment of the new order "history will begin". The point however, is that, absurd as it may be in terms of ordinary political development, for Winston Smith the idea that history has stopped is an important and devastating perception : it means that all avenues of escape are closed to him, he cannot even in fantasy run away from the present situation. If time has come to a halt there is no getting away from the "happening" or demand upon himself. For of course it is not true that in the world of *1984* nothing changes, even if the unfolding of history has ceased : on the contrary, the narrative is simply the story of a change, brought about in Winston as he is trapped in timelessness, pinned down under the awful eye of eternity. The change is that terrifying event which, as he knows, has always been waiting for him and which waited for his predecessors. In their case it was thrust off into the future, as with an Augustinian "Not yet", or else, in an attempt at reassurance, it is disguised as something else. At the end of

Keep the Aspidistra Flying we are told that "things were happening in the Comstock family", a new life is on the way. But that is where Gordon Comstock's story ends, and the thing itself is still in the future. Now it happens, and proves to be a painful birth indeed.

What happens to Winston, or rather in Winston, is the subject of *1984*, and not the external circumstances of its happening; although as has already been urged, in this above all of Orwell's books internal and external are hardly to be separated. The "political" aspects of the story are not unimportant, on the contrary, "politics", the demands of society and the state upon the individual, are shown as absolutely overpowering. But everything that comes under the heading of politics is so closely related to the internal process that it is impossible to say, in the movement of the novel, whether what happens to Winston is simply the reflection of events within him, or is to be thought of as bringing these about. It is Dorothy Hare who, reflecting on her loss of faith, perceives that "all real events are in the mind"; it is Winston Smith who, bringing the process round again to her starting point, carries the perception fully through. His world is a nightmare, but one from which he will never awaken; on the contrary again, it is one he wakes *into*. The clocks strike, as they strike at the beginning of the other novels; the alarm goes off. The nightmare is recognised as reality. The events within it are real, or become real, and there is no way to be sure whether they are taking place "within" or "outside", but it is of no importance. One view alternates with the other, and herein—"politics" as expression of dream—the political meaning of Winston Smith's history is to be sought. But first we must try to understand, if we can, the nightmare which assails and devours him.

It has a long perspective, not only in foreshadowings elsewhere, but in the story of Winston himself. At the beginning of *1984*, before anything "happens", he recalls a dream, "years ago", in which it is all foretold. He is passing through "a pitch-dark room" when someone speaks to him out of the dark; it is O'Brien, the Inquisitor, who later comes to haunt his thoughts and who tells him in the dream, "We shall meet again in the place where there is no darkness". The message is spoken "very quietly, almost casually"—as may be expected of the still small voice—and all that Winston knows on waking is that O'Brien "had spoken to him out of the darkness". He cannot even be sure later that he had met O'Brien at the time or knew of his existence : the Inquisitor speaks to him out of the darkness of his own mind. He does not know what the message means, but is certain that "in some way or another it would come true". As Orwell said elsewhere, "there are dreams that sometimes reveal to you the real state of your feelings", but how this state will work itself out is not immediately apparent.

We know of course that the place of no darkness is a cell under the merciless lights of the Ministry of Love, but the message is not really a deception. In its own terms it tells Winston exactly what will happen, that he will be brought out of the darkness of ignorance into the light. Let us look at the fulfilment of this dream from the point of view of the mysterious messenger, who is at once an external actor in Winston's fate and a spokesman for the unacknowledged part of his own mind.

Winston regains the faith that Dorothy Hare lost. As she loses her faith in dereliction, torment and nightmare so he, plunging far more deeply, finds his, which has been waiting for him, through the same process. Faith is indeed most cruelly forced upon him : so it must always seem to one part of the divided mind. The dream he remembers from seven years back (significant period !) tells him the truth which he cannot accept unless with groaning and much pain; unregenerate as he is when his story begins, he does not know what truth is, although he works in its Ministry. His history is concerned with Truth and Love, the two great commanding abstractions whose outward forms, in the enormous Ministerial headquarters towering over the city of men, are before his eyes but from both of which he is deeply estranged. Though he works in Minitrue the truth is not in him, he is in rebellion against it. He cannot accept truth until he is received into love; he cannot know love until, through its ministrations, he fully grasps and absorbs the truth. Truth and Love work together to make him a new man, and in the process the old Winston is destroyed. He is made over again, or re-born. He does not want to be, naturally—the natural man will always struggle against it—but supernatural love will not be denied.

1984, the history of Winston Smith's conversion, may quite properly be described as a love-story. It is so, however, on two levels, showing two kinds of love, the false and the true, the human and divine. The first must be exposed before the second is accepted; although it is by the agency of the partial and inadequate love that the erring soul is brought to the fullness of truth. Winston's human or earthly love is centred upon Julia, the girl who also works in the Ministry of Truth and, like him, turns out to be a rebel against it. The objection may very justly be made that Winston's love for Julia has very little of the genuinely earthly about it. From the beginning, with its reversal of the usual accepted roles—Julia's being all the initiative, Winston remaining passive all the way—it is an unconvincing affair, at least as an affair of flesh and blood; its supposed intensity, though feverishly asserted by both partners, has no other demonstration. Even they admit as much when it appears that they make love not so much from mutual desire as in an act of rebellion against the rule they both hate.

Hatred appears to be their primary motive. Their mutual declaration is that they "hate purity, hate goodness", are both "corrupt to the bones"; of course we know, or are supposed to know, that in their world where everything has been reversed this doesn't mean what it sounds like; all the same, since they use other emotional terms in their common sense—they do actually apply the word "love" to one another—it might seem ill-omened that they should speak so freely of hating its usual attributes of goodness and purity. It is even more ominous that they should rejoice in the dissociation which separates "it", their sexual gratification, from love. " 'You like doing this?' " asks Winston. " 'I don't mean simply me. I mean the thing in itself?' " Julia replies, " 'I adore it' ", and her declaration is "above all what he wanted to hear". He tells himself that "the thing in itself" is a primal force, "not merely the love of one person but the animal instinct, the simple undifferentiated desire", powerful enough to destroy the tyrannical unanimity of the Party. A more acute hearer might have noticed that un-differentiated is a misleading description of such a division of "it" from "me", and that lust, cut off in this way from distinction of persons, is a poor basis for the loyalty to individuals that is to restore the world.

Julia, whom Orwell is at some pains not to idealise, dwelling on her "practical" turn of mind, her ruthlessness and impatience with theory, is despite these difficult to believe in except as a fantasy of sexual relations cut off from responsibility and even, it may be said, from any deeply-felt sexuality : Winston's sadistic daydreams about Julia before he gets to know her, when he thinks of her hatefully as "young and pretty and sexless", are nearer the mark, perhaps, than Orwell intended. She is in fact a kind of intersex, her "swift, athletic movements" and "boyishness" especially in the act of throwing, being particularly noted (Orwell is recorded as having said in youth that "girls are no good, they can't play games"); the "atmosphere of hockey-fields and cold baths and community hikes" that Winston first perceives about her, the badge of the "Junior Anti-Sex League" that she wears, are more appropriate than they are meant to be. They remind one a good deal of Elizabeth, the conventional, cold young woman in *Burmese Days*, who rejects and destroys the unhappy Flory. In Julia they are intended, of course, to be no more than a disguise, beneath which her passions are hidden; but these passions are much harder to believe in than the cover they assume. In Winston they rouse resentment and hatred. He indulges in fantasies of violence upon her; even later, when he and she become lovers amid the "faint, sickly smell of bluebells" he feels an "incredulity" which we may well share.

At the beginning Winston suspects Julia of being an agent of the Thought Police, and perhaps, we may say, that is exactly what she is, a provocateur whose function is to trap the wary consciousness and lead it where it would not go, a shallow and false love which nevertheless makes Winston vulnerable to the true love that seeks him. She is, perhaps, no more than part of the process which (as Winston reflects) starts with the keeping of his illicit diary and leads inevitably to the cellars of the Ministry of Love; but she is the instrument by which he is brought out of his total isolation and comparative safety into the danger of feeling. She appears from nowhere, she has no history, and in her rather dubious femininity she is perhaps not much more for Winston than an extension of himself; but even if we think of her as a day-dream, she does represent the possibility of something happening in Winston's soul. She is the means by which the experience of suffering can be extended, even if it is still essentially Winston's own suffering; her existence, if thought of as fantasy, bears witness not to the actual birth of love in Winston, but at least to his longing for it. Perhaps she may be compared with that place in the "inner heart" of Gordon Comstock that "cared because he could not care". Thus a daydream, though false, may prepare the way for the truths of nightmare.

To encounter these Winston must leave "the surface of the earth" which Orwell often spoke of lovingly, and where, we feel, Julia belongs. To "love the surface of the earth" was for Orwell a way of expressing delight in life, named as the sign of sanity and energy in the writers he most admired, and claimed for himself. No doubt it is proper that men, who—whatever their technology now makes possible for them in going up and down—literally belong to the surface of the earth, should speak of their love for it. (Though sometimes their life there does not appear lovable; it may be wondered how often Orwell shared the King of Brobdignag's conviction that Gulliver's countrymen must be "the most pernicious race of little odious vermin that nature ever suffered to crawl upon the surface of the earth".) But as a symbolic formula for entering the whole of life to love the surface only is certainly inadequate; so, of course, Orwell found it.

Nearly all of his characters, as we have seen, make a descent at one point or another of their histories, subterranean and submarine expeditions that take them down, down, underground, underwater, in the lower depths, in the gutter, among the denizens of the deep; their downward plunge seen with continuously shifting feeling, sometimes as escape and entry into a safe refuge, sometimes as pure horror, a dive into the cesspool; sometimes deliberately undertaken, sometimes impelled, but never merely by accident; always by either inner or outer necessity. Elements of all these down-falls enter into Winston's experience: Dorothy Hare's, the most fully reported hitherto, at once flight and discovery, beginning with the total lapse of which she remembers nothing and ending in the phantasmagoria, the demons and arch-demons of Trafalgar Square; Gordon Comstock's self-willed blind and abandonment to misery; George Bowling's dive into Lower Binfield where, instead of a hoped-for respite from surface cares he fancies himself walking the ocean depths with "great crabs and cuttlefish reaching out to get him". But Winston goes much further and deeper than these; even, it may be thought, to the uttermost.

When he is betrayed, or betrays himself, he is taken first to a temporary lock-up very like the ordinary police-cell, full of a mixed bunch of drunks and petty criminals (only now with the addition of "politicals") in which Orwell back in 1932 made his experimental acquaintance with "clink". But when the inquisition begins he also begins his descent, deeper into torment, delirium and even unconsciousness, emerging intermittently as from "some quite different world, a sort of underwater world far beneath"; as he goes down further these depths engulf him until he is a part of them, walking "in a monstrous world where he himself was the monster". The preliminary torture cells are already "below ground level", but Room 101, the final destination, is "many metres underground, as deep down as it was possible to go". He goes down to the bottom; or at least far enough to see that the pit of himself he is forced to enter is indeed bottomless.

With the help of O'Brien he learns first about the truth, which is that in his own terms it doesn't exist. Orwell's hunger for the reality from which he so often felt himself cut off is here satisfied at last, and in a dreadful though expected way. Room 101, where all the prisoners of Miniluv are brought to the moment of truth, answers Orwell's lifelong expectation that "facts are apt to be unpleasant", that the underlying truth of anything is bound to be painful, that its painfulness is the actual test of validity : "the worst thing in the world" must always be the most painful truth about yourself.

When the torturers start Winston discovers that "nothing in the world was so bad as physical pain"; nothing in his world is so real. But the metaphysical torment proves to be more destructive. Winston's conversation with O'Brien in the cellars of Miniluv is very elementary metaphysics (Winston, as O'Brien tells him, is indeed "no metaphysician"), and contains at least one critical *non-sequitur*, but it is enough to cut away one of Winston's two precarious props to his own identity. Even for someone not so isolated as Winston (nor so attached as Orwell to the idea of "the autonomous individual") there is of course no logical refutation of solipsism : Winston, still at freedom and writing his "interminable letter" to O'Brien in his head, has already felt the threat implied in thinking that "both the past and the external world exist only in the mind", and has raised against it the desperate defence of "common sense". In his place of work he has already seen how all "manufactured" truths—the descriptive truths of human culture—are mutable and relative and therefore "lies". He might have reflected that this has always been the case, that historiography in particular doesn't deal in absolute truths, and that the only thing the Ministry of Truth does is (like the continual re-writing of the Soviet Encyclopaedia) to speed up the process and make it deliberate : where all is relative, truth and falsehood lie in the intention. But for him, in his isolation, the sticking point is more rigid and more fragile, a possession of the individual mind and memory within which it ought to be impossible to contain mutually contradictory "facts". O'Brien knows all these thoughts—as how should he not, being already an inmate of Winston's mind?—and has no difficulty in exposing the weakness of such reasoning; he shouldn't really have needed his torture-machine to convince Winston that the human mind is fallible. Winston, as the guardian of the truth, can now fall back only on a tautology, that $2 + 2 = 4$.

Orwell himself, in returning many times to this formula and his fear that tyranny might be able to make $2 + 2 = 5$ at command, seems to have used it both as a symbol of common sense, what everybody knows, and as an irreducible example of scientific knowledge. O'Brien's assault on Winston's mind is aimed at destroying both his trust in the "laws of science" (of which he knows nothing himself but which, like Orwell, he accepts as being "true") and his internal powers of judgment, his ability to put two and two together. O'Brien succeeds, not so much because pain drives Winston mad—as anyone's mind may be deranged by illness or drugs or mere lack of sleep to the point where sequential thought becomes impossible—as because he is in a sense mad already : he already believes that as guardian of "the secret doctrine that two plus two make four" he is the repository of reality.

Yet even in so formulating to himself the task of the intellect (his last meditation in precarious freedom, immediately before the Thought Police break in to arrest Julia and himself) he recognises the falsity of such a position. He has been thinking about the "proles", whose representative, a monstrously stout grandmotherly woman singing and pinning up washing outside, he watches with "mystical reverence", and from whose reality he feels himself entirely alienated. The proles (who are reckoned "animals" by the Party, and also by him, though in his case with yearning admiration rather than contempt) represent the body as he represents the mind, and the two are separate. As mind or intellect alone, his integrity based on the autonomous knowledge that $2 + 2 = 4$, he recognises at this point that he is cut off from real existence : he (and Julia also, as his extension) are dead. "We are the dead", he tells her; and at once the "iron voice" of the telescreen echoes him. The Thought Police have come; and truly we may say he has summoned them.

O'Brien's task in the destruction of Winston's "reason" is already more than half performed. "Reality is inside the skull", he tells him, and Winston (while recognising that it is death to think so) has already assumed it : that $2 + 2 = 4$, which merely formulates for the mind its own operations, is knowledge perfectly compatible with solipsism, and requires no reference to any external reality whatever. It is at this point, however, that O'Brien cheats, although neither Winston nor Orwell seems to have noticed it, in introducing the notion of "collective solipsism", which is of course nonsense. Solipsism, is obviously and irremovably dependent on "the autonomous individual", a solitary consciousness separate from all others and knowing, as certainty, only itself : as such it is logically unassailable. But what O'Brien is really saying is not a philosophical proposition at all, merely a social observation, that "truth" is the equivalent of received opinion, the opinion of the majority or of those able to enforce it; and that, socially speaking, there are collective delusions.

So much is certainly the case, but it is not an absolute condition, nor can it in any way impinge on a genuinely solipsist view : if reality is truly inside the skull, and if Winston had been truly convinced of it, he would have been given an immediate and irrefutable answer to O'Brien's sophistry. He need only say to O'Brien, "I do not believe in you or the whole apparatus of the Party". Only a madman could do that, it may be said, and Winston, though committed to the insane (though logical) proposition that his thought alone is the creator of reality, does not really believe it : for him, as for others caught in this metaphysical trap, the result has been rather the disappearance of any reality, either without or within. He cannot answer O'Brien with his own solipsist argument for an existential rather than a logical reason : his precarious sense of identity, clinging to nothing better than the most rudimentary of arithmetic statements for support, is already in so desperate a state that he is unable to say either "I believe" or "I disbelieve" about anything. He cannot really say "I" any longer, let alone make the positive assertion contained in "I believe".

From this intolerable state of nothingness he is shown the way out by O'Brien, and immediately, indeed inevitably, takes it. He can move in one direction only, which is to say "I believe in the Party"; just as the Berkeleyan demonstration of a thoroughgoing solipsism drives towards belief in God. For though in philosophical terms O'Brien's "collective solipsism" is nonsense, in theological terms, if the Party is the expression of the divine consciousness and will, it is perfectly good sense. The Party whose "mind", as O'Brien says, "is collective and immortal" fulfils exactly the same function in this process of reductive reasoning as does Berkeley's God. The solipsist, retreating always to a smaller and smaller point of inner certainty, must end by doubting his own existence—existence of any kind, therefore, as a personal possession : his doubts turn inside out and only the divine is left. Thus when Winston asks whether Big Brother ("the embodiment of the Party") exists " 'in the same way as I exist' ", O'Brien replies, "You do not exist' ". Only God has real existence, and his reality, of course, is eternal : " 'Will Big Brother ever die?' " asks Winston next, and is answered, very reasonably in terms of theological discourse, " 'Of course not. How could he die?' "

What is the Party, and Who is Big Brother, is by now very plain. Winston is not however ready to acknowledge it, not yet, as O'Brien says, having been humbled. He does not yet understand and accept the facts about himself, clinging to certain delusions which must first be removed. It is a hard struggle; indeed he gives up only at the very last the isolation which has been his refuge from the terrible solicitude of the Party. But love is all-powerful : it is love that is his undoing, and love that seeks him out. It is through his love for Julia that he is betrayed; as we have suggested, it is a false love, but it throws him into the arms of the true love where everything else is given up. At the time of his first meeting with Julia—while still thinking of her as an agent of the enemy and indulging in fantasies of murdering her—he acquires another possession. This is the old glass paperweight with its fragment of coral embedded in it that he buys from the bogus antique-dealer : an encapsulated piece of the past, and another expression (like Julia herself) of his longing and need. Similarly, it is thought of as property. It goes into

Winston's pocket as the symbol of his self-possession; the first thing he thinks of using it for, while yet imagining that Julia is a member of the Thought Police, is as a weapon to smash her skull. When he finds out his mistake—or rather when Julia "reveals herself" to him with her alluring declaration of love— he continues to hug both his hatred and his love to himself as *his*, the personal property of his conscious selfhood and the guarantee, indeed, of his integrity. In fact, like Julia, the paper- weight is only a bait in the loving trap of the Party.

As Winston puts it in his pocket (where, a guilty secret, it is "very heavy" though not outwardly visible) we may well wonder what has become of the crystal spirit which Orwell once glimpsed as a spirit indeed, its presence in another human being to be celebrated but not to be possessed. The answer is that what was once inviolable, beyond the reach of bomb or any other material force, is now smashed at once, broken on the empty hearth of the wretched garret in which Winston and Julia have made their delusory refuge. The paperweight, an antique, be- longs to the past as does the room, "a pocket of the past"; indeed it actually *is* the past, not an actual or acted past, the truth of which proves hard to remember, but an ideal past which is also a possession and an escape. It is a "tiny world" he can hold in his hand and yet in which he is contained : "The paperweight was the room he was in, and the coral was Julia's life and his own, fixed in a sort of eternity at the heart of the crystal." The "watery" glass concentrates the feelings stirred in him when he first sees the room, before he knows Julia : when the faint ghosts of a lost domestic affection wake in him "a sort of nostalgia, a sort of ancestral memory", and he imagines "what it felt like to sit in a room like this, in an arm-chair beside an open fire with your feet in the fender and a kettle on the hob". The memory seems to be of such an idyllic working-class family interior as Orwell described with such warm affection in *The Road to Wigan Pier*, but with a significant difference : Winston does not picture a family scene but only himself sitting there, "utterly alone, utterly secure, with nobody pursuing you" : not the warmth of human society but the absolute cosiness of the womb. Of this sort of nostalgia it can only be said, as is proved when the Thought Police break in to what has in fact been a trap all along, that those who thus live in the past perish in the present.

The crystal is broken; and what it might have told Winston, through his longing to be inside it, is forgotten, or never understood. For all this is only preliminary to the more shattering event in Room 101, which completes Winston's destruction, the discovery that he loves himself more than anybody or anything else. The "bottomless selfishness of the human being" when he is brought down there, "as deep down as it was possible to go", seems to be the final truth to be encountered in the Ministry of Love; yet just as Winston in his metaphysical exchanges with O'Brien misses a vital gap in O'Brien's argument, so now, even when he "betrays" Julia to save himself from the rats which he fears more than anything, he neglects a memory that might outbalance his betrayal. However well he is brought to see the operation of self-preservation in some, including himself, he already knows that in others, at least, love can transcend selfinterest. Right at the beginning he records in his secret diary something he has seen in the cinema ("all war films") : a cruel news-reel of massacre (the detail borrowed from one of the most mordant observations of Swift) in which there is a momentary glimpse of a Jewish woman trying, *uselessly*, to shelter a little boy in her arms, "as if she thought her arms could keep the bullets off him". Months later, asleep in bed with Julia, he has a "vast, luminous dream" in which, entered inside the glass paperweight, memories of childhood have returned; especially the memory of his mother making a similar protective motion, holding his dying baby sister. His mother's arm, *uselessly* sheltering the baby—for "something in the gesture told him that his sister was dying"—nevertheless encircles a whole world, himself, his life, the paperweight in which it is all taking place : "The dream had . . . been comprehended by—indeed, in some sense it had consisted in—a gesture of the arm made by his mother, and made again thirty years later by the Jewish woman he had seen on the news film, trying to shelter the small boy from the bullets."

The importance of the dream is not fully realised by Winston —nor, perhaps, by Orwell himself : the crucial thing being that in a quite unexplained but effectual way it includes forgiveness. Winston has until then known a terrible guilt towards his mother; his fragmentary memories include his callous behaviour towards her as a boy; the glimpse in the dream was his last sight of her before her disappearance into a concentration camp.

He has seen her in other dreams drowning in the depths together with his sister, and he has felt himself somehow responsible for her death. Now, even while recalling to memory his cruel and selfish behaviour as a boy, he is released from this guilt: "until this moment", he tells Julia on waking from the dream, "I believed I had murdered my mother." Reflecting on the dream, in which almost dried up sources of feeling have been touched, he sees how his mother's gesture of love and forgiveness, like the Jewish mother's in the horrible scrap of film, entirely transcends material circumstances: "a completely helpless gesture, an embrace, a tear, a word spoken to a dying man, could have value in itself." Could indeed, though he does not take his thought so far, be stronger than death.

Why does Winston not remember this when he comes to Room 101? One may say he forgets it by a voluntary act, by a consent to O'Brien already given. While meditating on the dream he thinks to himself that "the terrible thing that the Party had done was to persuade you that mere impulses, mere feelings, were of no account, *while at the same time robbing you of all power over the material world*" (my italics). This strange, broken-backed sentence is crucial, containing a sleight of mind that allows Winston Smith fatally to deceive himself. Its second half has no true connection with the first, neither qualifying nor qualified by it. It is irrelevant to the value of "mere feelings" that those who have them have or have not also power over the material world: the whole point of "mere feelings" in this context is that they have nothing to do with power. By robbing him of material power the Party doesn't force anyone to abandon belief in the value of "mere", or "powerless" impulses and the "helpless" acts that spring from them: the worth of such feelings is by definition outside the reach of force. The really terrible thing that the Party has done is wholly contained in the first part of the sentence: once a man has been persuaded that feelings, as feelings, are without value, it makes no difference whether he has power over things or not. We may suppose that such persuasion is easy because Winston already suffers from a rooted confusion between power and value. We may say further that when he comes to the test Winston is unable to make such a helpless and also inviolable gesture towards Julia or anybody else because his capacity for feeling has already been drawn out of him in another direction.

Winston's knowledge of his mother's forgiveness, which might have been a critical, saving realisation, does not help him; nor do the memories, or visions, of "the Golden Country", the ideal image of a childhood-Eden into which he longs to escape. Escape is impossible because he does not really wish it : whatever his conscious will may command, urging him to save himself and his mental possessions, the "few cubic centimetres inside your skull" which alone "was your own", another force has been at work in him from the start, impelling him like a somnambulist to the Ministry of Love, and finally to Room 101. He knows at the beginning where he will end : when he gets the deceptive message from O'Brien he is not really deceived, for he knows already that "what was happening was only the working out of a process that had started years ago". Although at the time he thinks he will be going there as a rebel, he is already drawn irresistibly to Miniluv. He has preserved himself, or been preserved, for this. He goes there with his possessions intact, his love, his hatred, his intellectual integrity, all thought of as the exclusive property of his conscious self—and they are all taken away from him. When his ego is faced with absolute destruction, the unbearable test, it is natural to give up these possessions to "save" his selfhood. Everything must be jettisoned to keep the balloon from sinking utterly into the depths. But this sort of saving is self-destruction : he that saveth his life shall lose it.

By this stage, if not before, it is impossible not to see *1984* as a religious parable, or rather as a monstrous parody of one. The Party is God, Big Brother the divine "embodiment" or incarnation. His tabernacle and dwelling-place is the Ministry of Love; his priests and messengers, the legions of his angels, are the agents of the Party and the Thought Police, ubiquitous and all-powerful; in himself, as his servant O'Brien teaches, he is immortal, all-seeing, all-knowing, and omnipotent. Through the device of "collective solipsism" he is literally able to do anything, with absolute power over "the laws of Nature". The Party can alter these "laws" at will, and perform the impossible : in such terms $2 + 2 = 5$ is simply the formula of a miracle.

God-Party seeks the individual soul, Winston, to make it absolutely his. The bodies of his subjects are already entirely in his power : he is everywhere, he hears and sees everything—the "telescreen", virtually Orwell's only technical innovation for the future, operates exactly like the Eye of God as represented in iconography. The sinful soul, full of guilt and immeasurable wickedness, desperately resisting the call to obedience, deludes itself with the belief that it can somehow hide from Omniscience : but "if I say, Surely the darkness shall cover me, even the night shall be light about me; yea, the darkness hideth not from Thee, but the night shineth as the day; the darkness and the light are both alike to Thee". So the fugitive soul will come inevitably to "the place where there is no darkness" in the cells of Omnipotent Love; will be made to confess all its errors, be humbled and brought to acknowledge its powerlessness, wretchedness, non-existence before God, who alone is reality. But God is not self-sufficient. The wages of sin is death ("Thoughtcrime does not entail death : thoughtcrime is death", writes Winston in his diary) but God desires not the death of any sinner, but that he should repent and live.

Winston is sought out by the emissary of divine power just as Job, the upright man, is drawn to the attention of God by Satan. O'Brien, though clearly related to Dostoevsky's Grand Inquisitor and other priestly ministers, and though at one point he does own to being mortal, is (to Winston, at least) himself a supernatural being, very like the Satan who is of the court of Heaven and is busy among the sons of men, going to and fro upon the earth and walking up and down in it. To Winston he is the Adversary, the Accuser; what he subjects him to in Miniluv follows the same course as the successive visitations upon Job, deprived of all possessions and supports, tormented by doubts, and reduced stage by stage to utter degradation, all his mortal pretensions taken away : like Job stricken with boils and scraping himself with a potsherd he is as O'Brien says, "nothing but a bag of filth . . . if you are human that is humanity". Like Job Winston still obstinately maintains his integrity in the secret places of his heart; like Job he is summoned to dispute (with all the cards stacked against him); and like him he is finally steamrollered by the manifestation of pure power, expounded by O'Brien as the divine dynamic, the central principle of the Party. He abhors himself and repents in dust and ashes. In one respect only is he unlike Job, that at no point until it is all over, can he say of Big Brother, Though he slay me, yet will I trust in him.

(Orwell's own feeling about the inextinguishable faith of Job, how far or near he came to sharing it, can be guessed from a remark in *Inside the Whale*. Discussing Henry Miller's posture of passive acceptance, he describes it as "a species of quietism, implying either complete unbelief or else a degree of belief amounting to mysticism", and goes on to say that "the attitude is 'Je m'en fous' or 'Though He slay me, yet will I trust in Him', whichever way you look at it; for practical purposes both are identical". Perhaps it does not need to be pointed out that they only look identical from the outside [for "practical purposes"] or from the point of view of scepticism. The unbeliever takes as an article of his faith that "nothing matters", and finds it a perpetual torment, because he does not really believe it—he knows that *he* matters. The believer who has reached the full "degree of belief" knows that nothing matters, under God, and is content. At their opposite poles they seem to be saying the same thing; but of course it is precisely for practical purposes, where the fruits of belief and unbelief are manifest in lives, that the difference shows.)

The final demonstration that God is Power is made through the rats in Room 101, where Winston's integrity or self-will, which is his secret hatred for Big Brother, has to be relinquished to save himself from the last horror. What is it that waits in Room 101, "the worst thing in the world"? The personal meaning for Winston (and Orwell) can be guessed at in terms of individual psychology, and will be touched on later; but Room 101 is singular among torture chambers in that it is both personal and general, one that everyone comes to in the end, and one that is unique for each person. It is the test that each must face, and fail. Death, as Orwell believed (and as O'Brien asserts) is "the greatest of all failures"; yet what awaits each individual in Room 101 is not death itself, universal and personal, although clearly related to it. Winston indeed has longed for death, thinking of it as escape; such a release is denied him—as it was denied Job, whose life Satan was forbidden to touch. Room 101 contains something that genuinely appears to be "worse than death"; it is rather the idea of death and what it may imply for the man who contemplates it.

We may note that this was something Orwell found great difficulty in doing. That man is mortal he certainly did not forget, and perhaps the most important way in which he must be distinguished from other Left-wing critics of society was his perception, repeated in many places and made the central theme

of *A Clergyman's Daughter*, that the decay of general belief in
"personal immortality" has been the chief mental event of
modern times, and has left a problem, social and psychological,
as yet unsolved. For him indeed it often seemed that the extinction of belief in "personal immortality" simply *was* the religious
problem, and whether that is in any way an adequate summary
leaves another question to be answered. In the meantime it is
necessary to remark that, unlike most of his contemporaries,
especially on the Left, he did think the fact worth some attention, that all men must die; but found it extremely hard (as who
does not, it's true) to think what death means for the
"autonomous individual".

The external circumstances of death, its sordidness and visible
horrors, he wrote about with fearful realism : the details of
bodily decay in, especially, *How the Poor Die*, not to mention
other accounts arising from his all-too close acquaintance with
sickness and death in hospital, can certainly be seen in the background as Winston looks at his "ruined body" in the mirror of
the Ministry of Love. But it is disease rather than death itself
Orwell was talking about in these places; the fact that "those
who take the sword perish by the sword, and those who don't
take the sword perish by smelly diseases" made him think
favourably of a violent death but did not make him think more
closely of death itself. When he tried to do so, recognising death
as "an absolute (the only absolute we know)" he tended, true to
his solipsist view of existence, to consider it in terms of outward
perception brought to an end, the individual's "world" (*his*
world, a personal possession) finished with him. The definition
offered in his bitterly compassionate account of *A Hanging*
is that when the victim's neck is broken there is "one mind less,
one world less". When he himself came near to death from a
wound in Spain he recorded it afterwards (in *Homage to
Catalonia*) as a "very interesting" experience, and the experience
is all external. His emotions, after a first "conventional" thought
for his wife, were of "violent resentment at having to leave this
world which, when all is said and done, suits me so well"; the
death he thought was a few minutes off was "a stupid mis-
chance", without meaning. Death (as it seemed to him on
another, more tragic occasion, the death of his first wife) is
"cruel and stupid".

Such thoughts are probably common, and may well be called

conventional. What is usually missing when one speaks of death's "meaninglessness" is an attempt to see what this lack of meaning means. It was one Orwell scarcely thought of, evidently; but at the beginning of Winston's story there is an odd remark that shows perhaps the first steps in trying to grapple with it. Winston, thinking of "the few cubic centimetres inside your skull" which are a man's only possession, goes on to reflect that in front of him "there lay not death but annihilation". On the face of it it is an absurd remark, since one can't suppose that for Winston the fact that his diary will be burnt and his body vaporised can make more absolute the absoluteness of his extinction. It is "the future" he is thinking of, and his inability to communicate with it after death through anything he might leave behind. But it is still a curious way to put it, and it is possible to think that Winston here is making a real attempt to look seriously at the void into which must fall everything that can be reckoned "your own".

Non-entity, the void, can only be described in metaphor, and in Room 101 Orwell may be said to have found one, a point at which something can be said about the meaning of death's meaninglessness. The end of life without meaning must be without meaning also : it is his life rather than his death that confronts Winston in Room 101. It is not an execution chamber, which Winston could presumably have faced with equanimity, preserving to the last the fantasy of dying with "his" hatred of Big Brother intact. It is the place where he is brought ineluctably up against his own nothingness : the truly bottomless abyss into which will fall all personal property, including the hatred which he hoped to cling to at the last. He calls for the torment to be transferred to "Julia", but by now Julia is transparently a figment, that part of his mind with which he has made a pact to die in "freedom", hating. Threatened with the most hateful torture he hates the hatred for which he is to be tortured; it is his last possession and he gives it up. He has nothing : he is nothing.

From this black night of the soul Winston is rescued by the divine power. "I shall save you, I shall make you perfect", O'Brien has already promised; "we shall squeeze you dry and then we shall fill you with ourselves". The heretic and sinner will be purged of all sin and self-will : "We burn all evil out of him." The command laid upon him is no longer that of the

"old despotisms", "thou shalt not" or even "thou shalt", but
the divine imperative, no longer social but direct and personal,
"thou art", the absolute demand made not upon behaviour but
on being. (In Imperial India and at school, those lesser imita-
tions of a divine order, Orwell had, as we recall, known long
ago that "you are not judged for what you do but for what
you *are*".)

Repentance first, until the sinners, empty of their selfhood,
are "only the shells of men" : then the making over again. So,
reconstituted, having put on the new man, Winston emerges
from the ministrations of Love, knowing salvation even in his
wretched, broken flesh : drunk with the special gin reserved for
penitents (which, like grace, is poured out free), and with the
vilest war propaganda, concentrated only on the divine will, indifferent to all other things and persons, he comes at last to see
the truth. He gazes drunkenly at a chess problem, too fuddled
to understand it, but grasping the symbolic meaning that "white
always mates", Good will always triumph over Evil. He gazes
at the ubiquitous holy image on the wall : "Forty years it had
taken him to learn what kind of smile was hidden beneath the
dark moustache. O cruel, needless misunderstanding! O stubborn, self-willed exile from the loving breast!" So, like the
mystic knowing that at last "all things shall be well and all
manner of things shall be well", he sees in gin-sodden ecstasy
that "it was all right, everything was all right" and that, the
struggle over, he loves Big Brother.

At the same time, to remind us where this journey started, it
is spring again, "a vile biting day in March, when the earth was
like iron and all the grass seemed dead". He meets and recognises Julia, and cares nothing for her, nor she for him. He sits
with his fellows, all sanctified by the same covenant of grace,
and sees himself and them as dead, "looking at each other with
extinct eyes, like ghosts fading at cock-crow".

What is this re-birth, this dreadful dawn? It is parody, as we
have said; though how much is conscious, how much has slipped
in against the writer's will, it is hard to guess. And it is no longer
possible to say what actually is being parodied : is it a parody of
religion in terms of the totalitarian State or of the State in terms
of religion? There is no doubt, however, about the intensity of
the feeling. There is no detachment now, no "objectivity" : the
writer is intimately, terribly involved in everything he is saying.

As we read *1984* we feel that, like Winston Smith, Orwell has never "until this moment considered what is existence", but that now—being, in fact, mortally ill—he is considering it with all the powers, intellectual and emotional, at his disposal, bringing to it all his experience of men and affairs, his memories and obsessions and his unsparing though limited knowledge of himself. If ever Orwell wrote a book in earnest, and there is no suggestion that he ever did otherwise, it is *1984*; there is no getting away from the effect of that profound despair by telling ourselves that he did not really mean it. At the end of his life, he put all of his life into it.

But though, as has been argued, the whole of Orwell's life-history as it shows in his writing leads towards Miniluv, the reception of Winston into its nethermost depths being only the last of many such descents, we should remind ourselves that the fall was not always seen in such absolutely negative terms. Let us look again at a couple of the earlier examples. When Orwell was working as a *plongeur* at the Hotel X in Paris ("a vast, grandiose palace with a classical façade, and at one side a little dark doorway like a rathole, which was the service entrance") he was already, we may say, collecting impressions and associations later to merge in Miniluv. When he gets the job there he is taken down "a winding passage deep underground, and so low that I had to stoop in places", and thence to "a tiny underground den—a cellar below a cellar, as it were", where he is to work. The prototype of Room 101 is easily recognisable, except in the atmosphere; for this underground cell is a cheerful place, remembered not only with a lively recollection of its discomforts but also with pleasure. Quite apart from the fact that he was glad to get work anywhere, Orwell was obviously happy in the cellar, and described it later with zest and a vivid sense of enjoyment in the work itself, rising at times to "a sort of delirium", and in the rough camaraderie. We get the same impression later on in *Down and Out in Paris and London*, when Orwell is making his first acquaintance with a London doss-house and goes down to the kitchen, "a low-ceiled cellar deep underground, very hot and drowsy with coke fumes". "I liked the kitchen," he says.

It is hard to believe, even without looking at other pleasurable descents, that this was simply a matter of being a young and comparatively fit man, and therefore of seeing things differently;

though differently Orwell certainly did see both the actual experiences of his adventures underground and the symbolic uses he made of them. The difference between the warm frowsty cellarage of the Hotel X and the Pennyfields lodging-house on the one hand and the frightful inner cell of Room 101 is principally one of acceptance. Orwell-Blair was a mate among mates, accepting and accepted.

To take it a step further, it is a question also, and perhaps more importantly, of self-acceptance. No doubt there was much in himself that Orwell found hard to accept; most of all perhaps in his bodily existence itself, the physical fact of being flesh and blood. In much of his writing can be observed traces of a sexual ambivalence which must have been quite contrary to the standards imposed on him and that he in turn imposed on himself, the value set upon "hardness" and the rejection of "softness"—of tenderness and femininity—expressed in many places, especially in *The Road to Wigan Pier*. The few but striking instances of feminine identification have been noted on the one hand; on the other, and complementary to these, there are the revulsion from and fascination by everything "dirty" or "smelly" pointed out by himself in Swift and almost as marked in himself; the evident obsession with blood, pain, and violence. All can be interpreted as evidence of sadistic and homosexual traits which Orwell severely repressed; the case has been argued, and could probably be taken further.

In particular, the rats which bring about Winston Smith's final surrender can reasonably be identified, rats being as it were animated phallic dirt, faeces made active and malevolent, as the central symbol of such a constellation of states of mind. The rat-torture, "a common punishment in Imperial China", says O'Brien, may possibly contain a memory of Octave Mirbeau's pseudo-oriental tale *The Chinese Torture Garden*, a collection of sadistic fantasies which Orwell might have come across in Paris. One of the tortures described is exactly that with which O'Brien terrifies Winston—only with the difference that the rats are supposed to gnaw their way into the victim's anus. The change by Orwell to Winston's face and mouth may be taken as a classic example of "transference upwards", and fits well enough with the very frequent references to "smashing in" faces and the oral symbolism recognised in male homosexual dreams. It is possible (and has been urged as a key) to view the whole climactic scene of *1984* as a narrowly averted homosexual rape.

(There is a striking parallel between the source of Winston Smith's supreme terror and the obsessional fantasy of Freud's "Rat Man", recorded originally in 1909. Freud's patient, a young man of high moral principles, was told by another man of a "specially horrible punishment used in the East", identical with that described by Mirbeau, and was thereafter haunted by it, and especially by the idea that the punishment was transferred from himself to someone else. The transferred torture, says Freud, was not thought of by the young man as being carried out by himself, but "as it were impersonally" : "the person to whom this 'idea' of his related was the young lady whom he admired." He was generally tormented by the idea that "something would happen to people he loved", not only in "our present life" but also "in eternity".

The interest of this case in relation to the terrors of Room 101 is enhanced by further remarks of Freud on his patient's life and character : how up to his fourteenth or fifteenth year he had been "devoutly religious", but from that time on had developed gradually into a "freethinker"; how he maintained that "self-reproach could only arise from a breach of a person's own inner moral principles, and not from that of any external ones"; how nevertheless he feared "disintegration of personality", and had been troubled by the conviction "from the age of seven" that his parents could guess his thoughts. "The moral self", he felt, "was conscious, the evil self was unconscious." Cowardice, Freud noted, was "peculiarly horrible to him"; he was also much concerned with becoming "too fat"; ideas connected with a small sum of money and also with dirt and dung played a large part in his obsessional neurosis.

The case-history is recorded in Vol. X of Freud's *Complete Psychological Works*, translated by James Strachey, and not published in English until 1955. Orwell could hardly have heard of it directly; apart from a possible common source in Mirbeau's story, the resemblances appear to be more of psychological than literary origin.)

If we accept that Orwell had such wishes and fantasies, which seems at least possible, and rejected them in himself as he vehemently did in others, it would account no doubt for much of the particular form which his obsessions took, but it would not take us much nearer understanding the essence of his work. The connection between an individual psychic development and a general attitude has still to be made; and here much may be learned from his account of his schooldays, *Such, Such Were the Joys*, written late in life and not published until after his death. References have already been made to this piece of autobiography, and it has been extensively discussed elsewhere; it is a source of information no student of Orwell can neglect. The relationship between the miseries of his preparatory school, "St Cyprian's", and the whole tenor of Orwell-Blair's adult life, and the special link between these miseries and the horrors of *1984* have been pointed out more than once.

The relevant points for the present study are to be found in the young Eric Blair's and the adult Orwell's attitudes to authority and love. The boy—already, it seems, an isolated child, who was conscious only of "dislike" for an elderly, remote father and, though loving his mother, too shy to trust her with his feelings—was sent to this school at the age of eight, an abrupt exile from home which was (and still generally is) a fixed feature of English upper-class boys' education, and which Orwell continued to regard as one of its worst features. Cut off from love, apparently rejected by his parents, subjected to the "spartan" conditions and bullying discipline taken for granted in schools of the kind, he was acutely unhappy and (as he interpreted his own feelings thirty-five years later) came to or confirmed certain conclusions about himself and the world. "I was in a world," he says, "where it was *not possible* for me to be good." He was guilty and deserved to be punished; governed by absolute laws "which it was not possible for me to keep", knowing that "the things you most want to do are always unattainable"; believing that "reality", epitomised by the feeling of his hard school bed on the first night of term, is always unpleasant and uncomfortable. Convinced of failure—"failure behind me, failure ahead of me"—and knowing his comparative poverty in a world in which money and worldly success were inextricably confused with moral virtue, he knew unavoidably that he was "no good"; there as elsewhere, moreover, he could have no hope of becoming better for there as elsewhere the affluence and social eminence that were the visible signs of virtue were valuable in proportion to their being unearned : "they all depended not only on what you did but what you *were*."

All this we recognise, and there is much more showing close correspondence between the child's attitudes and beliefs and the man's. The man may have exaggerated, or may have used hindsight to draw these correspondences closer, but that makes no difference, since it is the grown Orwell's beliefs we are interested in, and his beliefs about himself as a child are as important as any. The child (he tells us) was convinced that he was "no good", in other words that he was bad. He knew that he was unloved, feared that he was rejected as unlovable; had expectations of failure in the chief things looked for in him; even expected (since, as we have seen, death is "the greatest of failures") an early death. At the same time, and very naturally, the boy began to lose whatever of religious faith might be conveyed and cherished by the teaching and formal worship of an institution which commanded him "to be at once a Christian and a social success, which is impossible". He did not cease consciously to "believe in" God, but he knew that he did not love him : "on the contrary, I hated him, just as I hated Jesus and the Jewish patriarchs." Quite naturally, again, he identified with Satan as the enemy of God; but not so much with the defiant rebel as the doomed and desperate victim of divine omnipotence. A little later, he tells us (and we can infer therefore that this attitude developed and took root) that the last line of Meredith's poem *Lucifer in Starlight* struck him as exactly describing his own situation : Lucifer, revisiting the courts of heaven and recoiling from the sight of the stars which remind him of his overthrow by "the army of unalterable law". "I understood to perfection", Orwell says, "what it meant to be Lucifer, defeated and justly defeated, with no possibility of revenge." We may add to this his account from another source (*Why I Write*) of another verse-association : now at Eton, and enjoying a relative emancipation, he reads *Paradise Lost* with the eager appreciation of youth, and is specially struck by two lines which sent, he afterwards remembered, shivers of pleasure down his spine :

> So hee with difficulty and with labour hard
> Moved on; with difficulty and with labour hee.

His pleasure lay, he says, merely in the verbal effect, including the old spelling of "hee". But taking these lines in their context we may suppose also that his imagination was caught once more by recognition and sympathy with the Satan who at this point in the epic is fighting his way laboriously up from the nethermost Abyss.

Milton's Satan hopes here to make alliance with Chaos and ancient Night against the encroaching laws of Nature, and just as Meredith's Lucifer knew these laws to be against him, so also did the boy. He knew, however, that his own nature said otherwise, that the "instinct to survive" ran counter to the decrees of authority, absolute and just though they were. "To survive, or at least to preserve my kind of independence, was essentially criminal, since it meant breaking rules which you yourself recognised." Now we come to the crucial point. Orwell explains how he did in fact manage to survive : "I could not invert the existing scale of values, or turn myself into a success, but I could accept my failure and make the best of it." It sounds like stoical common sense; but there is a terrible contradiction here of which Orwell probably was not conscious, but which dogged him for the rest of his life. For to "make the best of failure" in the context of the absolute demands the boy thought of as being made upon him is not at all a matter of self-toleration, still less of challenge to ruling norms, but is to know that one is bad and make a virtue out of it : to say, in a word, Evil be thou my good.

That is an intolerable state of affairs within the soul, a verbal paradox which represents a deep division of impulses; yet many live in it. They learn to do so by fatigue and habituation, and chiefly by cutting themselves off from the feelings which threaten to tear them apart. Thus they become ghosts, detached from living, but unable to be at peace : ghosts are restless because they know that they are ghosts. There is always the inner heart that cares because it cannot care.

Such ghosts of living men are common, and have common desires. There are many points of resemblance between Orwell's self-disparaging sense of his own ghostliness and the shabby-genteel, mocking Devil who comes to torment Ivan Karamazov; perhaps the most striking (recalling Orwell's fantasies of being a woman, especially a fat one) is the Russian Devil's dream of achieving real existence by "becoming incarnate once for all and irrevocably in the form of some merchant's wife weighing eighteen stone, and of believing all she believes".

Orwell "got over" his childhood misery, recovered some of

his strength in the resting period given him by Eton—"a little quietude, a little self-indulgence, a little respite from cramming" —and grew into, perhaps, a not much more than normally unhappy young man. By his own account, his recovery was complete : he ends *Such, Such Were the Joys* by looking back in apparent tranquillity and seeing, not the torment he has just described, but "how incredibly distorted is the child's vision of the world"—thinking of oneself not as feeling creature but as "vision of the world" has become a rooted habit. He cannot quite laugh at his childish fears and misapprehensions, but he is far above them now : for, as he says, "the child and the adult live in different worlds". The child has learnt not to hope for communication—"not to expose your true feelings to an adult seems to be instinctive from seven or eight onwards"; and that applies most of all, of course, to the child surviving within himself. But the truth slips out : the child also knows that "all who have passed the age of thirty [Orwell was now forty-five] are joyless grotesques, endlessly fussing about things of no importance and staying alive without, so far as the child can see, having anything to live for. Only child life is real life".

So far as the child can see! He can see far enough, and deep into the life of the adult he has become. Orwell supposed he had rid himself of all those "fantastic mistakes". If he went back now, he asks, what would he make of his place of exile and separation, of the tyrants and persecutors who ruled over it? "What should I think of . . . those terrible, all-powerful masters? . . . I would be no more frightened of them than I would be frightened of a dormouse." So he declared early in 1947; he was in the middle of writing *1984*.

The fears, the hatreds and deprivations of the child transfer themselves to a larger stage; indeed to the largest stage of all, not less than the one on which man conducts his dialogue with God. Orwell, as we have seen, was a man of strong religious impulses who forced himself to "do without" religion; faith was something that had to be "cut off". The need remains, as he knew and said many times, the amputated abdomen which is the organ of feeling and belief aches like a phantom limb and the wretched wasp is indeed unable to live without it. The hunger for goodness and love, and for an absolute to give them reality, turns elsewhere : to the place where modern man has turned all his longing for absolutism—the State. Orwell's State is God, with no equivocation, no qualification whatever, but with all the ambiguities of his gropings for the divine, his yearning for acceptance and containment, his revolt against cruel and impossible commands, now focused upon it. But the State is not only Orwell's God, nor is the despairing alternation between defiance and submission his alone. The delusion which is expressed with such appalling conviction in *1984* is world-wide and issues not only in the metaphors and allegories of art, but in concrete act and fact, the political-divine states which men dream of and attempt to construct.

It is this epidemic delusion and its relation to Orwell's fantasy, that I wish finally to approach and attempt some analysis of. But first there is something to be said about another fictitious foreshadowing of the God-State, acknowledged by Orwell as one of the literary sources of *1984*, but not referred to hitherto; furnishing an element in the process which was neglected by Orwell but is essential to understanding of the phenomenon as a whole. This is *We*, the short novel by the Russian Yevgeny Zamyatin, first published in 1924; it will be discussed in the next chapter.

VII

Lucifer's Permanent Revolution

ORWELL ACKNOWLEDGED TWO books as influences in the writing of *1984*: Jack London's prediction of an anti-proletarian or fascist dictatorship *The Iron Heel*, and Zamyatin's *We*. In Jack London Orwell, who read many of his stories while still a boy, noted especially that he "excelled in describing cruelty" and also that he had enough insight into the mentality of totalitarianism to understand how it is maintained not in mere cynicism but with its own set of values and a "quasi-religious belief in itself". London, he said, was among those who could understand Fascism because "they have a fascist streak in themselves", an observation which not without some justification has also been turned upon him. (He also observed of London's anthropomorphic treatment of animals that "there seems to be good reason for thinking that an exaggerated love of animals generally goes with a rather brutal attitude towards human beings". Concerning pigs at any rate he and London seem to have felt the same; although the "pig-ethics" which London saw in the operations of capitalism Orwell extended as a description of political life in general.)

Further effects upon Orwell of early reading in Jack London may only be guessed at. When Orwell first came across London's early account of his life as a hobo, *On the Road*, or *The People of the Abyss*, London's description of life among the London poor in the early 1900s, is not recorded, though both were mentioned by him with approval and admiration. But it is difficult not to think that in these books—reminiscence in one case of becoming a youthful tramp by necessity, and a record in the other of what Jack London discovered by disguising himself in old clothes and entering the "abyss" of the East End—Orwell found examples for what he did himself. How far the motives were the same for both men can only be conjectured; but at least the reason given for Jack London's exploration in disguise—

to report, as he said, as "a correspondent writing from the field of the industrial war"—was exactly what Orwell claimed to be doing, especially when collecting material for *The Road to Wigan Pier*.

There can be no doubt that, hugely different though they were in skill and subtlety as writers, and in at least some of their habitual reactions, the two had much in common. The chief difference noted by Orwell himself was a temperamental one, that London had "an almost unconquerable preference for the strong man as against the weak man", whereas he would always be "on the side of the weak against the strong". It was a real difference, although it may be thought that such opposing attitudes both sprang from a similar preoccupation with the relations between strength and weakness, or between oppressor and victim. Even if that is so, there is no question which position allowed the greater sensibility. A typical example may be taken from London's and Orwell's description of an execution. In 1902 London watched, as an invited spectator, the hanging of a man in an American jail, and his account in a letter in some ways resembles Orwell's in *A Hanging*. His pretext for watching the execution, that "as a sentient creature" his only way of knowing about death was by observing the death of another, seems to arise from the same train of thought as Orwell's reflection on the fact of sudden, foreseen death—the live man who in a few moments would be dead, "one mind less, one world gone". To both writers the transition was something beyond intellectual grasp, for London "such a wonder in it all", for Orwell a "mystery". But what hit Orwell was not only the mystery but "the unspeakable wrongness of it all"; and it is his acute fellow-feeling, not only with the condemned man but with every living creature involved in the hanging, where London spoke self-justifyingly of necessity and consistency ("When you dare to walk home by sidewalks lighted by the Law, then you are party to the crime committed by the Law when it hangs a man") that opens a gulf between this celebrated essay, one of the most acute and memorable descriptions of an execution in any literature, and London's noisy sensationalism.

In style, in such characterisation as it contains, and in general implication London's most fully worked out (though still exceedingly slapdash) forecast of totalitarianism, *The Iron Heel*, is quite unlike *1984*. Nevertheless, the tyranny of the Oligarchs he described does in some notable respects resemble that of the Party (given the label by Goldstein of "Oligarchical Collectivism") in *1984*. The likeness is especially apparent in the Oligarchs' "high ethical standards", a point that Orwell emphasised when writing about Jack London in 1945. Both writers allowed a conviction of the relativity of morals to colour their presentation of a hateful system : London was committed by his social Darwinism to believe that might was right and in any case half wished to think so. Orwell went further, placing the Party "beyond good and evil" as the absolute arbiter of ethics according to its collective, or divine will.

Fascination by strength, or power, characterises both : at the beginning of *The Iron Heel* a spokesman of the coming Oligarchy describes his programme in words very like O'Brien's —power is "the king of words", "Not God, not Mammon, but Power". The Oligarchs, says this representative, "will grind you revolutionaries down under our heel, and we shall walk on your faces. . . . As for the host of labour, it has been in the dirt since history began . . .". But power for London's Oligarchs still has a definable worldly end, to defend "civilisation" against "the great beast" of the proletariat; the Oligarchy in fact spends much of its energy in continual class warfare, with bloody massacres of the workers. The purely abstract, even metaphysical notion of power for power's sake belongs to *1984*, whose collective oligarchs no longer fear the proles they oppress but look on them with contempt, as domestic animals. London's Oligarchy, though described in the main narrative as firmly in power, belongs to history and does not last for ever—supposed footnotes to the story inform the reader that its rule was maintained for 300 years and has been succeeded by a Socialist Utopia, "the Brotherhood of Man". (It may have helped to determine Orwell in his final choice of title that the greatest monument of the Oligarchy, in the building of which "a permanent army of half a million serfs was employed", was "not completed", according to one of the footnotes "until 1984 AD.")

The point about the date 1984, when Orwell came to use it, was, of course, that dates thereafter would cease to have any significance : after the destruction of "the last man in Europe" there is no more history. Orwell's scheme is deliberately designed to exclude any possibility of his oligarchs being overturned, and the kingdom of his Party-god is eternal. It is not merely the crudity of London's story that makes it so full of action, but the feeling that action is still possible : the almost continual scenario of individual murder and mass slaughter is schoolboyish enough, no doubt, but at least permits the preoccupation with violence and brute force to issue as conflict. In *1984* it is taken on to complete surrender.

Finally, we may conclude these brief remarks on the conflicts and ambivalences in *The Iron Heel* by pointing to something Orwell himelf ignored : it is curious that the whole of London's story, with its exaltation of the absurdly super-masculine he-men on both sides, is actually told, in the first person, by a woman, and it seems even more curious that Orwell, in his various observations on the book, never mentioned the fact.

With Zamyatin, a vastly more subtle and sophisticated writer, Orwell's sympathy was nevertheless probably much less than with Jack London, and he did not read *We*—though he had heard of it before—until early in 1946, when he was already engaged in writing *1984*. (*We* has a complex publishing history : it was written in 1920 and published outside Russia, first in English and Czech versions and subsequently in a re-translation into Russian, in the early 'twenties. It has never been published in the Soviet Union.) Orwell appears to have heard of it first in 1944, but was unable to get hold of a copy; he finally read it, in a French translation, two years later.

Although therefore *We* can have had no such place in the gathering together of ideas for *1984* as did London's story, it certainly supplied some identifiable elements, incorporated in the course of writing. More importantly, it may have influenced Orwell in a negative way. For in many respects *We* is the opposite of *1984*, and it is just for that reason that it is worth examining in some detail : whether or not as a result of conscious reaction on Orwell's part the two books in many striking ways— in outlook and fundamental assumptions about the world, in imagery and manner—complement each other.

We was described by Zamyatin himself as belonging to the genre of "socio-fantasy" pioneered by H. G. Wells, whom he admired; Wells, he pointed out, used his predictions of things to come largely as a form of social criticism, "social pamphlets disguised as science-fiction novels". His own fantasy goes very far beyond Wells, not in the detail or accuracy of the technical innovation envisaged, but in depth of psychological, and therefore of social understanding. Its interest does not at all depend on realistic scientific prediction (although Zamyatin, a naval architect by training, was well up in the technological possibilities of the age); there is none of the attraction by mere gadgetry shown by Wells even in the midst of his social-pamphleteering. But *We* may, unlike Orwell's novel, quite properly be classed as a species of science fiction, since it is in great part *about* science : its subject could be described from one point of view as the incarnation of science—especially of the "exact sciences" —in a totalitarian State.

The One State of *We*, set in the distant future, rules the whole world, and is about to set out in the conquest of new worlds : a rocket-ship, the *Integral*, is at the beginning of the story almost ready for blast-off into "universal space" to bring the inhabitants of other planets under "the beneficent yoke of reason". It is assumed that extra-territorial life, though certainly existing, may still be "in the savage state of freedom"; the task of the *Integral* will be to put an end to this and to bring about "the endless equalisation of all Creation". The earth itself is already a completely integrated society—or is believed to be one—the members of which, known only by numbers and accustomed to think of themselves not as individuals but as "we", lead lives ordered down to the last detail and under continual supervision. All live in the city, where the buildings are of glass so that everyone is continually visible except for a permitted "sex hour" when the selected and licensed parties are allowed to lower the blinds. A secret police known as the Guardians is perpetually on the watch; at the top of the Platonic edifice is a single ruler, The Benefactor, a being doubtfully human, though he does at one point conduct a conversation with the narrator, and appears at public executions, which are carried out ceremoniously by himself. The city, all glittering glass, is entirely self-sufficient (all food is synthetic), and the countryside is permanently cut off behind a glass wall through which nevertheless trees can be seen growing and wild animals moving about.

It will be seen that this is in no way a realistic tale—not even fantasy cast, like *1984*, in "the form of a naturalistic novel", but fantasy without disguise. It is set down in an expressionist, or more strictly a poetic mode admirably suited to exposition of the main theme : which confronts the regulated, obedient, rational-scientific view of man and man's possibilities with the wild claims of the imagination. The narrator, whose diary tells the story, is a mathematician-scientist, the designer in fact of the *Integral* space-rocket and an unquestioningly conformist member of the anonymous society of absolute equals. He falls in love, however, with a girl who is one of a widespread conspiracy against the rule of the Benefactor, and is drawn unwillingly into the plot. Unlike the bogus "Brotherhood" of *1984* the seditious underground movement of *We* is a real and powerful one; in the city itself (apparently a unified and universal Miniluv) it has many supporters, but it draws its chief strength from an unsuspected survival of free or savage human beings living like animals—they have actually developed a covering of fur and do not need clothes—beyond the glass Wall. They are not, it should be noted, domestic animals like the proles of *1984* and the livestock of *Animal Farm*, but wild, uncontrolled, and, so far as the regulated society of men goes, unknown : they may remind one of the men and women who survive beyond the reach of the Machine in E. M. Forster's story but they are a great deal more formidable than those Edwardian dwellers in the ferny brakes. They are dangerous, active, and disturbing; they do not passively wait for the accidental straying of conforming members of the One State but break in and lure them out.

They make their inroads upon the world of geometric unanimity through desire, through dreams—nobody in the One State is supposed to suffer from the "serious psychic disturbance" of dreams; nevertheless the narrator, to his horror, finds himself dreaming—and through the vital and lawless energy of the spring. The season at the beginning of *We* is the same as in the opening of *1984*, but the spring wind that blows from beyond the Wall, "from the wild plains that lie out of sight", bringing "the honeyed yellow pollen of certain flowers", is very different from the "swirl of gritty dust" in the April streets of Winston Smith's London. The pollen can be tasted on the lips and already "interferes with logical thinking"; later on sensation begins to merge in dream, when the narrator in sleep sees the same yellow colour all about and everything flowing with sap, himself included : "right then I myself felt the flow—and there was a certain lethally delectable horror about it all—." Spring may indeed be described as "seeping in like poison gas", but with far more powerful effects than Orwell was ready to imagine. It should be noted, too, that the erotic impulses roused by the spring, although much easier to believe in than those involved in Winston's love-making with Julia, are not separated from a more general upsurge of rebellious vitality; the rebels do not suppose, like Winston, that sexuality alone or, more specifically, lust will overturn Party and State.

The protest against the Benefactor's law of "compulsory happiness" is partly expressed in what may be described as a political act : on the ceremonial Day of Unanimity, when the Benefactor is expected to receive his annual universal vote of confidence, thousands of votes are openly cast against him, and this parody of a Soviet election, with one candidate only and any but one result unthinkable, ends in a riot. But the real threat to the One State comes when the Wall is blown up and the forces of the imagination, of instinct and desire, burst in on rational consciousness. Against this catastrophe the Benefactor has only one reply, the compulsory "Fantasiectomy" of all his subjects, a surgical operation to excise the imaginative powers altogether. It is performed on the narrator himself, and on all whom the Guardians can round up, but the issue remains in doubt : the book ends with armed mobs of insurrectionaries roaming the streets and the narrator, who has betrayed his rebel love and returned to complete servitude, can only assert, with the vehemence of desperation, that "rationality must conquer".

Their attitudes to "rationality" constitute the most significant difference between Zamyatin and Orwell, strikingly brought out in their common use of the formula $2 + 2 = 4$ as shorthand for rational certainties. The way they both use it may itself be regarded as a rather remarkable coincidence, since it cannot have been one of Orwell's borrowings from Zamyatin : his foreboding of the time when "two and two will make five when the Leader says so" antedates by several years his first reading of *We*. It is possible that both Zamyatin and Orwell recalled Dostoevsky's symbolic use of $2 + 2 = 4$, in more than one place : as the "mathematical" demonstration that Porphyry Petrovich, the investigating lawyer, looks for in *Crime and Punishment,* when the criminal himself will "prove his guilt as plainly as that twice two are four"; or as the exactly calculable goal of social advance which is passionately repudiated in the *Notes from Underground.* For Dostoevsky $2 + 2 = 4$ may be good enough for ants, but not for men : ". . . after all, twice two is four is not life, gentlemen, but the beginning of death . . . man has always feared this $2 \times 2 = 4$ formula, and I still fear it."

Zamyatin certainly shared Dostoevsky's distrust and dislike of attempts to fit mankind into $2 + 2 = 4$, and *We* exactly echoes the speaker in the *Notes from Underground* who declares : "I agree that two and two make four is an excellent thing; but to give everything its due, two and two make five is also a very fine thing." Rigidity and certainty, in *We*, are the tools of tyranny; uncertainty and the breach of the laws of arithmetic as of other laws are the signs of rebellion against it.

Thus Orwell's and Zamyatin's responses to the same idea are directly opposed. What for Winston Smith is a weapon against Big Brother (which fails him, or which he fails to hold on to) is part of the armoury of Zamyatin's Benefactor, and for the narrator of *We*, No. D-503, the chief prop of his orthodoxy and loyalty to the One State. The certainties of arithmetic which Winston clings to as a seditious secret in defiance of the God of the Party are repeated by D-503 as a charm against intrusive and disturbing thoughts : "The multiplication table is wiser, more absolute than the God of the ancients : it never (never —do you understand that?) errs." The message prepared for transmission by the *Integral* rocket to lesser breeds on other planets is that "the only things unshakable and eternal are the four rules of arithmetic. And only that morality which is built upon these four rules will prove great, unshakable, eternal." D-503 is a mathematician and a great many of his thoughts are set down in mathematical terms, even including the disturbing reflection that irrational numbers must correspond to some irrational reality; but even while thinking so he returns to the consoling conviction of the certainty and regularity of number : "mathematics and death are never in error."

Scientific "certainty" (which may not truly represent science, but was the element seized on both by Orwell, who knew very little of science, and Zamyatin, who knew quite a lot) was taken by one as subversive of absolute authority, and by the other as virtually identical with it. It so happens that in the actual course of events in Soviet Russia Orwell seems to have been more correct in his expectations than Zamyatin : Soviet scientists, restive under the restrictions placed on their work by the State, are often reckoned among the forces of dissidence. But in symbolic terms Zamyatin seems a good deal nearer the truth when he identifies the tyrannical State with the rational, orderly, and ordering faculties of man, and the irrational and emotional as the forces which constantly undermine and may even overthrow it.

Zamyatin's willingness to trust the "wild imagination" contrasts forcibly with Orwell's distrust and rejection of it : rejection is not too strong a word for Orwell's attitude if we remember that, with all his literary sensibility, he considered William Blake a "lunatic" and thought of "lunacy", madness, as being a disqualification for saying anything of real import. Orwell's attachment to rationality often, indeed, ran counter to his feelings about other writers : discussing Edgar Allan Poe, for example (in *Inside the Whale*), he allows that his tales carry conviction, *although* the "world-view" they spring from is "false and silly", and is puzzled by the contradiction. Why is it, he asks, that such stories, "which might very nearly have been written by a lunatic, do not convey a feeling of falsity?" The answer, he supposes, is because the writer himself believes in his creation; what such a belief in the products of a man's imagination may mean for him, and what it implies about the working of the imagination in general, he does not inquire further. The ambiguity of his feelings, his unwillingness to trust imaginative truth and at the same time his extremely sensitive ear for whatever rings true or false in literature drives him to the conclusion that "there are occasions when an 'untrue' belief is more likely to be sincerely held than a 'true' one"; but again, what might seem to follow therefrom is left unexplored.

When all trust is finally placed in consciousness and reason the unconscious (which may very well tell one sometimes that $2 + 2 = 5$, and be right to do so) becomes something to be feared, a destructive and terrifying "delirium" : so we find it, from Dorothy Hare's Walpurgisnacht in Trafalgar Square to Winston Smith's momentary visions of release in Miniluv, "roaring with laughter and shouting out confessions at the top of his voice", which are felt to be nothing more than traps of his own mind. (Zamyatin's D-503 on the other hand knows that "delirium" may contain truth, although he remains divided in his attitude towards it : questioning his contact with the forces of rebellion he says "No, fortunately, all this was not delirium. No, unfortunately, all this was not delirium".) It is interesting to note that Orwell, who had at times an acute appreciation of poetry and had formerly been used to express his strongest feelings in poetry, ceased to do so by the time he was writing *1984* and (in *The Prevention of Literature*, published early in 1946) showed an astonishing underestimation of the poet's role as prophet and accuser of tyranny. He describes poetry here as "an arrangement of sounds and associations, as a painting is an arrangement of brush-marks. For short snatches, as in the refrain of a song, poetry can even dispense with meaning altogether"—meaning being for him only that part of a poem that could be "translated into prose". Holding such a view it was perhaps natural for Orwell to suppose that "it is somewhat easier for a poet than for a prose writer to feel at home in authoritarian society ... It is ... fairly easy for a poet to keep away from dangerous subjects and avoid uttering heresies".

The fate of poets in the Soviet Union does not support this conclusion; and before their persecution and involvement in ideological manoeuvre began Zamyatin knew what was likely to happen. True, the poet who has a minor role in *We* appears at one point reciting an official ode he has composed to celebrate a public execution, but it is made clear that this use of his talent sickens him; he is one of the first to join the revolt and is killed in the course of it.

It is poetry, the poetic vision, and not science that will destroy the rigid beehive society of the One State; even D-503, transformed by erotic passion, becomes aware of the volcanic forces inside himself :

The idea had never come into my head before—but then the thing is precisely thus : we who live on this earth are constantly walking over a burbling, blood-red sea of fire hidden there, deep within the maw of the earth. But we never think of that. But now suppose that this thin shell under our feet were suddenly turned to glass, that we were suddenly to see—

I had turned to glass. I saw into myself, deep within me. There were two I's ...

It is a very different feeling from that of Orwell, who allowed himself to love only the surface of the earth and who (in the person of Winston Smith) was paralysed by the fear of what lies beneath. Against the rational power of the State it is this seismic, unquenchable fire, emerging as "wild", "savage", untamed, no longer under rational control, that will restore the world, as Zamyatin sees it, to sanity.

At this point however we must note that Zamyatin himself, in *We,* is in a moral dilemma, and though it does not seem so crippling in its effects as is Orwell's split between the tyrannical Good which is bad and the Badness which is never allowed to be good, it shows the same contradictions at work. The forces of revolt in *We,* both the primal energies outside the Wall and their allies within, are specifically identified as demonic—and, we may say, not without reason. Zamyatin himself, a man of fierce courage, was not unwilling to have himself cast as "the devil of Soviet literature"; in his extraordinary letter to Stalin in 1931, asking permission to live abroad, he was completely unrepentant about what others had found "harsh and offensive" in his writing, and it seems quite likely that under the not yet absolute rigidity of dictatorship at the time this bold defiance was one of the reasons why Stalin did in fact allow him to emigrate. Lucifer here has no doubts about being Lucifer; he is not yet the Father of Lies but on the contrary the champion of truth, and truth is something positive, not merely a matter of saying No. There is a subtle but real difference between the attachment to truth of Orwell and Zamyatin. The former, expressing himself with conscious conventionality, commented on the tergiversations of the Popular Front about Stalinism in Spain: "I hold the outmoded opinion that in the long run it does not pay to tell lies." The latter, writing to Stalin himself, said positively, "I have the very awkward habit of saying not what is expedient at a given moment, but what seems to me the truth."

In *We* the men and women who have refused to submit to the crushing benevolence of the One State call themselves mysteriously "Mephis", and a pseudo-footnote (supposedly added to D-503's manuscript by a learned Venusian) completes the name for us as Mephistopheles. On his single adventure outside the Wall D-503 glimpses a rock-painting "of a winged youth with a transparent body, and in the place usually occupied by the heart there was a dazzling ember, glowing with a dark-red glow". Clearly this is Lucifer, and also doubtless Prometheus, who in the passion of his "holy glowing heart" is (in Goethe's poem) joyfully defying God and getting on with his business of making and remaking mankind. And yet earlier in the story one of the poems recited at a public execution (which has all the trappings of religious ritual, with appropriate feelings in the devout congregation) names Prometheus in another aspect as symbol of the One State : the victim whose crimes are recited in the poem has endangered order,

> But at this point Prometheus (by which we were meant, of course) came on the scene :
> And harnessed fire to steel machine,
> And forged on Chaos Chains of Law!

Prometheus can be discerned at the back of the rebels, defying the deified omnipotence of the One State; Prometheus, maker, inventor, and harnesser of natural forces (which include the forces of human nature, harnessed and domesticated) is also the One State's actual embodiment.

Such divided motives produce an unavoidable confusion, the complete and riotous confusion, with the fate of the One State still undecided—the wild forces of the imagination loose in the streets, D-503 merely clinging to the hope that "rationality must conquer"—in which the tale is no doubt intentionally left at the end. Before that, however, there is an episode, actually irrelevant to the main working out of the story, which reveals very well Zamyatin's ambivalence concerning the Promethean, Luciferian (and specifically anti-Christian) drive of the insurrectionary Mephis. The Integral rocket is about to take off; its preparation is described at the beginning, and the projected flight, with D-503 obediently in charge, remains an underlying motif throughout. But the Mephis have a plot to take the rocket over themselves and use its power to destroy the One State; they are actually on the verge of carrying out this coup in the middle of the *Integral*'s test-flight. But the Guardians circumvent them, the attempt fails, and the flight ends tamely enough and indeed, so far as furthering the story goes, pointlessly, in the *Integral*'s scheduled return to earth and the arrest of the conspirators.

We feel here strongly Zamyatin's own self-doubt, the attractions of scientific power fighting against knowledge of what is done in the name of science; the realisation that to escape from the tyrannical purposes of state-rocketry—the *Integral* being destined, as the active principle of the One State, to subdue the universe—by Valkyrie-flights of rebel-rocketry is a delusion. The Mephis who propose to seize the *Integral* have already fallen into its megalomaniac power. It is interesting to note, as an example of Zamyatin's grasp of psychological processes, that at the meeting of Mephis outside the Wall at which, in an atmosphere of feverish excitement, the plan to take over the rocket is discussed, somebody protests against the scheme as "madness", and it is D-503, formerly the most rigid and obedient of members of the One State, who, beside himself, replies : " 'Yes, yes—precisely! And we must all go mad, it is imperative for all of us to go mad—as speedily as possible!' " It may be supposed that the degree of madness or dissociation espoused here, consciously recommended, is in proportion to the rigidity which preceded it; and it may be expected that the extremity of exaltation, or inflation, that carries the subject away—"all this was extraordinarily strange and inebriating", says D-503; "I felt myself superior to all, I was I, a world by itself, I had ceased to be an item, as I had always been, and had become an integer"—will lead in due course to self-defeat and fall.

We must not forget that the whole story, though set in the distant future, was written in the immediate aftermath of the Revolution, concerning which Zamyatin, a former member of the Bolsheviks, must have had painfully conflicting feelings. The revolt of the Mephi-supporters within the city—men, hitherto silent and subservient, "who had crawled out from under the murky overhangs of their foreheads", and who are now roaming the streets, "tipsy, gay", casually swinging their weapons—clearly owes much in its fragmentary description to scenes of the October Revolution itself, the rising in the name of peace and freedom which already, as Zamyatin's prescience saw it, was congealing into a cast-iron dictatorship. We may perhaps guess that Zamyatin's conflict during October—when he had returned to Russia, but was no longer a Bolshevik, having left the Party before 1917—is directly reflected in a brief exchange between D-503 and one of the insurrectionaries, who is already using the collective pronoun, the Party's first person plural, for the rebellion against collectivity : " 'We sure are active!' " D-503, accustomed to speak in exactly this way in the name of authority, asks himself in bewilderment, "Who were *we*? Who was I?" An entire complex of the ethical contradictions involved in every social revolution, carried out by awakened individual consciences in the name of a collective good, is concentrated in this momentary self-questioning.

Once again we may be reminded of Blok's poem *The Twelve*, describing a similar scene, both historical and mythological, in which the patrol of the Red Guards marching the streets, shooting at random and apparently lost in the whirling snow, is an amalgam of anarchic individual impulses and collective "solidarity" ("Keep A Revolutionary Step!"); but which, as the Red-Apostles go through the storm, "abusing God's name", "prepared for anything,/regretting nothing", resolves the contradictions, through the cross-fire of the Revolution, in the vision of Christ.

Such a resolution was not possible for Zamyatin, whose view of Christianity, expounded at various points in *We*, seems to have been a strictly conventional hostility (the Benefactor himself is half-identified with the Christian God, an Almighty who declares that "true, algebraic love for humanity is infallibly inhuman, and that an infallible sign of truth is its cruelty". Against the Luciferian energy of the Mephis Christianity is represented as pursuit of a "beatific quietism", or spiritual entropy: "It was entropy which . . . the Christians worshipped as a god."

Zamyatin tries to find a symbolic way out of the contradiction by other means, a projection of successive rebellions which is a kind of echo in his fantastic-mathematical terms of Trotsky's "permanent revolution". D-503 protests against the Mephi-girl E's proposal of revolt against the One State in precisely the terms of Party orthodoxy, that everything has already been accomplished and the State is inviolable: "our revolution . . . was the last. And there can't be any other revolutions. Everybody knows that." She mocks him, the mathematician: "name the ultimate number for me"—

"Come, E—that's preposterous. Since the number of numbers is infinite, what number would you want to be the ultimate one?"

"Well, and what revolution would you want to be the ultimate one? There is no ultimate revolution—revolutions are infinite in number. The ultimate revolution—that's for children."

In a moment, however, in reply to D-503's objection that there is no sense in further revolutions, "since everybody is already happy" (the One State having "subordinated Hunger" and "mathematised Love") E—invokes childish wisdom herself, asking What comes next?—" 'that's what we must always ask, precisely like children, "But what comes next?" ' " Against D-503's "full-stop", the "equable" state of social entropy, she calls for violent innovation, "fire, an explosion, Gehenna".

This is clearly in line with Zamyatin's general attitude of trusting to boundlessness, the unlimited—or the unconscious— to redress the killing restrictions of rational law. The idea of the infinite, with infinite scope for humanity, reappears many times as a principle of life in answer to the static condition of "absolute happiness", which is equated with absolute zero. But it will not escape notice that this take-off into the infinite, a universe of unlimited space and time, is precisely what the One State has been planning in literal fact, what the resources of the One State have made possible in the building of the *Integral*, and what is to be undertaken in the name of scientific uniformity and domination, bringing to all creation "a mathematically infallible happiness".

Such an apparently insoluble opposition of imperatives, the acute sense that although "obligation and crime cannot coincide" they do in fact appear to do so, interpenetrates *We* from beginning to end. What makes Zamyatin's novel a document of such great interest is that he could see these ancient problems of *can* and *ought,* the old Platonic stumbling-block that "liberty and crime are . . . indissolubly bound together", raised in fearful and perhaps unprecedented form by the Russian Revolution, and it gives *We* a unique place in Utopian literature as an anti-Utopia written, with profound understanding, in the midst of an actual Utopian enterprise. It must be said, bearing this in mind, that *We* has an authenticity, as evidence of the underlying motives of social revolution and of the ideological superstructure that revolution creates, much beyond that of *1984.* If *We* is a fantasy, Russia was in the first years after the Revolution "the most fantastic country in all present-day Europe" :

Zamyatin's own comment (in an essay on the "socio-fantasies" of H. G. Wells) shows how well he was aware of the connection between fantasy and fact, between the imaginative formulation of human aspirations and conflicts in art and their projection in act, the process of what the actors involved in it believed was "making history". Orwell, too, had his contact with revolution and history-making, in Spain; but penetrating though his analysis of the Civil War was, his insight into the moral issues involved never had the depth nor the power of generalisation shown by Zamyatin. (Indeed Orwell seems seriously to have underestimated *We,* despite its acknowledged influence on him and though he urged its publication in Britain; at many points his comments on Zamyatin show a rather limited understanding. In particular, remarking on Zamyatin's account of "diabolism" and "atavism" as something which appears to be "part of totalitarianism" he completely misses the point of the Mephis, or Lucifer, as representing the revolt *against* totalitarianism. But perhaps, considering the trap his own feelings about Satan had led him into, that is not surprising.)

Nevertheless *We* and *1984* are, as has been said, complementary. Both depict a State with divine attributes, centred or incarnate in a ruler who, whether invisible like Big Brother or personally present and active among men like the Benefactor, is explicitly God-like in the sense of presenting an absolute demand upon man; both show the law of God, conceived in terms of power, as ending in the annihilation of man, and it is noteworthy that the motive for the exercise of this crushing power, thought of by Orwell as being for its own sake, power for the sake of power (which is not actually a motive at all), or more plausibly by Zamyatin as "cruelly loving", the benevolence of "the Jehovah of the ancients", does not in the least affect the result. In each case man surrenders his humanity, *voluntarily* —an essential point—to an authority which will relieve him of volition and the agony of choice; in each case the longing to be rid of uncertainty and ambiguity in obedience to an absolute is satisfied at the price of love. Both fantasies make use of that prototype of all argument between the individual and the absolute, the Book of Job; in the case of *1984,* as we have seen no more than inferentially and perhaps unconsciously; in the case of *We* quite explicitly, in D-503's interview with the Benefactor, who invites him to "dispute with me" in the same words that God spoke out of the whirlwind, challenging D-503 to "talk as grown-ups".

The difference between the two (which again perhaps lies in Zamyatin's more conscious borrowing from the Book of Job) is that in *We* the Almighty speaks to a scientist, not this time showing him how puny is his knowledge—for man by this time has answered nearly all God's rhetorical questions, Canst thou, Knowest thou, in the affirmative—but how meagre are his emotional resources. The Benefactor in this short interview speaks chiefly as did Ivan Karamazov's Grand Inquisitor, explaining once again that freedom and happiness are incompatible, that if men are to be happy their rulers must "weld them to this happiness with chains". In this of course he has no need of persuasion; D-503 already, as an instrument of mathematically determined happiness, merely submits. His real destruction is brought about much more simply, merely by rousing his suspicion and jealousy: the Benefactor suggests that the Mephis have courted D-503 not out of regard for him but only to gain entry to his rocket, the *Integral*—and immediately D-503 is convinced. From now on he repudiates the rebels and, in helpless confusion, is ready for "fantasiectomy"; after which, in the name of rationality, he betrays all that he knows about the "enemies of happiness".

If a mathematician-scientist, designer and navigator of spaceships and aspirant to the stars has no more feeling in him when put to the test but hatred and jealousy, then he will be as well to throw down his arms and give in to Reason: there he will be safe. But for a moment he thinks of another kind of refuge. After the interview with the Benefactor he goes out to find himself again in the midst of violently contending forces, the Benefactor's execution-machine, "ponderous, sinister", standing in the street, and the rioting Mephis calling on him to "join us". He is torn by contrary impulses and actually weeps, a thing unknown in the One State where everyone smiles all the time: he then, with one of those leaps of association which make the poetic narrative of *We* so remarkable, suddenly thinks, "If only I had a mother—as the ancients did: a mother of my own— yes, precisely, *my own* . . .". But science has abolished motherhood and knowledge of identity along with it.

Science has become a god, who offers refuge from suffering: the Benefactor unites science and the state in one person, a holy duality. That this is not (even allowing for the extreme compression of Zamyatin's symbolism) a just view of science will readily be granted : the irrational, creative, imaginative side to scientific pursuits is given to the Mephis, the permanent revolutionaries. But the modern state, of course, is able to use both urges—that towards safety and certainty, and that towards unlimited expansion—to underpin its claim to divinity. If scientific thought is essentially nonconformist, the powers of control that it confers and the very idea of control itself command obedience and worship. The divine state merges with the divinity of science as, in the history of religions, one idol combines with another. Such a hybrid idol Orwell and Zamyatin show between them; when we look at both their fantasies together we have a view of the actual prospect—of the real possibility—that lies before us.

VIII

Jonah and the Lord

BOTH *1984* AND *We* describe a gross idolatry. By way of summing up we may try to see what it means to say so : what it meant for Orwell, whose lifelong road to confrontation with this idol we have been tracing; what it means for us.

It is needful first to understand that the "idolatry of the State" is not only a common turn of phrase, indicating undue regard for centralised government, but can bear the full force of meaning attached to the word idolatry; in some degree perhaps it always does so. An idol is a false god, but it is god : idolatry is not deference or obedience given to something "as if" it were divine, but worship, the actual devotion due to God— although to say so is of course begging the question, since in the absence of God nobody knows what devotion is due to him. The idolater knows at least that his god *must* be obeyed : the idol's commands and demands are absolute, because he is god, and he is god because they are absolute. In the hunger for absolutism one fantasy supports the other.

When God is present among men he supplies their chief end, to love, honour and obey him; when he is not, men have no chief end, nor indeed any end at all, except the end of their individual lives. No play on words is intended, for death, in the absence of any other, does in truth become an aim. As Orwell said, death is "an absolute, the only absolute we have left"; but, again, it is clear from all that he said, and didn't say on the subject—among the rest, it is implied in the context of this particular remark—that though much obsessed with death he could think of it only in one way, as the absolute extinction of an isolated consciousness. It could be thought of therefore as the aim of life, as the terminus is the aim of a railway, but not as conferring meaning on the way thither, being itself meaningless. It was an event to which the only attitude in anticipation was "simple resentment". Death was not a mystery, for Orwell, a child of his generation, would not allow there to be any mysteries, there were only problems to be solved. He did however allow that there were problems; his importance, at least among the writers of the Left, is in his readiness to admit it.

Many times over he drew attention to the inadequacy of socialist thinking about the questions that would still be "left to be answered" when the political-economic objectives of socialism were attained. A useful example may be taken from the essay on Arthur Koestler written in 1944; as was often the case, Orwell used discussion of another writer to say things about himself. A fairly long quotation is necessary. Orwell is dealing with Koestler's wartime novel *Arrival and Departure,* a story about a European revolutionary whose motives are revealed by psychoanalysis as fundamentally neurotic; the conclusion (at least as Orwell interprets it) is that though the hero finally returns to the struggle, as a British secret agent against the Nazis, he has no good reason left for doing so. Orwell continues :

> But after all, this does not invalidate the Socialist case. Actions have results, irrespective of motives. Marx's ultimate motives may well have been envy and spite, but this does not prove that his conclusions were false. In making the hero of *Arrival and Departure* take his final decision from a mere instinct not to shirk action and danger, Koestler is making him suffer a sudden loss of intelligence. With such a history as he has behind him, he would be able to see that certain things have to be done, whether our reasons for doing them are "good" or "bad". History has to move in a certain direction, even if it has to be pushed that way by neurotics. In *Arrival and Departure* Peter's [the hero's] idols are overthrown one after the other. The Russian Revolution has degenerated, Britain, symbolised by the aged consul with gouty fingers, is no better, the international class-conscious proletariat is a myth. But the conclusion (since, after all, Koestler and his hero "support" the war) ought to be that getting rid of Hitler is still a worth-while objective, a necessary bit of scavenging in which motives are almost irrelevant.

This passage is quite remarkable—though also typical—for raising issues of real moment and for inadequacy in dealing with them. It is perhaps not necessary to point out that although actions have results whatever the motives behind them, the nature of these results is *not* irrespective of motive, and that the effect of motives upon actions is the implicit, if not the obvious subject of Koestler's novel; that, having mentioned Marx, to go on to say that "history has to be pushed in a certain direction" without inquiring what the direction may be, or caring whether the reasons for pushing are good or bad, is a surrender to the most crass aspect of Marxism, the idolatry of history or history-as-moving-staircase; that to suppose "motives are almost irrelevant" in the war against Hitler is actually to give up thinking about motives altogether, and to fall back on blind obedience. It is especially noteworthy here that, speaking of "getting rid of Hitler" as "scavenging" Orwell lapses into the most dubious aspect of his reliance on "decency" (the Nazis are refuse, or dirt, to be cleaned up) and, in fact, into the very way of thinking about enemies, real or supposed, which the Nazis carried to such logical conclusions as the Final Solution.

After this demonstration of confused reasoning—hardly, indeed, of reasoning at all—Orwell goes on to say that "to take a rational political decision one must have a picture of the future", and in due course gives his own. It is not a cheerful one, a sufficient instance indeed of his view that "facts are apt to be unpleasant"; it does, however, say more than that:

> Since about 1930 the world has given no reason for optimism whatever. Nothing is in sight except a welter of lies, hatred, cruelty and ignorance, and beyond our present troubles loom vaster ones which are only now entering European consciousness. It is quite probable that man's major problems will *never* be solved. But it is also unthinkable.

And, finally:

> The only way out is that of the religious believer, who regards this life merely as a preparation for the next. But few thinking people now believe in life after death, and the number of those who do is probably diminishing. The Christian churches would probably not survive on their own merits if their economic basis were destroyed. The real problem is how to

restore the religious attitude while accepting death as final.
Men can only be happy when they do not assume that the
object of life is happiness.

What comes out of these remarks is that Orwell, his own idols
being as he believed irrevocably overthrown, thought seriously
about the need for religious faith—and, as we know, he had
been thinking about it for many years, perhaps ever since he
formally "lost his faith" as a boy—but hardly at all about
what faith might actually consist in. Here and elsewhere he
identified "religion" (presumably the Christian religion) with
belief in personal immortality, the either-or that Dorothy Hare
wrestled with at the end of *A Clergyman's Daughter*; but he
evidently made no real effort to understand what religion might
have to say about the here and now as well as "the hereafter".
Perhaps, considering the conventionalities of religious instruc-
tion and the fear and misery with which it was associated, along
with everything else, at his prep school, it is not surprising that
it should have been so. It is more remarkable that he retained
an affection for and interest in "that peculiar feeling that we
used to call 'Church' ", the decaying institution, redolent of
"powdered corpses", which reappears again and again in his
writings, from the cold, dilapidated, and more than half-empty
edifice within which Dorothy Hare's father disdainfully admini-
sters the Sacraments to a dwindling congregation he patently
despises, to the now frankly ruined shell, not far from an atomic
bomb-site, in the bell-loft of which, thick with pigeon-dung,
Winston Smith and Julia meet to make unreal love and to
daydream about an impossible future.

It was probably only when he thought of the Church as
ruinous and empty that Orwell was able to tolerate the idea
of it. He did not mind, when he was on the run from the
Stalinists in Barcelona, spending an extremely uncomfortable
night among the rubble of a burnt-out church; but some years
earlier, on one of his down-and-out expeditions, he refused to
take shelter in the crypt of St Martin-in-the-Fields because he
had heard that those doing so were asked "searching questions"
by "some woman known as the Madonna". The alternative was
the nightmarish attempt to sleep in the Square recorded at length
later in the person of Dorothy. In his own person, as both Eric
Blair and George Orwell, he was buried, by his own wish, in

the country churchyard of Sutton Courtenay, in Berkshire, but by that time he was dead.

Are we to say therefore that Orwell's interest in religion was no more than nostalgia, the symbolic summing-up of his longing for a past less terribly demanding than present or future? In a way that would be true, since undoubtedly he did think of organised religion as belonging irretrievably to the past. (It caused him, among other things, grossly to underestimate the importance of the Church, Orthodox and otherwise, in the Soviet Union : the role of Moses the Raven is the main thing that would have to be altered if *Animal Farm* were re-written today.) But the lack of faith he did know about, as something affecting his own and other people's lives, in the present and in the dreaded future.

Orwell was one of the few people to remember that Marx, when he said that religion is the opium of the people, preceded it with another definition, that "religion is the sigh of the soul in a soulless world". Orwell's own comment was approving, if not very penetrating : "What is he [Marx] saying except that man does *not* live by bread alone, that hatred is *not* enough, that a world worth living in cannot be founded on 'realism' and machine-guns?"

Marx was saying rather more than that, surely, and perhaps not altogether that at all. What can be seen (for instance in the *Theses on Feuerbach*) in Marx's discussion of religion is the idea that "religious self-alienation" has been succeeded by a secular self-alienation much more radical, a split between subject and object which has truly de-animated the world, and that to put a soul back into the world remains "the chief thing to be done". The *Theses* go on to criticise Feuerbach's identification of "the human essence" as "an abstraction inherent in each individual", and to propose another definition, that the "human essence" capable of restoring a soul to the soulless world is "the ensemble of social relations". Thus, discarding Feuerbach's "contemplative materialism", the "contemplation of single individuals in 'civil society' ", Marx declares the standpoint of the "new materialism" based on "human society, or socialised humanity".

We scarcely need to complete these quotations with the celebrated slogan the young Marx enunciated at the end of his Theses—"the philosophers have only interpreted the world, in various ways; the point, however, is to change it"—to see the bearing they have upon the world both of *We* and of *1984*. The object of attack in both these books is totalitarianism, not Marxism; Zamyatin as we have remarked was too much in sympathy with much of the Bolshevik revolution to make his satire other than a double-edged one; Orwell insisted that *1984* was not to be understood as anti-socialist. Nevertheless (and whether or not we suppose Zamyatin and Orwell to have been familiar with these Marxist texts) Marx must be given the credit for understanding and in a manner for laying down the programme of both their dreams and nightmares.

Marx believed in the force of scientific activity, as part of the Promethean enterprise which impinges upon and transforms the world; but he also recognised its drive to "objectify" or alienate the world; he saw that this alienation was the fundamental wrong, whether considered as the separation of man from man in the division of classes or man from what he makes in the division of labour. Concerning Feuerbach's "dissolution of the religious world into its secular basis" he pointed out that self-alienation and "duplication" of the world into a "real" and an "imaginary" one still remain. He named the reason : "the fact that the secular foundation detaches itself from itself and establishes itself in the clouds as an independent realm is nearly only to be explained by the self-cleavage and self-contradictoriness of this secular basis" : in other words, science and the philosophic atomism of the detached observer that goes with it have already brought about a de-realisation which, by the overwhelming prestige and power of scientific discovery and application, is imposed on the world at large. To redress it Feuerbach invoked the "human essence", an abstraction (said Marx) supposed to be "inherent in each individual" which was to be the equivalent of the "religious essence". It could not, however, be an active principle, but could be "comprehended only as 'genus', as an internal, dumb generality which merely *naturally* unites the many individuals". He, Marx, therefore proposed another definition of the human essence : it is to be looked for in "socialised" or collective humanity.

This is, so to speak, where Winston Smith, Marx's "isolated human individual" par excellence, comes in; to find that he, the "autonomous" human being, the consciousness that in the last resort has only itself to rely on, is in fact the only one left. The redeeming value that he needs, the restoration of reality or soul to his world of ghosts, has been invested in socialised humanity, i.e. the Party. He, as a lost soul—hardly that, since he isn't allowed by his beliefs to have a "soul", but most certainly lost—is inexorably impelled, both pushed and drawn, towards the collective repository of the real and the good : to losing himself in the social substitute for God. The social god through his servant O'Brien has no difficulty in showing Winston what he is : how "the spirit of man" manifests itself in him, physically rotten and mentally corrupt. He has thought of the "human spirit" or essence precisely in Feuerbach's terms, as an "internal dumb generality", in some undefined and inactive way the natural property of the species : generalised and entirely dumb, or unconscious, in the proles, and when it reaches consciousness in him, lifeless, isolated, and perverse.

If his reliance is upon this genetic quality, O'Brien only has to show him himself in order to disillusion him—for, as he is a man, it must belong to him too. His person as he sees it in the mirror is broken and revolting. What is left of his body (as in many ascetic nightmares) is a mere "bag of filth", no more than the tripes of humanity : the bowels which as organs of feeling he has tried to repudiate take their revenge and declare themselves to be the whole man. His mind, the exiguous remaining corner of motive and intention, is no better. His own litany of hatred, recited in supposed commitment to "the Brotherhood" and opposition to Big Brother, is revealed with its programme of murder, destruction, treachery and lies as the mirror of Big Brother's own kingdom. Finally he is shown the hungry and filthy rats of his own desires and, refusing to face them, his nothingness. As God, who has no objective existence, has long ago been dismissed as worthless, not due any consideration, so he himself, God's image, is of no value whatever. All value has been taken over by "socialised humanity", which Winston knows is a crude and brutal cheat but which, where there is no other value to be seen, draws his allegiance with a force not to be resisted. The torture in fact, as O'Brien says, is quite unnecessary. It is used, not to persuade Winston, but to satisfy his need for punishment, the only contact with reality left to him : for as nothing in a bad world is so bad as physical pain, so nothing is so real.

All this is implied in Marx's *Theses*. For if God is a myth, socialised humanity is just as much so, and of a kind that lends itself unavoidably to idolatry. All the questions asked about God by the sceptical inquirer, where is he, what does he look like, how does he speak, are answered by faith with the maddening but sufficient reply that nothing can be known about him except in direct experience which can never be described : that he is "a spirit", or a mystery. Socialised humanity on the other hand is expected to be describable, as any idol may be, and actually is so, in terms of what humanity does : "All mysteries which mislead theory to mysticism," says Marx, "find their rational solution in human practice and in the comprehension of this practice." So social man in action is given an identity and name as the Party, or Big Brother, or the Benefactor, or Science : and into this personified generalisation (while denying the very possibility of such a notion) flows everything that is due to God. The abstraction is made concrete in deeds, which are all the deeds of the Party, concentrated and raised to the skies in the structure, made with men's hands, of Miniluv.

To a living, invisible God lives are due, and can be paid because he himself provides the coin, in the endless exchange of giving and receiving. But to idols, which are visible and dead, the gift must similarly be visible and completely defined : not the worship of living spirits, but of captive bodies; not lives, which are free and continually unfolding, but deaths, which are a full stop. It is typical of idols that they demand human sacrifice; in fact it may be said that until they do so they are not idols at all. A representation of God in the shape of an animal, or a man with wings or twelve arms, or wielding a thunderbolt, or sitting in his mother's arms, is a metaphor, and can receive metaphorical gifts, visible and tangible as food or wine, firstfruits, the light of candles, the smoke of incense : all are metaphorical expressions of what is due the whole time in prayer, which is not metaphorical. But Moloch, who is not a metaphor or representative, but *is* God for those who insist that God must be visible, demands gifts that are not metaphorical but actual. Moloch, literal god, must have literal offerings : the deaths of his subjects, which are thought to be no surrogate or way of saying "as if", but absolutely themselves. The proof of real belief in real Me, says Moloch, is real blood; to be prepared to kill, as Shaw's Moloch, Andrew Undershaft, says, is the final proof of sincerity.

Poor idol ! He is deceived, for death is not a thing, it does not exist, it is simply a Not; the lives with which, taking this absolute short cut, he hopes to be fed finally and all at once, merely vanish; and though he can stuff himself with all the appurtenances of death, the blood, the agony, he is as empty as before, and always hungry. He, lifeless, is famished for lives, and receives only deaths, for that is all he will take. Only in such a way can one make sense of the reply given by the idol's attendant and executioner, O'Brien—that God is power and also that, being all-powerful, he must constantly demonstrate his power, his jackboot "stamping on a human face—for ever".

As we have noted, the idea of permanent power, and fascination by its violent exercise, were found by Orwell in Jack London, but he took them a crucial stage further. The Iron Heel is not yet God (indeed is by no means all-powerful), its power is used for recognisable, though extravagant political ends. The power of the Party-god expounded by O'Brien is divine and all-sufficient; but not all-satisfying. For power is not a self-sufficient entity, but purposive, it is always power *for* something. Energy can be thought of as being without direction, but power, which is energy harnessed and controlled, is always pointed, and pointed by somebody; power for power's sake is nonsense. And in fact the power of the Party-god has a perfectly well described purpose, to enforce love and fill its empty belly with death. Both are needful from its point of view, because to be sure of love, absolutely sure, it must be forced—otherwise who can be certain that it will not be withdrawn again, or that you really have it, as a possession, at all?—and to satisfy hunger absolutely not gifts, through people's lives, but the seizure of the whole of them and all at once, in their deaths, is the only way of being certain of food. But, once again, unhappy idol!—the more it grabs to itself and screams its needs, the less it gets, for love by definition—it is almost the only way of defining it, when all else has been pared away—is free, it cannot be compelled; and lives, as soon as they are brought to an end, are no longer there.

Moloch, and his attendants, are as hungry as unfed and uncherished infants; his worshippers, of whom there is no lack, are hungry too, and equally unsatisfied. They are starved of meaning, purpose, value, reality : guilty of being such starvelings, they hunger most and first for forgiveness. When Winston Smith is arrested he is aware first of gnawing hunger; his eyes are drawn painfully to the scrap of bread which, being forbidden as a gift between prisoners, lies untouched on the cell floor. But he hungers even more for the bread of heaven : after his torment has begun he dreams not of escape but of acceptance, a time when "everything" should be "all right, there was no more pain, the last detail of his life was laid bare, understood, forgiven".

All Orwell's life, on the evidence of his writing, he longed to be understood, and it is clear from the way this is described— whether in Flory's unsatisfied yearning for complete understanding in his relations with Elizabeth, or Winston's gratitude even to his torturer for his knowledge of Winston's own thoughts —that something quite different from intellectual comprehension is meant. Orwell most fully explains his meaning in *Inside the Whale*, where one of the great merits for the reader of Henry Miller is named as "the peculiar relief that comes not so much from understanding as from *being understood*" (Orwell's italics). " 'He knows all about me,' you feel; 'he wrote specially for me.' " Orwell goes on to describe the effect of Miller's writing as of hearing "a friendly American voice, with no humbug in it, no moral purpose, merely an implicit assumption that we are all alike. For the moment you have got away from the lies and simplifications, the stylised, marionette-like quality of ordinary fiction, even quite good fiction, and are dealing with the recognisable experience of a human being".

Such "understanding", not *of* the writer by a critical detached intelligence, but *by* the writer as fellow human being, appears to give Orwell a kind of absolution. He goes on to ask what is the "experience" Miller is talking about, and admits that though he deals with the man in the street, it so happens that the street is full of brothels; he allows that what elsewhere he calls, with a shudder of disgust, "the WC and dirty handkerchief side of life" has, thanks to Miller's position in Paris, an undue prominence. (Miller, he explains, is an expatriate and therefore cannot help writing in *Tropic of Cancer* about a world of outsiders and riffraff, bounded by "the cafe, the church, the brothel, and the studio". It does not really seem to follow, but it is easy to see how it would help to establish rapport with Orwell, who felt himself an exile wherever he was, and who was impelled, more by internal needs than anything merely circumstantial, to seek out and share low life of different sorts.)

Reference to *Inside the Whale* has been made at various points already; but a final look at what Orwell says there may be taken, so to speak, from inside Miniluv. Miniluv, it has been argued, represents the last and deepest of Orwell's descents but, being made in the terror and bewilderment of complete dereliction, it cannot be recorded critically by the subject. In the essay, however, Orwell came his nearest to examining his own *nostalgie de la boue* with judicial candour, and what is interesting is that in the context of his admiration for Miller his feeling about the gutter undergoes a marked change. He describes Miller's attitude to life in general as one of "acceptance" and this, he is careful to say, means accepting *everything* : it includes not only the dirty handkerchiefs and frozen school latrines, but "concentration camps, rubber truncheons, Hitler, Stalin, bombs, aeroplanes, tinned food, machine-guns, putsches, purges, slogans, Bedaux belts, gasmasks, submarines, spies, *provocateurs*, press censorship, secret prisons, aspirins, Hollywood films, and political murders". This often quoted list of hated things, it should be noted, is not Miller's—he has already mentioned Miller's complete indifference to politics and public affairs generally—but his own. It is much like one of Swift's catalogues of loathsome people, objects and qualities, and may even have been deliberately modelled on them; it is also like many other assemblages of pet hates elsewhere in his own writing—notably in *Coming Up For Air*. It is perhaps the most extensive of them, although the crowd of hateful persons whom George Bowling fancies in pursuit of him as he sets out for Lower Binfield is almost as comprehensive.

All such lists are, one may say, of the unacceptable parts of human life which, even when one forces oneself, with fascinated revulsion, to acknowledge them as one's own, continue to be repudiated and projected elsewhere; whence they return, of course, with accusing hate, to hound one down. But here they are all accepted. Not finally, and only by proxy : Orwell wishes his burdens on to Miller and assumes that he, saying "I accept" in a general way, will include these too. But is this not very like forgiveness of sin, the absolution received at the hands of another? Even in this one place, inside the whale, it does not last, nor is it ever quite wholehearted : "to accept civilisation *as it is* practically means accepting decay", it is entirely "passive" and "even 'decadent', if that word means anything". Whatever it means, it is not rejected here with anything like the over-emphatic disgust Orwell showed for "passivity" and "decadence" elsewhere. It is not taken to the point at which, through acceptance, the sinner may be freed from his sin; the point where grace and the law cease to seem in contradiction of each other. But though Orwell is (like most of us) far short of that point in the essay, and would in any case have repudiated any such formulation, some interim respite is granted him here; the moral Orwell, angrily looking for dividing lines, is for once almost at peace.

It is by no accidental transition that he proceeds, *via* a general sketch of contemporary thought as exhibited in writing between the wars, and the different prospects of delusion or despair that it seems to offer, to the image which gives the essay its title—the idea, circuitously arrived at, of being in the "visceral prison" of the whale's belly. Miller himself found nothing horrible about such a notion, but on the contrary thought it attractive; and Orwell in turn seizes on it as "probably a very widespread fantasy". It was certainly one he entertained, as we have seen; we may go a little further now in asking what it meant to him.

To be inside the whale was the most complete restoration of what had been lost, the bowels of emotional life, not indeed attached to the subject, but as his entire environment. The whale is, as Orwell says, "a womb big enough for an adult"; it is the maternal body, fat and receptive—half spurned, half longed for in the world above, on the surface of the earth—but coming back now in the deep with such complete forgiveness that the subject, with all his insatiable hunger and hateful desires, is simply ingested. He is safe in there from "a storm that would sink all the battleships in the world"—all the violent, armoured forms of hate—and also from himself.

But the great fish that swallowed Jonah is also the instrument of the Lord, prepared for the purpose—something that Orwell never mentions in all his references to the story. He does not even mention the opening of it, although one might suppose that the figure of Jonah, the unwilling prophet, outcast and victim, would have had a strong appeal for him. It is yet more striking that he forgot the end, even if his reasons for doing so are easy to see. To remain safe and untroubled—and indeed as good as dead, though not actually so—Jonah should stay permanently inside the whale, a child who refuses to be born; and that is where Henry Miller (and George Bowling) wanted him to be. George Bowling, it will be remembered, thought of an ordered and untroubled society as one in which, among other things, Christ is permanently on his cross and Jonah is always in the whale. The incompatibility of these two images, let alone the truncation of scriptural narrative, seems never to have occurred to him.

Jonah did not stay in the whale; did not even wish to, but prayed to God from the depths of his affliction, from the abyss where the weeds were wrapped about his head, and from the bottom of the mountains (all places visited by Orwell's imagination), and God heard him and ordered his release, vomited forth by the fish upon dry land. He had a task as a prophet, moreover, which he was now able to accept and actually to perform.

It is remarkable, looking again at this ancient and highly compressed little story, almost the shortest of the Prophetic Books, to see how closely its symbolic happenings bear upon Orwell's career; and to reflect again on his familiarity with it and fondness for it, together with his evident unawareness of its import. Orwell was not, of course, accustomed to think of such stories as having any real reference to human lives; they were fairy-tales and, as such, like the works of poets, which were for him lunatic or impossible, not to be taken seriously. It was a part of his whole upbringing, and his reaction to it, to think so : those who hear the Lessons read out as obligatory formal observance seldom expect actually to learn anything from them. The prophet against his will, angry, frightened, and taking to his heels, a fugitive from God who prefers rather to be selected as a victim of men than to obey the Lord, should surely have been recognisable to him; so too might Jonah when he finally acknowledges his calling and sets off to put the fear of God into Nineveh. But Jonah's recovery he resolutely kept his eyes from : that people are swallowed by whales or find their way back to the womb in order to be born a second time did not occur to him, until at the end the story reappeared in bitter travesty.

Miniluv is a dry-land parody of God's great fish, turned into a hard and glittering monster, the visible form of Leviathan; which, after swallowing up Winston Smith and subjecting him to its unspeakable digestive and regenerative processes, vomits him forth again, if not exactly re-born, certainly transformed. Winston's emergence from Miniluv is rather like the supposedly factual incident (one of the oddments read out by George Bowling's father from the pre-1914 or antediluvian newspapers) of a man swallowed by a sperm whale and regurgitated later, still alive but bleached perfectly white by its gastric juices and, of course, stark mad. It is not a restoration that bodes any good to anybody except to Big Brother, whose demand it fulfils that all shall love him absolutely, and without any reason.

But comparison of *1984* with the Book of Jonah picks out a critical point at which something other than this ghastly process of digestion might have begun and the whole direction of the apparatus of parody and negative equivalents might have been reversed. It is, after all, Jonah who sets his own deliverance in motion, crying to the Lord out of the depths; whereupon his cry is heard, and he is delivered. It is something Winston Smith cannot do, either in terms of the ostensible relationship between tormentors and victims or those of the underlying parallel, of the individual soul under the trials of the divine. He is, however, given the chance. It is so quickly passed over that one scarcely notices it, and it is hard not to feel that Orwell was hurrying past a place he felt bound to go through on his way but in which there lay a threat to all the assumptions of his story. The point is where O'Brien, engaged in knocking away all Winston's moral props, asks him, Do you believe in God? Winston answers simply No, and O'Brien moves on quickly to the next question, to pin down "the spirit of Man" and to show what in Winston's terms it amounts to. He plays back Winston's vow to murder and lie in opposition to Big Brother, and demonstrates that hatred has engendered hatred in the ordinary and foreseeable way; that greed and fear will not miraculously be transformed into righteousness, but of themselves will only produce greed and fear.

It may be thought that Winston gives up his belief in "the spirit of Man" a little easily, but he has already surrendered a much stronger position without a fight, and it is an oddity that opens a great chasm in the story. Not that Winston's atheism is inappropriate in terms of his supposed life-history—he could hardly be anything else but atheist. But within the terms of the novel not Winston's answer but O'Brien's question is a glaring anomaly. First we must ask, what is this word "God" doing in a vocabulary already so drastically pruned of doubtful and thought-stimulating speech? True, O'Brien has used it already, and has perhaps a special licence to speak in obsolete terms; for others it is of course taboo. (Ampleforth, the translator, has allowed the word "God" to stand in a re-jigged poem, and concludes that this is the crime for which he has been arrested.) Winston himself has already confessed that he was a religious believer, along with being "an admirer of capitalism and a sexual pervert", but that was under torture, and is mentioned only as an example of the crude lies told in an attempt to satisfy his torturers. When O'Brien asks the question later it is no longer a frivolous one but requires a serious and sincere answer; and how does he know even that Winston will understand it? Even supposing that Winston may have been familiar with the word God, how should he know at once exactly what O'Brien means by the question, what at least some of its implications are for his present predicament, and why he is bound to answer it in the negative? He, after all, hasn't had the kind of religious education which made Orwell react to "the word God" with "frozen disgust"; for him it should mean nothing at all—or else a mystery which O'Brien would indeed be hard put to it to explain.

For now we come to the second, and stronger objection, that within the scheme of *1984* as a caricature-portrayal of divine tyranny, or the tyrannical-divine, to introduce one half of the parody in, so to speak, *propria persona*, causes the entire structure momentarily to collapse : as though an actual domestic beast were to walk into the society of *Animal Farm*. Since the Party clearly is God, and has been unequivocally defined as such by the one divine attribute, power, what or who is this other God that Winston might believe in?

O'Brien's question makes so awkward a hole that one wonders why Orwell allowed it to be asked at all, and perhaps he should be given credit for the honesty that forced him to do so, even if in his embarrassment he had forthwith to plunge on and forget all about it. Indeed, although it cracks the story apart, the question about God has to be asked, if we are thinking in "Naturalistic" terms, because to complete the destruction of Winston every possibility of salvation except the dreadful upside-down salvation of surrender to Big Brother must be shown as useless or delusory. Perhaps also it has to be asked even within the framework of parody in order that the parody should stand out, as it were, against a background of the real thing. But if so it must be asked as a genuine question, with a real possibility of being answered with a Yes; and the implications of that are so disconcerting for all the assumptions of *1984* that it is not surprising to see Orwell taking fright and changing the subject like someone who has committed an appalling solecism.

Suppose that Winston had said Yes. Either his affirmation would have to be demolished along with Winston's other beliefs, a task which O'Brien, already positing a system of thought only tenable by "faith", must find difficult; or it must be accepted, in which case all the pretensions of the idol he serves must vanish. The question and its possible answer show up, in a flash of clear light, the nonsensical position Winston (or Orwell) has got himself into : that, because he has no faith he can acknowledge, he transfers faith to a monster; because he can't believe in a God beyond his own reason he is brought to believe in a construction deliberately and grotesquely insulting to reason.

If we may imagine such considerations fleetingly occurring to Orwell, we see his "reply", which is to reach for the instruments of torture. Pain, he says, can make anybody believe anything. But pain, though it weakens and confuses Winston, is not what destroys him; Orwell makes it clear that his destruction is not primarily due to physical torment, nor even to the brain-surgery by which, like the consenting hordes of *We*, he undergoes a variant of "fantasiectomy", but to his own want of any principle except hatred with which to oppose his persecutors. And hate is not opposed to the Party's theology at all but is the main point of its doctrine.

It will be said, nevertheless, that to show how a state is based on hatred will not cause it to disappear; that there have been, and are, states that compel their subjects' allegiance by all the methods of violence; that if their manifest evils are to be faced or their rise prevented means must be found.

1984 is not about practical politics; it is not, as a satirical fiction, even about political theory—although, especially by the interpolation of extracts from "Goldstein's" supposed account of "The Theory and Practice of Oligarchical Collectivism", a caricature of politico-historical generalisations is included in the narrative and made a part of Winston Smith's subjective experience. *"The book"*, being actually the forged invention of the Party's priesthood—or at least presented as such; O'Brien tells Winston later that he wrote some of it himself—has an ambiguous and somewhat anomalous position in the story, a parody within a parody and, as preliminary to Winston's discoveries in Miniluv, an apparently truthful account which is in fact all lies, or a pack of lies which tells the truth. Marxist theory, or more strictly the Machiavellian-Marxism of James Burnham (which Orwell both strongly disliked and was obviously influenced by) enters the story with a peculiar effect, as a kind of burlesque; very much as theoretical and supposedly rational discourse is distorted, rearranged and, it may be, brought to reveal its underlying motives in dream. The sections of *"the book"* which Winston has time to read are only partially taken up, even as parody, with the sort of theorising Orwell found in Burnham—the hierarchies and division of power in the world of 1984, the so-called "political realities" of the society he predicated. The official ideology of this society is only mentioned in passing—though it may be thought significant that only one is described at all, that prevailing in "Eastasia", where it "is called by a Chinese name usually translated as Death-Worship but perhap better translated as Obliteration of the Self".

But the underlying thought is analysed at some length; in fact the principal subject of Goldstein's supposed theories, so far as Winston Smith is able to learn them, is the system of self-deception known as *doublethink*, "the power of holding two contradictory belief in one's mind simultaneously, and accepting both of them". The exposition of *doublethink* is an effective satire upon the hypocrisies and dishonesties practised by Marxist orthodoxy in the name of "the dialectic", but it is more than that : in Goldstein's account of it, as a process both "conscious" and "unconscious", a form of deception carried out with "the firmness of purpose that goes with complete honesty", it is the formula for a permanently divided mind. Such division brings separation from the real ("tampering with reality"); and whether this is thought of in the way that Goldstein describes it, as a deliberate aim, or as the ghostly effect that Orwell experienced in his life, does not matter. The place of value, or the self where contradictions may be held in balance has, as personal property, been obliterated, and selfhood now belongs to God the Party, which consequently controls reality and can "arrest the course of history".

Typically this "vast system of mental cheating" is most fully practised by those of the highest intellect : "those who have the best knowledge of what is happening are also those who are furthest from seeing the world as it is." The disease of *doublethink* is an intellectual one : "In general, the greater the understanding the greater the delusion : the more intelligent, the less sane." But it is far from being merely a disorder of the intellect : as *1984* and indeed the whole of Orwell's writing shows, it is a moral disease, a sickness of the soul. Goldstein's description itself recognises that *doublethink* is itself the effect of something deeper, "the original motive" which brought everything else in its train, "the never-questioned instinct that first led to the seizure of power and brought *doublethink*, the Thought Police, continuous warfare, and all the other necessary paraphernalia into existence afterwards". What is this motive—an original sin which, since it serves the needs of the Party, has become virtue— we are not told, for Winston's reading breaks off at that point : the discovery is only made by implication, and painfully, in the cellars of Miniluv. *"The book"* remains as intellectual superstructure, the rationalisation that floats on the surface of a dream. It is also, as generalisation, a way of showing that the dream is more than Winston Smith's; it is of long duration and wide extent. Both in its unreasoning depths and in the accompanying intellectual dissociation the system of "controlled insanity" is universal.

Here we return to the main theme. The novel is a fantasy, and it may well be called a sick fantasy, the product of personal neurosis. Much of what has gone before has attempted to interpret Orwell's writings in this way and to show how their development was related to emotional needs and failures, recurrent obsessive fears, and a consequently distorted view of "things as they are". Those who are very sure they know and understand things as they are may be disinclined to pay much attention to these gloomy inventions, with their obviously partial grasp and presentation of human nature. If Orwell, when he thought he was writing about "politics", was all the time writing about himself, it makes a good excuse for ignoring the political implications of what he said.

I do not think they can be so easily set aside. Politics, whether thought of as the art of the possible or as the working out of Lenin's "who, whom" (who uses whom), cannot be separated from the state of people's minds; the fears and delusions of individuals as well as their hopes and desires issue in the affairs of state. If Orwell is seen as writing out a neurosis, public affairs may be taken as acting out the same thing, the fruit of disquiets and emotional hungers shared by many and taking political form as much as the hunger for bread. All writers are, as he himself said of Henry Miller, "symptomatic"; his own books are the symptoms—the expression, that is to say, in terms of internal or subjective events—of what is made grossly visible in the various institutions and actions of the modern state and men's reactions to it; especially of the hypertrophied state we call totalitarian. Applying the same terminology, we can say that if writings such as Orwell's are the symptoms, the state itself is the visible sign of the same disease : the emptiness and atomisation of men's lives, the intolerable situation of the "autonomous individual" without faith in anything but that nonentity, his conscious reason; and the consequent flow of faith, trust, and worship into a merely contingent structure, the relative and pragmatic product of multiple human interests which thus becomes absolute and divine.

Nothing in this is new, needless to say, but as human needs and responses repeat themselves in evolving forms, the worship of the state is more complete and demanding today than, perhaps, ever before, and threatens more absolute demands in the future. Similarly, the "autonomous individual" has doubtless been a way man can think of himself ever since the emergence of consciousness; but as the recognised unit of all social relations he belongs to modern times, the creation especially of the growth of scientific thinking and (as has been extensively argued) of Protestant culture. Orwell's place in this tradition has been well demonstrated in a recent commentary (by Alan Sandison) with the implication that he stands very near the end of it, indeed almost as "the last man in Europe", the title he originally intended for *1984*. Man so viewed is an individual or he is nothing; and now the autonomous individual, who was always on his own and has become desperately aware of his loneliness, looks forward to the time when the threat to his autonomy shall become overwhelming. It is the function of writers like Orwell, feeling within themselves with singular intensity the conflicts that beset many, to show not only how things are but what they may become. Fantasies and delusions are not one man's property, nor do they die with him; their forms persist from generation to generation, as it were biding their time. What in one time appears as a fantastic invention, a "mere fable", may emerge in another, far beyond the dreams of the fabulist, in literal fact. If anyone doubts the connection between personal fantasy and public actions, let him turn (to take an instance remarked by Orwell himself) to the last and least "realistic" of Swift's inventions, the most obvious product of identifiable neurotic disorder, and then look beyond the life and opinions of the Houyhnhnms to those of Nazi Germany. The fantastic projections of Orwell and Zamyatin, we have said, look equally towards the destruction of man, and envisage the immolation of humanity on the altar of the state. But although they show it thereby in a more "advanced" stage, in the context of a fully developed state apparatus, they do not show the consequences of self-hatred more exactly than Swift. The Yahoos, who are dirt, useful only to rational beings as slave labour, are only waiting for history to get into motion before they can all be herded together, to be expelled from existence in "the arse-hole of the world". The Houyhnhnms have already been debating the final solution of the Yahoo problem. Gulliver himself, an honorary Houyhnhnm, prefigures some of the incidental diversions of Auschwitz, building for himself a coracle covered with Yahoo-skins.

Winston Smith is the direct heir of Gulliver, but his situation is different. Gulliver, the free voyager, could take his autonomy about the whole surface of an imaginary earth, which was still a place of infinite possibilities. For Winston there is scarcely any freedom of movement left, either in his private fantasy or within the cage of unpleasant fact which his author's fantasy has made for him : fact rigidly circumscribes his individual existence at the beginning and by the end has destroyed it. But the fact that destroys him is a falsehood just as his autonomous freedom is false, or delusory : out of a conspiracy of such delusions is the world of modern man constructed.

How much of a delusion is the idea of the "autonomous individual" can be seen well enough in Orwell himself, a man permanently divided against himself. The unity of many such self-separated persons, suffering the further separation from each other of industrial organisation and social atomism, is the collective delusion of all. The State, in a word, doesn't exist, there is no such thing, as Auden said; but out of the need for something undivided all these fragments conspire to invent and

then to make the impossible "thing". They make it in the image
of themselves : a cruel and frightened Reason, with reason of
state as its guiding principle, tyrannising precariously over the
divisions of the rest. It is a metaphor, Hobbes's giant "artificial
man", that has been forced into concrete existence; a convention so formulated in terms of coercive institutions that its
"members", as they automatically think of themselves, are
constrained to behave as though it were an actual being. The
Emperor has no clothes, he is simply naked man like everybody
else : but everybody else, terrified of nakedness and clothed in
his own conventions, agrees to dress him in superhuman majesty
and power. *The Emperor's New Clothes* was a favourite story
of Orwell's, and he thought of adapting it to modern times; but
the vision of the child, whose eye penetrates the bogus panoply
of state with candour and faith, was not possible for him. It
does not seem possible for us; although the story promises that
"at last" all the people will shout : "He has nothing on."

In the meantime we consent to be deceived by the unreality
of the State, and build an enormous shell about its nonentity, the
solid outer casing of an inward nothing. The "apparatus of
state", the machinery of power, is tangible and all too credible,
and that is just what we demand, since we no longer believe
myths but wish to be told lies. To the reality which is expressed
through myth, the oneness and supremacy of the divine, that
which is everywhere and nowhere, and is only to be described
in metaphors and fables, the lie bears the relation not of an
opposite (although that is how the secular State is thought of
by its devotees) but a gross, bad copy, a botched up manufacture,
in fact a parody; for which reason the description of it is a
parody of theology. (Of course if one begins to speak in this way
it is hard to avoid the further comment that much, if not all,
theology parodies itself, just as much religious observance makes
an idol out of religion. But theologians know that what they are
doing is impossible, and believers that their worship is not more
than the visible covering of an invisible activity, in spirit and in
truth. It takes a statesman actually to believe in his make-
believe.)

The way out of these prisons of almighty reason is to be sought
through the imagination and its fictitious creations; for there
is a close analogy between the power of authority, of the state
as religion or religion as the state, of science (or the popular idea

of science) wielding its weapons of "natural law", of any or all
of these, ruling the apparently helpless subject with indisputable
force, and the knockdown arguments of fact against the pleas
of fiction.

The State compels, its actions are the exercise of power, its
servants may even come absurdly to think, as does O'Brien, that
power is the reason of its being. So God conceived as power
dragoons the universe into order, with no other purpose but
domination. Arguments of fact are similarly supposed to compel
consent, as the impossible Houyhnhnms thought that Reason
alone, with sufficient demonstration, must be followed by agree-
ment. But fiction, the free device of the imagination, neither
compelled nor compelling, acts in quite a different way, not by
the false compulsion of lies that masquerade as facts and
attempt to impose themselves by force, but the persuasion of its
beauty. So works of fiction are like works of love; imitating the
beauty of the world they draw the soul into communion with
reality. Nothing is forced on the reader of fiction, nothing is
compelled, the author is helpless; in his helplessness and defencelessness, offering himself through his work, and not in his
delusions of grandeur, is the true way in which the author can
be said to imitate the work of God. Graven images are not idols
so long as they are recognised as the work of men's hands and
imaginations, beautiful but powerless to do more than move men
to love what is present, but invisible, in the world and each
other.

If Winston Smith had said that he believed in God, O'Brien
would have told him that he believed in a fiction, and he could
have agreed : if a fiction is a statement that is not covered by
"the facts", then God is a fiction. There are other statements
of this kind, as that there is a Self which is not that of the
autonomous individual; that men are brothers; that two and
two make five, or that there is a whole greater than its parts.
Their truth is not verifiable, for it rests in the whole of existence.
Believing therefore in what cannot be held in the hand or put
in one's pocket, but can through the fragments of a life express
and elicit love, Winston might have been killed, or tortured into
imbecility, or into denying his belief, but whatever he suffered,
the effect would have been different. And he might have persuaded O'Brien, by the defencelessness of his belief and by its
unspeakable beauty, to come down off his ridiculous high

priestly horse, stop acting the fictitious role of the Grand Inquisitor, and share acknowledgment of the fact that he, and
Winston, and Caesar, are all men, the sons of human parents
in the flesh and in the spirit the sons of God, and one neither
less nor more than any other. The frightful edifice of Miniluv
would have vanished like the bad dream that it is. True, the
concrete walls and the torture-cells, the locks and electric lights
would remain, but only as a building raised by men, capable of
being demolished by men; as they will demolish it when they
come to know themselves in each other.

Should we think of George Orwell as a prophet, and if so of
what kind? His vision was shadowed by the sufferings of his life,
and by his different efforts to defend himself against these sufferings, of loneliness and fear and want of love. It emerges, even in
the deformations inflicted by self-torture, in his books, and it is
recognisable too in the still half-formed outlines of political institutions and practices coming into monstrous being. The world
of *1984* is preposterous, but perfectly possible, for what men can
do to each other in daydreams of omnipotence they can find a
way to carry out. It will not necessarily come to pass, and if it
does not that will be partly due to Orwell, who thought of his
last book as a warning—even if its warning is not altogether
what he thought. Perhaps he did not fully realise its nature,
but concerning that we have no right to speak. A writer's life
and his work, even in those able to achieve far greater objectivity than Orwell, are so intimately and subtly interrelated
that it is never possible to say how much he knows of what he is
doing. Nor can we expect to know it all ourselves.

This inquiry has not been concerned with Orwell as a man,
except insofar as his life illuminates his writings; we have the
right to question the work only. But if, for personal reasons, it is
painful to think of him dying in the despair which is so elabor-
ately laid out for inspection in *1984*, it can be remembered that
every book is an offering, a gift. In the last period of his life, and
in his last completed essay, his *Reflections on Gandhi* (with
whom, needless to say, he had little sympathy) he turned, as
always, to speak of himself, disguised in a generalisation:

> The essence of being human is that one does not seek per-
> fection, that one *is* sometimes willing to commit sins for the

sake of loyalty, that one does not push asceticism to the point
where it makes friendly intercourse impossible, and that one
is prepared in the end to be defeated and broken up by life,
which is the inevitable price of fastening one's love upon other
human individuals.

And a little further on :

If one could follow it to its psychological roots, one would, I
believe, find that the main motive for "non-attachment" is a
desire to escape from the pain of living, and above all from
love, which, sexual or non-sexual, is hard work.

Certainly he found it so; certainly he was broken. In the depths
of Miniluv O'Brien tells Winston : " 'We have broken you up.
You have seen what your body is like. Your mind is in the same
state. I do not think there can be much pride left in you.' "
Writing his last book Orwell was allowing himself to be broken,
and how the pieces are brought together after that necessary
process is not in the author's hands.

But for a final word we may return to the Book of Jonah, the
proud, contumacious, and fearful prophet who did everything
back to front : the "mere Jonah" the main point of whose story
Orwell persistently forgot. After being ejected from the terrible
shelter of the whale Jonah at last obeyed the call of God and
went to summon Nineveh to repentance; when he did so effec-
tively, so that king and man and beast put on sackcloth and
turned away from evil and violence, God himself repented of
his destructive purpose and spared the city. And Jonah, who
had not forgotten his quarrel with God (which he continued,
we may say, where Job left off) was furious at being made a fool
of, and a whole further cycle of life and death had to be shown
to him, and even then he maintained that he did well to be
angry, even unto death. But his story is left behind to tell us not
of God's anger but his mercy, which may extend even to
Nineveh, that great and sinful city, now co-extensive with the
bounds of the shrunk and interconnected earth, wherein are so
many millions of persons that cannot discern between their right
hand and their left; and also much cattle.

Index
by
Michael Gordon